Reasoning draws a conclusion and makes us grant the conclusion, but does not make the conclusion certain, nor does it remove doubt so that the mind may rest on the intuition of truth, unless the mind discovers it by the path of experience . . . . Therefore reasoning does not suffice, but experience does.

Roger Bacon, Opus Majus (Burke)

Contents

List of Figures

Foreword

The history of my connection with the Voynich manuscript is as follows: in 1951 Mr. William F. Friedman introduced me to the manuscript and I spent my spare time in studying the combinations of the most commonly occurring symbols. I wrote a report of my work for Mr. Friedman. I should mention that the only part of the manuscript which was available to me at the time was the twenty pages at the end which contain no illustrations. In fact he deliberately used me as a control—he told me nothing other than the information about the manuscript contained in the book *The Cipher of Roger Bacon* by Newbold. On the strength of this study I came to the rather definite conclusion that the text could not have been arrived at merely by the substitution of single symbols for letters whatever the language involved.

Subsequently about twelve years ago I read a paper to the Baltimore Bibliophiles covering the history of the manuscript and some of the attempts to decipher it. This paper, almost unaltered, was printed in an internal office journal.

In the fall of 1975 I read a paper on the subject to a group of colleagues. As this occasion was rather widely advertised within the organization, it attracted quite a large audience and the attention of some of those who attended was drawn to the study of the manuscript.

From the time when Mr. Friedman's health began to fail. I have acted as a sort of unofficial coordinator of the work of some of the people who have been working on the problem, and when Miss Mary D'Imperio told me of her interest. I suggested that she should assume this responsibility.

She has written a far more comprehensive and more scholarly survey of the problem than mine and it will. I believe. become the definitive background of future work in this field.

To my knowledge there have been three rather extensive analyses of the script of the manuscript. by Mr. Friedman, by me, and by Captain Prescott Currier. Of these, I believe Captain Currier's to be far the most complete. All three have reached similar conclusions at any rate in some aspects, and I find myself quite unable to accept any suggested solution unless it takes account of these analyses.

John H. Tiltman

24 November 1976

Introduction

The reader may well wonder, "Why still another paper on the Voynich manuscript?" So much has been written already on that most studied, most curious, and most mysterious manuscript upon which so many researchers have exhausted their faculties in vain. Perhaps a few words of explanation might be useful in setting the stage for the reader, and in presenting the motivation for this monograph.

As a relatively recent newcomer to the ranks of Voynich manuscript students. I have unwittingly retraced the steps of all my predecessors, rediscovering their sources, repeating their experiments, growing excited over the same promising leads that excited them, and learning only later that all these things had already been tried and had failed, often several times. I have no wish to imply that I regret any of my efforts. In fact, I little suspected, when I was first introduced to the problem of the Voynich manuscript at Brigadier Tiltman's lecture in November 1975, that I would spend all my spare time for the next year on an intellectual and spiritual journey spanning so many centuries and ranging over so many aspects of art, history, philosophy, and philology. I have thoroughly enjoyed every moment of my investigations, and would not give them up at any price.

The fact remains that, in spite of all the papers that others have written about the manuscript, there is, to my knowledge, no complete survey of all the approaches, ideas, background information and analytic studies that have accumulated over the nearly fifty-five years since the manuscript was discovered by Wilfrid M. Voynich in 1912. Most of the papers have been written either to advance or to refute a particular theory, providing in passing a brief glance at others' efforts, primarily to sweep them out of the way. Some presentations provide good treatments of some aspects of the problem, notably those by Voynich (1921), Newbold (1928), Tiltman (1968), and Krischer (1969). Much vital information, however, is to be found only in unpublished notes and papers inaccessible to most students. I have felt that it would be useful to pull together all the information I could obtain from all the sources I have examined, and to present it in an orderly fashion. I hope that the resulting survey will provide a firm basis upon which other students may build their work, whether they seek to decipher the text or simply to learn more about the problem.

This monograph will be arranged in four main sections. First, I will present a survey of all the basic facts of the problem: the "givens", as it were. Second, I will try to cover all the primary avenues of attack and the information relevant to each: the external characteristics of the manuscript itself, the drawings, and the text. Third, I will survey the major claims of decipherment and other substantial analytic work carried out by various researchers. Fourth, I will provide a rapid sketch of collateral and background topics which seem likely to be useful. An extensive bibliography is included, comprising books and papers on the Voynich manuscript itself and on a variety of related topics.

I wish to express my appreciation for the generous aid of John H. Tiltman, without whose encouragement this monograph would never have been completed. I wish also to thank Stuart Buck, Edwin S. Spiegelthal, and Stuart MacClintock, who proofread my manuscript and offered many helpful criticisms and suggestions.

Chapter 1

The Known Facts

1.1 The Manuscript As Found

It seems important first of all to distinguish clearly between the givens—the incontrovertible facts available to all students of the manuscript—and the lush growth of conjecture that has accumulated around the few meagre certainties we have. A clear physical description of the codex itself is provided by several authors. The entry in the catalogue of H. P. Kraus (antiquarian bookdealer and owner of the manuscript for a number of years) provides an excellent, compact sketch (see figure 1). In brief, the mysterious manuscript consists in a small quarto volume, with leaves of varying size but of an average nine by six inches, some multiply folded. Most pages contain, in addition to copious text in the unknown script (which I will call the "Voynich script" throughout this paper), colored pictures of considerable variety, whose meaning is open to conjecture. Most appear to represent plants, astrological or cosmological material, and pharmaceutical recipes, while a few show human figures surrounded by bizarre objects in scenes of undetermined import. The text and drawings will be studied in considerable detail in Chapters 3 and 4.

The manuscript has no cover; the first page contains only four brief paragraphs of text without pictures, but with an apparent crude attempt at rubrication by means of enlarged and embellished initial characters in red ink. The last page shows a few lines of writing near the top, in a different script or mixture of scripts than the bulk of the text, along with a few symbols from the Voynich script, and a scattering of sketchy drawings of animals, people, and other unidentifiable objects in the upper left corner. Some leaves in the body of the manuscript also contain jottings (largely illegible) in scripts and hands apparently differing from the majority of the text. These atypical scraps of writing will be dealt with more fully below.

We have one other bit of concrete data to exploit: a letter, found between the pages of the manuscript by Wilfrid Voynich. Figure 2 shows this letter, and figure 3 provides its translation from Latin as prepared for Voynich and published by him (1921, p. 27). The letter was written by Joannus Marcus Marci in Prague to accompany his gift of the manuscript to Athanasius Kircher, S. J., in Rome. The letter adds the following solid facts to our knowledge (as fleshed out by the research of Voynich, who he describes in interesting detail in the work cited above):

The manuscript was in the hands of Joannus Marcus Marci (A.D. 1595–1667), official physician to Emperor Rudolph II of Bohemia (A.D. 1552–1612), in the year 1665 or 1666.

It had previously been in the possession of one or more other persons, otherwise unidentified, probably associated with the court of Rudolph II.

It passed from the possession of Marci to Athanasius Kircher in 1665 or 1666, and remained in his hands for an unknown period of time.

It had been sold to Rudolph by an unidentified person at an unstated time for the large sum of 600 ducats, according to information provided to Marci by a Dr. Raphael Missowsky (A.D. 1580–1644), who was a familiar at the courts of Rudolph and his successors.

Another nugget of information was wrested from the enigmatic pages of the manuscript itself as a result of a fortunate accident. A mishap during photographic reproduction of the manuscript revealed a partially erased signature on the first page. Examined under infra-red light, this signature was found to be "Jacobj à Tepenece", that of a man identified by Voynich as Jacobus Horcicky de Tepenecz (d. 1622). This man was director of Rudolph's botanical gardens and alchemical laboratory. He did not acquire the patent of nobility with the title "de Tepenecz" until after 1608. Thus, we have one additional fact: the manuscript was in the hands of another familiar at Rudolph's court at some time during the period from 1608 to 1622.

The last bit of concrete evidence we have is the place where the manuscript was found by Voynich in 1912; this source was kept secret for some years, in the expectation that Voynich might wish to return and purchase more manuscripts there. It was ultimately revealed to be the Villa Mondragone, in Italy not far from Rome. The following is a précis of information concerning Mondragone, gathered by John Tiltman:

"....A villa in Frascati near Rome, built by Cardinal Altemps about 1570. In 1582 Pope Gregory XIII issued from Mondragone the bull reforming the calendar. The villa apparently continued in the Altemps family, as in 1620 a later member bequeathed the Mondragone library to the Vatican Library. In 1865 the villa became a Jesuit College which was finally closed in 1953." (Tiltman 1968, p. 2.)

This, then, is all we really know for certain about the enigmatic codex: what observant students have seen in the book itself, and the letter that accompanied it when found. (So far as I can discover, no scientific study of any kind has ever been carried out on the inks, pigments, or parchment; and no attempt has been made to examine the pages under special light for hidden writing.) Upon this meagre foundation of fact, an imposing edifice of deduction and guesswork has been erected through creative research and persistent scholarship, first by Wilfrid Voynich, and then by a succession of later students. Later sections of this paper will deal in fuller detail with these conjectures, many of which seem well founded and of certain value to future students of the manuscript.

1.2 The Known History of the Manuscript

A set of solid bench marks can be assembled from the sources described above, and summarized as follows:

The manuscript was in the hands of some unknown person who brought it to Rudolph's court some time before 1608.

It was in the possession of Jacobus de Tepenecz for some time after 1608 and before his death in 1622.

It was held for some time by another person, unidentified, who willed it to Joannus Marcus Marci sometime before 1665 or 1666.

It was sent by Marci from Prague, during 1665 or 1666, to his old teacher, Athanasius Kircher, in Rome.

It did not then reenter recorded history until it was discovered by Wilfrid Voynich at the Villa Mondragone, Frascati, Italy in 1912.

After the death of Voynich in 1930, the manuscript remained in the estate of his widow (author of a well-known novel, *The Gadfly*, which enjoyed great popularity in the Soviet Union). Mrs. Voynich died in July 1960. Miss A. M. Nill, a close friend and companion of Mrs. Voynich over many years, was co-owner of the manuscript.

It was purchased on July 12, 1961, by Hans P. Kraus, New York antiquarian bookseller, for $24,500.

Kraus valued the manuscript at $100,000, and later at $160,000; he tried repeatedly to find a buyer for it at those prices. Finally, in 1960, he presented it to the Beinecke Rare Book Library of Yale University, where it now remains, catalogued as manuscript 408, and valued at $125,000 to $500,000, according to different sources. (Information concerning the modern history of the manuscript was obtained from Tiltman 1968 and from unpublished notes kept by Miss Nill for herself and for Mr. and Mrs. Voynich.)

Chapter 2

Avenues of Attack on the Problem: A Survey

In this chapter I will attempt to cover as much as possible of the great variety of conjecture, reasoning, research, and investigation that has been carried out by a wide range of scholars, from Voynich down to those of recent years. I have arranged this material under a selection of topics relating to important characteristics of the manuscript, (its provenience, date, original language, authorship, etc.), which have excited the curiosity and exercised the ingenuity of all its many students. I can lay claim to a knowledge of only a small part of the work that may now be in progress or that may have been done in the recent past; many people have undoubtedly carried on their work alone, and their ideas and results have become known only to their immediate colleagues and acquaintances. Any day now, a new announcement of success could break upon the world from one of these students. I hope that the present summary, however incomplete, may serve to gather together more information about the manuscript and its researchers than has hitherto been available in one place.

2.1 Conjectures Concerning the History of the Manuscript

Soon after his discovery of the manuscript, Voynich undertook a very competent and thorough investigation of its history. He turned up a wealth of interesting data, and succeeded in piecing together a plausible sequence of events to fill in most of the blank spots between the known benchmarks. He traced the origin of the manuscript to Roger Bacon (1214?–1292?), a learned Franciscan scholar and philosopher, renowned in later times for his occult powers. Of Roger Bacon much more will be said below (see Sections 2.2.2, 5.1 and Chapter 7). Voynich stated that he had fastened upon Bacon as the most likely candidate for authorship by a process of elimination, assuming, as he did, a thirteenth century date for the manuscript even before he saw the letter from Marci mentioning the similar belief held by someone at the court of Rudolph II. Voynich's statement of his reasoning while examining the manuscript at the castle where he found it is worth quoting in full.

> "Even a necessarily brief examination of the vellum upon which it was written, the calligraphy, the drawings and the pigments suggested to me as the date of its origin the latter part of the thirteenth century. The drawings indicated it to be an encyclopedic work on natural philosophy. I hastily considered the question of possible authorship of the work and the names of only two thirteenth century scholars who could have written on such a variety of subjects occurred to me: first, Albertus Magnus, whom I at once eliminated from consideration because his ecclesiastical and political position was such that it could not have been necessary for him to conceal any of his writings in cipher, and secondly, the Franciscan Friar, Roger Bacon, an infinitely greater scholar, who had been persecuted on account of his writings and whose scientific discoveries had been misrepresented as black magic. Moreover, for many years he had been forbidden by his order to write, and he himself referred in his works to the necessity of hiding his great secrets in cipher." [1921, pp. 415–416.]

Voynich continues, relating his discovery of the Marci letter as follows:

> "It was not until some time after the manuscript came into my hands that I read the document bearing the date 1665 (or 1666), which was attached to the front cover. Because of its late date I had regarded it as of no consequence, and therefore neglected it during the first examination of the manuscript." [P. 416.]

He must have been gratified indeed to find his conjectural attribution of the manuscript to Bacon thus dramatically corroborated.

Next, Voynich turned his attention to teasing as much additional information as he could from the facts at his disposal. He uncovered a quantity of fascinating detail concerning the personages mentioned in the letter and otherwise suspected to have been associated with the manuscript, many of them familiars of Rudolph II and members of his court. The subject of Rudolph, the scientific and pseudo-scientific movements that grew up around him, and the astonishing flock of scientists, spies, charlatans, and other flamboyant personalities that converged upon Prague during Rudolph's reign, is in itself a valuable area for study. The work published on this topic by Bolton (1904) is quite out of date, and while enjoyable reading, fails to do justice to the subject in the light of today's scholarship. Evans (1973) provides a detailed, up-to-date presentation on Rudolph and the elaborate and interesting culture surrounding his court. Evans makes a tantalizingly brief mention of the Voynich manuscript, but does not add anything to our knowledge of its origin.

Here, in brief, is my chronological outline of the hypotheses Voynich put forward to fill the gaps in the known history of the manuscript, and to suggest further lines of investigation to complete the picture (all information in the outline below is from Voynich 1921).

3

Latter half of the thirteenth century. The manuscript was penned by Roger Bacon, as a record of his secret discoveries of science or magic.

—1538? The manuscript rested in some monastic library in England until the dissolution of the religious houses at the time of the Reformation; this destruction began in 1538.

—1547? Many Bacon manuscripts (some say as many as 1200 all told) were collected by Dr. John Dee, Elizabethan mathematician and astrologer (of whom more will be said below in Chapter 8). He obtained these, Voynich suggests, through his association with John Dudley, Duke of Northumberland, who amassed a large fortune through the rapacious spoliation of religious houses during the Reformation. Our manuscript could have come into Dee's hands as early as 1547, according to Voynich. While it was in Dee's possession, he made vigorous attempts to decipher it, as attested by a remark in a much later letter (dated 1675) quoting Arthur Dee, John Dee's son, to the effect that he had seen his father spending much time over a book "all in hieroglyphicks" (on this matter, see also Section 8.9 below).

1584–1588. John Dee, failing in his attempts to decipher it, carried the manuscript to Prague on one of his visits to Rudolph's court between 1584 and 1588. It was, then, to Dee or someone representing him that Rudolph paid the 600 ducats which was his price for the manuscript. It was probably also Dee who convinced Rudolph or others at the court of Roger Bacon's authorship; Dee was to a considerable degree obsessed with Bacon throughout a large portion of his life, and had a large part in disseminating knowledge of Bacon's work and refurbishing the reputation of the thirteenth-century friar, condemned by the Church and his contemporaries to centuries of neglect. Dee even claimed to be a descendant of Bacon (whose real name, Dee claimed, had been "David Dee" and not Roger Bacon at all).

—1608? Rudolph made various attempts to get the manuscript decrypted by his stable of scholars and experts. In this endeavor, he may have committed the manuscript, for working purposes, into the keeping of Jacobus de Tepenecz, whose name was written on it, and who may have kept it after Rudolph's abdication in 1611 and the subsequent looting and dissolution of the Emperor's extensive museum and collections. Since de Tepenecz was ennobled in 1608, he could not have written his name on the manuscript in the form we see before that date.

—1622. de Tepenecz died in 1622, and we have no evidence for the history of the manuscript between that time and its appearance in the hands of its next known owner, Marci.

—1644? According to the Marci letter, the manuscript was in the possession of an unknown owner, mutual friend of Marci and Kircher, for some unknown period; indeed, it may have passed through several hands during that time. It must have come into Marci's possession sometime before 1644, since Marci was able to discuss it with Dr. Raphael, who died in that year. Voynich suggests (p. 419) that "research into the Bohemian State Archives will lead to the discovery" of the intimate friend of Marci and also of Kircher who had the manuscript between 1622 and 1644.

—1665/6. During the time between 1644 and 1665 or 1666, we are reasonably certain that the manuscript was in the possession of Joannus Marcus Marci, and that it then passed into the hands of Athanasius Kircher. What Marci and Kircher did with it while they had it, we do not know.

—1912. Voynich says, "my own impression is that Kircher left the manuscript to someone at the court of Parma, where he had patrons and friends, and it probably remained in the possession of a member of the Farnese family until, with other manuscripts, it was removed to the collection in which I found it." (p. 430.)

Later researchers have added only a few details to this chronology so ingeniously ferreted out by Voynich. Brumbaugh (1975, p. 347) suggests that Kircher himself may have deposited the manuscript directly into the Villa at Mondragone. John Manly (1921b, p. 188) claims that "it is clear that Marci did not possess the manuscript in 1640, when he was with Kircher in Rome", since he would naturally have given it to Kircher then. He also reports that Marci, in the preface of a work entitled "Idearum Operaticium Idea", mentions as his mother-in-law one Laura, daughter of Dionisius Misserone, who became director of Rudolph's Imperial Museum. Manly implies that Misserone could have been the unknown friend who bequeathed the manuscript to Marci. Finally, Manly provides the interesting bit of information that the 600 ducats, Rudolph's payment for the manuscript, would be the equivalent of $14,000 in 1921, and he contributes some new data regarding de Tepenecz: this scientist was obliged to flee the country during disturbances that took place in 1618, and may well have parted with the manuscript then, since it apparently remained in Prague.

Robert Steele, an eminent historian and Baconian scholar who has edited many of Roger Bacon's works (Bacon 1909–1940), concurs with Voynich in connecting the manuscript with John Dee. He says, "Mr. Voynich is, we believe, right in his conjecture that it was sold by Dee to the Emperor Rudolph at the close of the sixteenth century, attributing it to Roger Bacon, and that it was probably 'the book containing nothing but hieroglyphics' of which Dee's son spoke to Sir Thos. Browne." (Steele 1928b, p. 563.)

4

2.2 Authorship and Purpose

2.2.1 A Hoax, a Forgery, or Nonsense?

Many students have had, at times, an uncomfortable suspicion that the mysterious codex upon which so much fruitless effort had been spent might be a fabrication, its text representing nothing meaningful or orderly enough to be capable of decipherment and translation. Wilfrid Voynich seems to have felt that the manuscript was unquestionably a genuine production of a thirteenth-century author, and specifically of Roger Bacon. Dr. Albert H. Carter (one time technical historian of the Army Security Agency) states the opinion shared by most students who have grappled with the elegant puzzle when he says, "So much time and so much expense in vellum of excellent quality went into it, it cannot be a hoax. . . . It is conceivably the work of a wealthy and learned, if deranged, person, but not a hoax" (1946, p. 1). In an early report, John Tiltman, one of the most faithful and thoroughgoing of the manuscript's students, expresses his considered confidence in its authenticity: "I do not believe the manuscript is completely meaningless, the ravings or doodlings of a lunatic, nor do I believe it is just a hoax—it is too elaborate and consistent for either. . . . About the worst thing it can be is a deliberate forgery for gain. . . . I regard this as rather improbable. . ." (1951, p. 1).

In a more recent presentation, Tiltman reiterates these judgements, refusing to accept suggestions that the manuscript contains only "meaningless doodlings". He continues, "There is more sense to the idea that the work is a forgery. This I think is highly unlikely, especially if Captain Currier's ideas are correct." (Tiltman 1975; the reference to Captain Currier concerns his findings of multiple "hands" in the text, for which see Section 6.8 below.) Erwin Panofsky, a prominent scholar of medieval and Renaissance studies, added the weight of his learning to this view: "I should like to reiterate my opinion that the Voynich manuscript, whichever its place of origin, date and purpose, is certainly a perfectly authentic document" (1954, p. 3). Finally, Elizabeth Friedman, wife of William Friedman (prominent cryptologist and student of the manuscript) and a distinguished scholar and cryptologist in her own right, expresses a similar opinion: "All scholars competent to judge the manuscript . . . were—and still are—agreed that it is definitely not a hoax or the doodlings of a psychotic but is a homogeneous, creative work of a serious scholar who had something to convey" (1962).

At least one recent researcher has spoken out in favor of an opposing view, stating that the manuscript is in fact a forgery, and may contain a considerable quantity of meaningless "dummy" text intended merely to fill it out to an impressive length. Robert Brumbaugh (1974, 1975, 1976) claims that the book was expressly and calculatedly designed by some sixteenth-century opportunist in order to fool the Emperor Rudolph into parting with the large sum of money that he did, indeed, spend to obtain it. To this end, the text was provided with a wealth of apparently easy "keys", and just enough easily decipherable material on the last page to convince Rudolph's experts that it would prove to be readable with the expenditure of a reasonable amount of effort. Faked "evidence" was also planted on the last page, according to Brumbaugh, to associate the secret book closely to Roger Bacon—that exciting and mysterious possessor of impressive scientific and occult powers in whom John Dee had been busily raising interest to a fevered pitch at Rudolph's court.

In spite of all this, Brumbaugh shares the view that the manuscript is not totally meaningless. He says, "There is an underlying text . . . and sooner or later, by collaborative work, it will be read. There is no way of predicting what it will say; it could be anything from a standard botany textbook to formulae for the Elixir of Life deriving from Roger Bacon" (1975, p. 354). Father Theodore C. Petersen, another dedicated long-term student of the manuscript who possessed a wide background of learning in history and philology, expresses his view thus: "There is agreement that the text of the Voynich manuscript obeys uniform rules which are constant and unchanging throughout the whole 246 extant quarto pages of writing—indicating that the script contained an intelligible meaning for its writer" (1953, p. 1).

Newbold, Feely, and Strong, the three other principal claimants (besides Brumbaugh) to some degree of success in deciphering the manuscript, all accepted it as a genuine and serious production either of the thirteenth or the sixteenth century. William Friedman also, while not to my knowledge associating the manuscript with any specific author, regarded it as a valid document with some content capable of being deciphered and read.

Some students of the manuscript, and others who disclaim any interest in it, have advanced the view that its content can have no value for science or for the study of human thought. Tiltman, in his early report to Friedman, says, "I do not in any case imagine there is anything historically or scientifically important contained in the manuscript" (1951, p. 1); this, in spite of his deep and long-continued interest in the problem and his firm rejection of the theory that the manuscript is completely meaningless or fraudulent. Elizabeth Friedman indicates that the lack of serious interest in the manuscript on the part of scholars was, on at least one occasion, a cause of disappointment to her husband in his research: "It appears to be gibberish to many serious-minded academics, who are apt to scoff at the idea that its solution would be of any value to science or learning—as did a great foundation to which Friedman once applied for a grant for the detailed study of the manuscript. In the opinion of the board, a solution would not advance human knowledge. The manuscript probably contains only trivia, the board said." (1962)

5

I must confess that I can see little justice in the reasoning of those "academics" who dismiss the Voynich manuscript out of hand, after what can only be the most superficial attention. Even if it is, in fact, a fabrication associated with the court of Rudolph II, an understanding of who wrote it, its passage from one to another of Rudolph's familiars, and the part it played in the remarkable congeries of religious and political activities at Prague in those times could prove to be of great interest. In the history of thought, it is not the intrinsic importance of a work that matters so much as its place within a larger pattern of events and meanings. If the manuscript is a compilation, however "deranged" or idiosyncratic, drawn from earlier magical, alchemical, or medical works, it has at least as much intrinsic interest and "scientific" import for the history of Western thought as do other similar manuscripts which are readable, and concern only one topic (i.e., they are either astrological, or alchemical, or medical). Reputable scholars apparently see no waste of time in studying "plaintext" manuscripts of this type, and may spend much of their lives so occupied.

The Voynich manuscript appears to be unusual in that it combines in one book at least four different medieval disciplines, apparently with some attempt to integrate them into a single system. If read, it could provide a highly interesting picture of a theory or doctrine interrelating all these disciplines, at least in the beliefs or practices of one individual or school. Finally, even if the text is totally meaningless (a possibility that seems to me highly unlikely), a decipherment of the text in some manner permitting an understanding of the code, cipher, or other concealment system employed should be of great interest for the history of cryptology, and perhaps also for the study of alphabets and writing systems. In summary, I could accept a finding that the manuscript was a hoax or a forgery; I might also accept the presence of a large amount of dummy or filler text, to pad out the length of the document or to act as "cover" text within which a shorter message is hidden. I cannot, however, see any justification for dismissal of the manuscript as trivial or unworthy of careful and systematic study. We can assess its value for human knowledge only *after* we have read it, or at least learned quite a lot more about it.

2.2.2 *Who Wrote It, and Why?*

Roger Bacon (A.D. 1214?–1292?) as Author. Voynich, as we have seen above, was certain of Bacon's authorship from the outset. His reasoning, presented above (Section 2.1) need not be recapitulated here. William R. Newbold, the first would be decipher of the secret book, maintained that Bacon wrote it, as a diary of novel scientific researches unacceptable to the Church. He intended the book, according to Newbold, for his favorite pupil John, or for some other disciple or friend, providing the recipient with an oral key subsequently lost. The first chapter of the book describing Newbold's findings presents an excellent sketch of Roger Bacon's life, writings, and thought, indicating that he had made a thorough study of the thirteenth-century friar and his works (1928, pp. 1–28). J. Malcolm Bird (1921) accepts Newbold's decipherment, and the attribution to Bacon, in favor of which he provides a lengthy justification.

At least two other objective and painstaking researchers agree that there is no conclusive evidence against the original authorship of the manuscript by Bacon (whether it is in his autograph hand or represents a later copy of his work). John M. Manly (prominent literary scholar who later refuted Newbold's solution) expressed his opinion thus in an early comment: "That the manuscript is Bacon's, or even that it dates from the thirteenth century, cannot then be proven by documentary evidence, but there is no evidence against this tradition, and the appearance of the manuscript itself confirms it. . . ." (1921, p. 189). Tiltman concurs with this view: "There is as yet no solid evidence that the manuscript is not by Roger Bacon, or a copy of a work by him" (1968, p. 13). A number of prominent Baconian scholars accepted, indeed hailed with enthusiasm, Newbold's claim to have proven that Bacon was the author (Carton 1929; Gilson 1928). For further discussion of this question, see Chapter 7 below.

Roger Bacon Not the Author. Others are just emphatic in their rejection of Bacon either as the scribe or contributor of any content in the manuscript. The objections of some revolve around their rejection of an early date for the book, and their apparent unwillingness to consider it as a later copy of Bacon's work. They cite opinions of experts dating the manuscript around 1500, and therefore much too late to have been a work by Bacon, or even likely to have been a copy (most copies of Bacon's works that have come down to us were made in the fourteenth and fifteenth centuries). Still others reject Baconian authorship not, apparently, in general, but specifically as a part of their emphatic rejection of Newbold's decipherment and his attribution of the manuscript to Bacon, along with such impossibly anachronistic activities as the invention of the compound microscope and telescope, and their use to observe events within a frame of reference completely foreign to Bacon's times. Erwin Panofsky has stated flatly that "The Roger Bacon theory is in my opinion at variance with all the available facts and has been convincingly disproved by Mr. Manly" (i.e., in Manly's articles demolishing Newbold's theories) (1954, p. 2). Dr. Charles Singer, eminent historian of science, said in a letter to Tiltman (12 November, 1957), "I came to the conclusion that all suggestion of a knowledge of the microscope [again referring to Newbold's decipherment]

6

was simply nonsense." Finally, Lynn Thorndike has, with characteristic emphasis, stated his opinion that "There is hardly one chance in fifty that Roger Bacon had any connection with the production of the Voynich manuscript." (1929, p. 319).

Anthony Askham as Author. Dr. Leonell C. Strong (whose claims to a decipherment of the manuscript are discussed in Section 5.3 below), insisted that the author was a sixteenth-century physician named Anthony Askham (or Ascham), who had published several almanacs, astrological works, and an herbal. (Tiltman has ferreted out references to a number of these, as early printed books: see Askham 1548a, 1548b, 1550, 1552, and 1553.) Strong claimed, further, to have deciphered Askham's name on folio 93 of the manuscript. No other student has accepted this theory, and Strong's proposed readings of the text have been emphatically rejected.

Other General Suggestions Regarding Authorship. Dr. Carter claimed to see evidence of "a copyist at work" (1946, p. 1). He mentions duplication among the zodiac diagrams, there being in fact two leaves showing the Ram, Aries, and two showing the Bull, Taurus. (These diagrams are, in actuality, quite different when examined carefully, and the apparent "duplications" are only superficial; the pairing of diagrams for these two zodiac signs clearly had some definite purpose known only to the author of the manuscript.) Dr. Singer, in a letter to Tiltman (12 November, 1957) expresses the opinion that the origin of the manuscript was somehow related to Rudolph's court and to John Dee. While he does not further specify the nature of the connection, one gains the impression that he may have had in mind an idea similar to Brumbaugh's discussed above. Panofsky states the following view: "My idea always was that the manuscript was written by a doctor or quack trying to impart what he considered secret knowledge to his son or heir" (1954, p. 2).

2.3 Provenience and Underlying Language

England, Medieval Latin. Voynich, as we have seen, traced the manuscript to Roger Bacon, in the England of the late thirteenth century. He probably also, therefore, assumed the underlying "plaintext" to be the medieval Latin of the Schools, used by Bacon in all his surviving works. Newbold (1928, p. 44) also gives the manuscript an English origin, claiming to rest his opinion on "the judgement of experts" not further identified, based on the parchment, ink and style of the drawings. His proposed decipherment produced a form of medieval Latin. The language which Feely (1943) claimed to have discovered in the manuscript was also Latin, but in a system of abbreviated forms not considered acceptable by other scholars, who unanimously rejected his readings of the text.

England, Medieval English. Leonell Strong (1945) maintained that he had deciphered the text as medieval English; as we will see in Section 5.3 below, other students have rejected his theory and the plaintext he produced, both as valid medieval English and as a correct decipherment of the Voynich text.

Unspecified European, Latin. Elizebeth Friedman (1962) states that her husband, William Friedman, agreed with other qualified experts that "the country of origin is definitely European; it might be England, France, Italy, or what is now Germany." She adds, further, that "the text is based upon a written language that is probably Latin, the language of all learned and scientific discourses of that period, but may be medieval English, French, Italian, or Teutonic." These views seem to leave us with a discouragingly wide choice, indicating that the "experts" could fix upon no definite evidence to narrow the area of their search.

Italy. Hellmut Lehmann–Haupt, Bibliographical Consultant to H. P. Kraus (owner of the manuscript between 1962 and 1969), suggested in a letter to John Tiltman dated 1 November, 1963 that Italy was a likely country of origin. He states, "While both paleographically and historically speaking, Italy is as likely a place of origin as any other country of Europe, there is no evidence that the manuscript must have been made in Venice, or elsewhere in Northern Italy. The possibility that it comes from Central or Southern Italy is still open, and this could very well mean exposure to the Arab world." He proposes that Arabic should be considered as a candidate for the underlying language. Robert Steele suggests that some of the writing on the last page may be "perhaps in a North Italian hand" (1928b, p. 564). Brumbaugh draws evidence from details in some of the drawings for his theory of a relatively late date and a European provenience. Thus, in one of the zodiac-like circular diagrams, he says "Sagittarius wears a fifteenth-century Florentine archer's hat in his medallion (though it is retouched over the month name)" (1975, p. 349).

Germany or Eastern Europe. Charles Singer, in a letter to Tiltman dated 12 November, 1957, states his feeling that the manuscript is "of Germanic origin", and "connected with John Dee and that sort of movement." He gives a somewhat fuller statement of this view in another letter to Dr. G. M. J. Flemming, undated but obviously written at about the same time: "The judgement that I formed upon the manuscript was that it was of the sixteenth century, of South German work and possibly related to Prague and John Dee." Singer also suggests that Czech, Polish, or some other East-Central European language should be considered to underlie the text. Fortunately for students of the manuscripts, whose difficulties are already sufficiently burdensome, he considers Magyar "highly unlikely."

Both Singer (in the letter to Flemming) and Panofsky (1954, p. 2), mention a reading of some scattered phrases on the last page as High German; this reading was proposed, apparently in a private communication, by Richard Salomon of Kenyon College. Dr. Salomon suggests that a portion of the text in a mixture of scripts should be read: "so nim geismi | 1 | ch o.", representing a medieval prescription meaning "(If such and such a condition prevails), then take goat's milk or ..." This "prescription", which breaks off in mid-sentence, Salomon sees as continuous with the preceding text on the line. He suggests an interpretation in German also for the brief words found on folio 66r, near a figure of a man lying on his back as if sick or dead, and surrounded by several ambiguous objects. He reads the text as "der mussteil", referring to the obligatory endowment of a widow with household goods on her husband's death.

2.4 *Date of Origin*

Thirteenth or Fourteenth Century. Voynich (1921, p. 415) assigned the manuscript to the latter half of the thirteenth century, as we have seen above. Newbold stated that "in the judgement of experts," a study of parchment, ink, and style of drawings placed the manuscript in the thirteenth century. (1928, p. 44). Petersen says, "I agree with Mr. Tiltman that the juxtaposition of a herbal with the kind of astrological tables found here indicates a fairly early date for the manuscript. The thirteenth century manuscripts of St. Hildegarde of Bingen show drawings illustrating the influence of the heavenly bodies and elementary celestial forces upon the vegetative and animate life of the earth. The fourteenth century manuscript Vatican 1906 has somewhat similar astronomical drawings" (1953, p. 2). Steele provides the following interesting comments, with the benefit of his expert knowledge and personal familiarity with medieval manuscripts (and in particular the works of Roger Bacon): "The usual methods of dating a manuscript fail us; the writing cannot be placed, the vellum is coarse for the thirteenth century, but not impossible, the ink is good. Only the drawings remain, and owing to their complete absence of style the difficulty of dating is but increased. It is strange that the draftsman should have so completely escaped all medieval or Renaissance influence" (1928b, p. 563).

Fifteenth Century. Hugh O'Neill, a prominent American botanist, published an identification of certain plant drawings as New World species: "The most startling identification...was folio 93, which is quite plainly the common sunflower, Helianthus Annuus L. Six botanists have agreed with me on this determination. This immediately recalls the date 1493, when the seeds of this plant were brought to Europe for the first time (by Columbus on his return from his second voyage). Again folio 101v shows a drawing which does not resemble any native European fruit, but suggests plainly Capsicum, a genus strictly American in origin, known in Europe only after the above date. ... It seems necessary to consider this manuscript as having been written after 1493" (1944, p. 126). Other scholars, however, completely reject O'Neill's identification of the sunflower and pepper plant, and are as emphatic in their claim that *none* of the plants pictured in the manuscript are of New World origin. Helmut Lehmann-Haupt (bibliographical consultant to H. P. Kraus) stated in a letter to Tiltman dated 1 November, 1963, that "there is a near agreement on the date of the CIPHER manuscript as around, or a little after, the year 1400."

Sixteenth Century. Panofsky adds his voice to these suggesting a late date for the origin of the mysterious codex: "Were it not for the sunflower | as identified by O'Neill | ...I should have thought that it was executed a little earlier, say about 1470. However, since the style of the drawings is fairly provincial, a somewhat later date, even the first years of the sixteenth century, would not seem to be excluded. I should not go lower than ca. 1510–1520 because no influence of the Italian Renaissance style is evident. The above date is based on the character of the script, the style of drawing and on such costumes as are in evidence on certain pages, for example folio 72 recto | probably referring to the costumes in the Gemini representations |." (1954, p. 1). Elizebeth Friedman states the consensus of expert opinion at the time as follows: "Paleographic experts agree that the nature of the drawings, the writing, the ink and vellum, etc., indicate that the manuscript is certainly of later origin than the thirteenth century. The female figures, for example, are not the angular forms characteristic of that period but are of a later, rotund, period. Some experts suggest that the probable period in which it was written was 1500, plus or minus twenty years" (1962).

A. H. Carter reports the similar judgement of Miss Nill (a friend of Mrs. Voynich who accompanied him when he examined the manuscript in (1946): "The style of the drawings, especially the conventions of the line drawings in the women, suggest to Miss Nill, quite properly, that the manuscript is far later than the thirteenth or fourteenth centuries. There is nothing 'Gothic' or angular about them. They are fat and rotund and suggest in their style the influence of the realism of a later period. The coloring of the illustrations may well support a later date than the thirteenth century" (1946, p. 2).

Among those agreeing on a sixteenth-century date for the manuscript is Dr. Charles Singer, who states in his letter to John Tiltman (12 November, 1957), "The date of the manuscript would, in my opinion, be somewhere in the neighborhood of 1520 or perhaps a little later...." We have already seen that he connects the origin of the manuscript with John Dee and Prague. Leonell Strong makes an interesting suggestion, that "The format and use of certain peculiar symbols (mirror images of the Italian d or di and el, respectively) are evidences that the author was probably familiar with the manuscript of Leonardo da Vinci's 'Anatomy' (written about 1510)" (1945, p. 608). Strong's identification of Anthony Askham as author of the manuscript also leads him to place it in the sixteenth century, since Askham's known works were published from 1525 on.

Robert Brumbaugh presents perhaps the most detailed and specific evidence for a sixteenth-century date: "...it seemed plain to me from the outset that this is not a thirteenth century manuscript, and I doubted whether Rudolph II or any of his experts ever had accepted it as an autograph work by Roger Bacon. Detail after detail pointed to a later date closer to 1500 than 1300....Sagittarius wears a fifteenth-century Florentine archer's hat in his medallion (though it is retouched over the month name). A clock, tucked away in folio 85r, has a short hour and long minute hand, a style not developed until the fifteenth century....In short, this manuscript is at earliest a compilation of about 1500" (1975, p. 349). (A number of the points Brumbaugh employs to bolster his argument depend upon his own decipherment and associated specific identifications of the symbols with numerals, etc.; I have omitted these, retaining only his more objectively based comments. For further discussion of the "clock", see 3.3.6.)

Finally, Jeffrey Krischer obtained, in the course of his research, the opinions of a number of experts at Harvard University concerning the date and provenience of the manuscript (see Section 6.7). He reports their judgement as follows:

"Professor Giles Constable (professor of medieval history, Harvard University), in looking over photostats of the manuscript, dated the manuscript as sixteenth century and suggested that the script might be a form of private language motivated by the desire to keep such a powerful document from the general public. Science in this period represented power and if one assumes the manuscript is indeed describing plants and biological and astrological phenomena, then this line of reasoning is quite acceptable. The date of the manuscript was again placed in the sixteenth century by Mr. Rodney Dennis (curator of manuscripts in Houghton Library of the Harvard College Library). Mr. Dennis identified the script to be in the style of the sixteenth century humanist script. Another dating of the manuscript was due to Dr. Franklin Ludden. Dr. Ludden determined the date as being in the period 1475 to 1550. His method of dating is based upon analyzing the style of the drawings; the features of the nude figures; the stylization of the botanical drawings." [Krischer 1969, pp. 51–52.]

In consideration of this review of many pronouncements made by scholars and experts, I have made a rough "box score" summarizing their opinions. It is crude, but it may aid the reader in bringing some order out of the multiplicity of judgements that have accumulated over the years during which the mysterious manuscript has been studied. In the tally shown below, I have arbitrarily assigned a score of "2" to such statements as "in the judgement of experts", or "the consensus of opinion", and a score of "1" to the opinion of a single writer, without attempting to weight them in any greater detail.

dates	score
1250–1399	5
1400–1550	12

To my mind, this summary of expert opinion does, in fact, lend considerable weight to a relatively late date for the manuscript.

Chapter 3

Avenues of Attack: The Drawings

3.1 Relationship of the Drawings to the Text

It has been suggested by some students, baffled and exasperated by repeated, futile attempts to make sense out of the pictures as a way of cribbing into the text, that there may be no necessary connection between the writing and the illustration on any given page. The pictures, some have proposed, may be a "blind", introduced to mislead the would-be decipherer and further conceal some dangerous secrets of a totally different character. Most serious students of the manuscript appear to be certain, however, that text and pictures were drawn together and form a related whole. Elizebeth Friedman states, for example, "There can be no question that the same scribe wrote the text and made the drawings, as any handwriting expert would readily agree" (1962).

Dr. A. H. Carter concurs in the above opinion: "Because the same ink and the same kind of penstrokes appear in the illustrations and because the text forms an integral and unified part of many of the illustrations, it appears probable that the same person wrote the text and drew the illustrations" (1946, p. 1). Tiltman feels that we have a right to expect that the text belongs to the illustrations, "in the complete absence of evidence to the contrary" (1968, p. 11). In the view of those who have studied the manuscript with care, the text seems to be intricately interwoven in and around the pictures in such a way as to have rendered a close collaboration necessary between scribe and draftsman if they were, in fact, different persons. In some cases, text strings are written on parts of pictures (for instance, as labels on the objects called "pharmaceutical jars" by many students in folios 99r and 102v2, and in the segments and cells of the intricate diagrams on folios 85–86 as well as many astrological and cosmological drawings.

3.2 Nature and Characteristics of the Drawings

The impression made upon the modern viewer first coming upon a photocopy of the manuscript (the form in which it has most frequently met the eye of students), is one of extreme oddity, quaintness, and foreignness—one might almost say unearthliness. To the reader who has seen pictures of more typical illuminated medieval manuscripts, these pages look very different indeed from what he expects to find in such a book. For me, at least, after working with the photocopy intensively for some weeks, the initial impression of "queerness" lost its prominence and gave way to other, more considered reactions which may be summed up as follows:

Homogeneity of Style. The drawings and text of the entire manuscript seem to me to form a consistent whole, the product of one school or group of closely related persons if not of a single person.

Craftsmanship and Pragmatism. The scribe (or scribes) seems not to have been motivated by design or esthetic criteria any more than by what we, today, would consider realism. Many of the plant folios and some cosmological designs (notably 9r, 11v, 16v, 33v, 41v, 49r, 68v2, 67r1, 67r2, and 68v1) present a stalwart, bold felicity of composition that is almost architectonic in its quality, and (to me) quite pleasing. The impression which I receive is emphatically one of craftsmanship rather than art.

Structural Regularity. I gain a persistent impression of the presence of rules and relationships, a definite structure with its own "logic", however erratic and bizarre it might appear when compared to present-day concepts. The intricate compound forms in the script and its matter-of-fact, rather austere style all confirm this impression of craftsmanlike and logical construction in my mind. As I will try to show below, there appears to be a similar quality in the diagrams, as if conventionalized forms are used almost as symbols and combined to build up more complex symbolic statements. As a part of this quality of "constructedness," there is a persistent tectonic element of style in the drawings, emphasizing three-dimensional forms, symmetry, and connectedness of parts.

Idiosyncratic, Individual Quality. As has been noted by others, the manuscript seems to stand totally apart from all other even remotely comparable documents. No one, to my knowledge, has so far discovered anything else at all like it. It strikes the viewer as a very strong and definite statement, completely independent of any known style or doctrine. It seems to be deliberate, designed production of an individual or a small group working alone. (This apparent isolation may, of course, be due simply to our failure to discover the other documents or philosophies related to it, but it seems unlikely that no trace of such parallels would have been recognized by the many eminent medieval and Renaissance scholars who have examined the manuscript). In Section 3.2.3 I will discuss some other manuscripts that have been mentioned as possibly comparable to the Voynich manuscript.

The above are my own impressions of the visual qualities of the manuscript; we will see below how some other students have reacted to it.

3.2.1 Provenience and Style

Voynich communicates his impression of the contrast between this manuscript and the other, more typical medieval manuscripts with which it was found: "It was such an ugly duckling compared with the other manuscripts, with their rich decorations in gold and colors, that my interest was aroused at once" (1921, p. 415). Dr. Carter provides a detailed description of the manuscript, with considerable emphasis on the draftsmanship, pigments, and style; his personal reaction is as follows: "The illustrations are done with great care, not with attention to providing a pleasing picture but rather with attention to accuracy of detail. They are, as Miss Nill pointed out, the kind of drawings that a scientist would make for himself, not illustrations designed to enhance the beauty of the book" (1946, p. 1).

Students disagree to some extent on the quality of the drawings as accurate portrayals of their apparent subject matter. There is also considerable disagreement (not surprisingly) about their esthetic quality. To some, they are pleasing; to others, they seem clumsy, inept, and childish. An anonymous author in Scientific American takes a critical and contemptuous view: "These pictures are crudely drawn in by a person who obviously was somewhat lacking in artistic ability, even for a thirteenth-century scribe" (1921, p. 432). Again, the same author expresses a similar opinion a few pages later: "The scribe was not a great success as an artist; his efforts sometimes remind us of the crude outlines we produce in impressing upon a draftsman what we want and how we want it" (p. 439). Charles Singer, in his letter to John Tiltman, 12 November 1957, expresses a similar contempt for the representational and artistic quality of the plant pictures: "The figures of plants are not botanical at all but of the kind one makes when doodling or the children make of plants."

As will also be noted in the discussion of the script below (4.1.1), while many students have briefly mentioned the style of the drawings as a factor in their judgements concerning the date and provenience of the manuscript, none of them provide any real facts to back up their remarks beyond a vague reference to "experts" not further identified. As we have seen above, Steele remarks, "It is strange that the draftsman should have so completely escaped all medieval and Renaissance influences" (1928b, p. 563). Carter (1946) refers to the "rotundity" of the human figures and the lack of "Gothic" style as evidence for a date later than the thirteenth or fourteenth centuries. Panofsky (1954, p. 1) assesses the style of the drawings as "fairly provincial"; he also states that there is no evidence of influence from the Italian Renaissance style. In sum, it appears as if no one has made or documented a really careful and systematic attempt to contrast and compare the style of the Voynich manuscript drawings to other manuscripts of various origins and dates such as could answer some of our questions.

3.2.2 Pigments and Inks.

Dr. Carter provides a detailed description of the pigments. This deserves to be quoted in full, in spite of its considerable length, since few students ever get to see the manuscript in any other form except black and white photocopies.

> "Some of the colors appear to be colored ink or water color, some a kind of crayon, and some an opaque kind of paint like poster paint. There are many colors; the ink is good strong brown; there is an amber-like ink, like British-tan leather goods; a bright, not quite brilliant, blue ink or water color; an opaque aquamarine; a good strong red, carmine rather than scarlet or vermillion; a dirty yellow (the yellow and browns of the sunflower illustration are like those, only a little faded, of the Van Gogh sunflower picture; the greens are less brilliant); a red that looks like a bloodstain about a week old; a dirty green; an opaque green; a kind of green crayon; and several other greens of various hues, intensity, value, and texture; a red that looks like face rouge in color and texture; a thick red that makes dots of color that you could scrape with your finger nail; a red ink just like ordinary red ink today; a blue that sparkles with tiny fragments (not apparently by design).
>
> "Some of the colors are flowed on as with a brush; some have left pigment-borded contours as where a little pool had stood unblotted. Some may have been blotted (with cloth?). Some were applied with strokes of the quill, and some were scrubbed into the vellum with a blunt quill which had become furry on the end as a wooden stylus does after repeated use." [Carter 1946, p. 2.]

3.2.3 Relationships to Some Other Illustrated Manuscripts.

My sources have disappointingly little to say on this topic. One gains the impression, whether justly or not, that the bizarre quality of the pictures and the difficulty of identifying with any certainty what they portray, has caused most scholars familiar with more conventional medieval manuscripts to throw up their hands in disgust after the most cursory glance. The "herbal" pictures of complete plants and the astrological diagrams associated with recognizable zodiac figures offer perhaps the most immediate promise for comparisons to other herbal or astrological drawings. Panofsky (1954, p. 1) addresses the problem as follows: "Manuscripts in plain language remotely comparable to the Voynich manuscript are, unfortunately, of at least four kinds: first, herbals: second, cosmological and astrological treatises; third, medical treatises in the narrow sense of the term; fourth, possibly, treatises on alchemy." He suggests that the mystical drawings of a thirteenth-century monk. Opicinus de Canistris, may be worth examining as comparable astrological and cosmological works. Father Petersen (1953, p. 2), mentions the visionary writings and drawings of St. Hildegarde of Bingen as possibly comparable, and he recommends the fourteenth-century Vatican manuscript 1906 as similar to some of the astronomical drawings.

Tiltman states his considered opinion: "To the best of my knowledge no one has been able to find any point of connection with any other medieval manuscript or early printed book. This is all the stranger because the range of writing and illustration on the subject of the plant world from the early Middle Ages right through into the sixteenth and even seventeenth centuries is very limited indeed" (1968, p. 11). Elizebeth Friedman expresses her own and William Friedman's views when she states flatly, "So far as is known, there is no . . . key or crib." (1962) (For those unfamiliar with the term as used by cryptanalysts, a "crib" is a parallel or comparable text in a known language that can be used to break into an unknown text as the three parallel inscriptions in different scripts on the Rosetta Stone were employed in the decipherment of Egyptian hieroglyphs. A crib can also take the form of a guess as to the subject matter, or individual words that might be found at certain places in an unknown text.)

Opicinus de Canistris (A.D. 1296–ca. 1336). R. Salomon (1936) describes the visionary and mystical drawings of this monk and shows extensive illustrations of them. Born in Pavia, Italy, Opicinus had a difficult and unhappy life; he fell and injured his head as a child, a mishap which may have had a central part in the later episode of illness and visions which he recorded in the remarkable book of drawings studied by Salomon. The draftsmanship is very delicate and beautiful, with an artistic quality totally different from that of the Voynich manuscript. The designs are extremely dense and intricate, with many concentric circles, intersecting arcs and lines, and bands densely packed with tiny sets of numbers and letters. Many of them show carefully-drawn human figures with well-drafted maps of the world and other, smaller human figures inside them or interlocking with their outlines.

Maps and architectural plans are a prominent feature of Opicinus' productions, as are Biblical symbols such as animals standing for the Four Gospels, and the signs of the zodiac. One drawing shows his entire autobiography, from his birth up to the year 1335 or 1336 (when he drew the pictures), all packed onto one page. They are all closely overwritten with Latin text, in very tiny, neat letters; the text is primarily about Opicinus himself (his feelings, his sinfulness and unworthiness, events in his life, etc.) represented in symbolic ways interwoven with religious symbolism and quotations from the Bible and patristic writings. The only real similarity to the Voynich manuscript drawings is the encyclopedic quality, in combining so many disparate elements symbolically within a structural and semantic unit. The appearance and style of Opicinus' productions are totally at variance with those of our manuscript; Opicinus was a trained artist and draftsman, and had produced an earlier book of beautiful architectural drawings of his native town. Pavia, as well as a number of devotional religious tracts.

St. Hildegarde de Bingen (A.D. 1098–1179). St. Hildegarde, abbess of a convent in Germany, was gifted with powers of prophecy and mystical vision. She produced several books describing and illustrating these visions, as well as a book about the causes and cures of disease. Her drawings appear considerably more like those in our manuscript on the face of it; they are relatively "provincial" and "crude," and have none of the delicacy and professional quality of Opicinus' drawings. Hildegarde's drawings have some of the same symbolic, "constructed" quality as those in the Voynich manuscript. They show rather different elements of content, however: animal heads and recognizable figures of Christ and the Virgin, for example. Some of the drawings appear to have banks of rays, clouds, or flames similar to those on some Voynich manuscript folios.

There is little or no text or labelling within any of the illustrations I have seen of Hildegarde's works; their meaning is explicated in connected text elsewhere in the books. Their symbolism, as explained there, is entirely Biblical and Christian (a sun-like ball of flame represents Christ's burning love; three smaller stars above it are the Trinity; heads spouting vapors are people preaching the Gospel or using words to do the work of the devil, etc.). The designs have a highly symmetrical, abstract quality similar to many Voynich pictures, and some have similar arrangements of small cells or radiating lines in bands around a circle. It is amusing to note, after all the pontifications of experts about "rotund" figures and the absence of "Gothic" style in the Voynich manuscript, that Hildegarde's twelfth-century human figures are well-filled-out, vivacious, plump, and lively. (For a good discussion of Hildegarde's works and reproductions of many drawings see Singer 1975, pp. 1–58.)

In spite of all the above points regarding general similarities. I cannot see any really close kinship between these drawings and those of the Voynich manuscript. The main import of the comparison with Opicinus' and Hildegarde's productions is to demonstrate that such individualized, encyclopedic, symbolic works were by no means uncommon in the Middle Ages. The astrological manuscript (Vatican 1906) referred to by Petersen is not really very similar to the Voynich pictures either: a careful study of the numerous illustrations of this and other similar manuscripts (in Saxl 1915 and 1927) shows very few parallels to the cosmological or astrological diagrams in our manuscript. Most such medieval astrological pictures feature human figures, figures of animals, and other clearly recognizable graphic elements which are much less prominent in the abstract style of the Voynich drawings.

3.3 *Content of Specific Classes of Drawings*

At the risk of boring some readers, I will go into the appearance of the drawings in some detail in the following paragraphs: for various reasons, it is not possible to reproduce many of these folios for inclusion in this paper, and so a verbal description must suffice to convey some idea of their content to the reader who cannot obtain access to a photocopy of the manuscript. None of the sources I have studied has accorded much attention to most of these diagrams, or discussed their content in any way, excepting for a few passing mentions of details on this or that folio which some student happened to find useful or suggestive in connection with a particular theory of his own. Therefore, I hope the reader will bear with me through the following somewhat lengthy discussion of individual drawings, and my attempt to come to grips with their specific content and detail. Figure 4 provides an overview and classification of the folios according to their apparent subject matter.

3.3.1 *Herbal Drawings.*

At first glance, the numerous illustrations of whole plants, usually accompanied by one or more paragraphs of text, seem to offer the best hope of a successful attack on the enigma. Other students have bent their efforts vigorously to the task of relating some, at least, of these drawings to known plants or to illustrations in other herbals, with results that can only be described as disappointingly vague and ambiguous. Elizabeth Friedman summarizes the most substantial of the identification attempts as follows: "Although a well-known American botanist. Dr. Hugh O'Neill, believes that he has identified two American plants in the illustrations, no other scholar has corroborated this, all agreeing that none of the plants depicted is indigenous to America. Sixteen plants, however, have been indisputably identified as European by the great Dutch botanist Holm. The remainder are composite; i.e., the root system belongs to one plant, the stem system to another, the leaves and flowers to still others. A few show imaginary root or flower structures." (1962) Unfortunately, since Mrs. Friedman's article appeared in a newspaper, there was no citation of the reference to Holm's substantial discoveries: I have not, so far, been able to turn up a published source for this information. Petersen appears to have obtained a detailed list of Holm's identifications from some source, and noted many of them on his transcript. In spite of Mrs. Friedman's emphatic and convincing statement of Holm's findings, later writers such as Tiltman (1968, 1975) do not seem to accept them as any more final than those of O'Neill.

Many scholars seem to question O'Neill's dramatic identification of the sunflower plant on folio 93r (1944, p. 126). I can see good reasons, also, for questioning his "capsicum" or pepper-plant identification; the picture involved, on folio 100r, is among the small, sketchy drawings arranged in rows next to a "pharmaceutical jar", possibly representing a recipe for an herbal mixture. (For a discussion of these "pharmaceutical" drawings, see Section 3.3.2 below.) The objects O'Neill sees as pepper fruits could as easily be leaves, drawn according to the curious, blocky convention habitually adopted by the scribe of the manuscript, to be discussed further below. This impression is supported by the fact that they are colored green, and not red. The "pepper" identification was exploited by Brumbaugh in his decipherment; he suggests that the coloring of the "pepper" green rather than red was a matter of deliberate concealment (1974, p. 546). Many students have taken a stab at identifying the plant pictures; they are probably the most closely-studied drawings in the manuscript. The list of plant identifications compiled by Petersen in his hand transcript includes identifications he attributes to Mr. and Mrs. Voynich. O'Neill, and Holm (Petersen 1966).

At this point, I would like to pursue a brief digression concerning the idiosyncrasies of style in many plant structures shown in the herbal folios. For what they are worth, I will present my own subjective, and admittedly personal, reactions, in the hope that they may stimulate others to examine these drawings more closely and reach their own conclusions. The plant parts frequently have a curious blocky, chunky, rough-hewn look, with platform-like structures surrounded by hard outlines

14

defining a sharp change of plane. To my eye, this characteristic convention causes some of the structures to appear as if they had been molded out of plastic; see, for example, the root crowns in folios 44v, 45r, 45v, 37v, 27v, 23r, 9r, 11r, 13r, 16v, and many others too numerous to list. They seem to be provided with one or several circular platforms, consisting of tubes or inverted cones with flat, disk-like tops, from which the stems protrude, often encircled by a ring like a washer or gasket at their point of emergence (see figures 5-7 for some typical details from these drawings).

An analogous structural peculiarity may be seen in the leaves of folios 15r, 88r, 100r, 101v2 (some of which are "pharmaceutical" rather than "herbal" drawings); they seem to end in similar platform-and-gasket-like swellings. In the root structures of folios 3v, 22v, 45r, 45v, 54v, 65r, and others, tubers are shown strung along the root fibers in a similar blocky arrangement, like sections of pipe fitted together. In folio 53r, they even seem rectangular, like a string of wooden blocks (figures 5-7 show some examples of these forms). I cannot guess at the significance which may lie behind this pervasive element of style, but an understanding of it may well be important in interpreting the drawings and in tracing their origin. The same stylistic convention is apparent in the "pipes," "tubes," and cloudlike structures in the mysterious folios featuring human figures (folios 75r and following), to be discussed more fully in 3.3.5 below.

A somewhat similar blocky, rough appearance is seen in some herbal drawings in other manuscripts, that have been copied over and over again from some much earlier source by successive scribes. This is the case, for example, in some early Anglo-Saxon medical manuscripts based on the drawings of Dioscorides. Illustrations I have seen of some plant pictures in an herbal attributed to Arnaldus of Villanova, entitled "Tractatus de Virtutibus Herbarum", have the same chunky look as some of the Voynich manuscript folios (cf. also Tiltman 1968, figure 6). If, as this would imply, our herbal drawings are copies at many removes from some earlier source, we should still be able to recognize them by their general composition on the page and their structure (number of stems, fruits or flowers, rough shape of leaves and roots, etc.), especially since, as Tiltman pointed out (1968, p. 11), the different sets of illustrations for early herbals were relatively few and the same sets of pictures were used again and again over many centuries by successive compilers.

I think, rather, that this angular quality is a feature of the scribe's personal style, and may even have some symbolic significance. It is executed quite boldly and uncompromisingly, and does not seem to be an unintentional result of ineptness or clumsiness; the scribe definitely intended the plant parts to appear as he showed them. I offer the suggestion that the draftsman of these pictures was more accustomed to, and interested in, making mechanical or structural sketches than in illustrating natural objects.

Another point should be raised here, concerning the presence of animals and human faces attached to or intertwined with the roots of some plants: for animals, see folios 25v, 49r; for faces, see 33r, 55v, 89r1. Some root structures have the appearance of animal or human bodies, with the main plant stem emerging where the neck would be: see folios 99v, 90v1, 89v1 (lions?), and 46v (a bird with spread wings: an eagle?). Some roots resemble the foot or feet of an animal, with claws and toes (e.g., 89r1). There are known parallels to this practice in a number of early herbals. Frequently, if a plant was supposed to provide an antidote to or protection from the bite of some venomous creature, the animal was shown under or near the plant, almost as a mnemonic device to emphasize the association. The Voynich manuscript examples may have a similar purpose, except that in many cases the animal seems to be eating, hanging from, or burrowing in the plant much too happily to be a target for its ill effects. Perhaps the intent is horticultural, implying that the worm, bird, etc., is frequently found with the plant, and feeds on it. Alternatively, and most probably (to my mind), the meaning is purely symbolic, as is common in alchemical manuscripts. (For examples of animal forms, see figures 8 and 9.)

The faces attached to some plant roots (see 33r, 89r1), and the suggestions of eyes, horns, snouts, etc., on other plant parts (see 38r, 28r, and figure 9 for examples), are considerably harder to explain. Tiltman (1968) cites the examples of the "barnacle goose" and the mandrake, well known to all students of early herbals. Some such personification of plants, or mingling of plant and animal life into one form, may be involved in the Voynich manuscript. The plant may be considered to engender or nourish an animal, or to possess some animal or human qualities like those imputed to the mandrake. In any case, I would like to suggest that these two signal oddities—the curious sculptural modelling of plant parts, and the presence of animal and human forms among plants parts—should receive more systematic study in comparison with similar practices in known herbal and alchemical manuscripts (an interesting parallel in an alchemical manuscript dated to the sixteenth century will be noted in Section 8.8 below).

Another curious structural feature of many plant folios is the rigidly and mechanically symmetrical arrangement of plant stems and leaves. For example, the stems rising from the root crowns in folios 5r, 22r, 35v, 40r, and 90r2, and the arrangement of the main roots in folios 2r, 11r, 11v, 14r, 14v, 22v, 45v, (and others) all exhibit a strange reentrant form, crossing one another or twining together in a curious knot-like manner (see figures 5 and 7). Leaves are arranged on stems in a rhythmically symmetrical pattern, for example in folios 3r, 13v, 22v, 29r, 41r, etc., which seems highly contrived and

15

mechanical. in harmony with the architectonic quality, exhibited elsewhere. This quality is present even in the flowers or "fruits" that grow from these strange "molded-plastic" plants: the flower on folio 90v1, for example, looks like a set of metal spikes, rigidly fixed together; flowers in folios 3v, 6r, 56v, 90r2, and 96r look like the hoods of vent-pipes (see figure 8). (Again, some striking parallels will be mentioned in the alchemical manuscript discussed in Section 8.8).

3.3.2 *Pharmaceutical Drawings.*

The pages in this section of the manuscript show rows of small, sketchy plants or plant parts, which seem to emphasize one structure—roots or leaves—at the expense of the remainder. They are so abbreviated as to appear almost like mnemonic or shorthand symbols referring to plants already illustrated more fully in other folios, or to plants otherwise familiar to the scribe and his colleagues. A determined effort by several students to relate these sketches to the herbal drawings has not been very successful, however.

The other salient feature of these pages is the presence of objects that have been said to resemble pharmaceutical jars or drug containers. On some folios (e.g., 99r and 102v2), the jars are "labelled" with phrases or words in the Voynich script, unfortunately almost illegible in the photocopy at my disposal because the pigment filling the body of the jars in many cases tends to obscure the writing. In other cases, a "label" seems to appear near the jar which probably relates to it, or to the "recipe" it stands for. A similar "label" appears near each small plant sketch in the rows; it is hard to tell, in some cases, which of several neighboring plants is meant by each "label". One or more paragraphs of text are present between the rows of pictures. The jar is usually at the left margin of each such row, irresistibly suggesting that the plants in that row were to be used to make up the compound prescription symbolized by that jar. The design of the jars is very ornate and florid, with many fitted cylindrical sections decorated by geometric designs, fancy embellishments around the edges, curly feet, and elaborate finials or handles on the top (some of the latter resembling, to the irreverent modern eye, the central ornaments on an automobile hood); see figure 15. The ornamentation and the "pipe-section" structure is similar in style to that of the "cans" from which some figures emerge on astrological folios (see below, 3.3.3) and to some of the fancy platform or pipe structures in the folios featuring human figures (see 3.3.5).

3.3.3 *Astrological and Astronomical Drawings.*

Prominent among the drawings are a series of circular designs apparently clearly related to the months of the year, and each provided with a central medallion showing a zodiac symbol. A recognizable, if oddly-spelled, month name has been written in what most students agree is a different and later hand than that of the Voynich script. Figure 10 shows details of these month names. The page for January and February (Aquarius and Capricorn) is missing, having been removed before the manuscript was found by Voynich. The student's first hope of getting anywhere through the known association with months or zodiac signs is soon disappointed, since there is apparently little else in the diagrams that can be remotely associated with conventional astrological diagrams and horoscopes.

Most of the diagrams have approximately thirty female figures shown around the periphery in one, two, or three rows: some of the figures are free-standing, while others appear to emerge from vertical or horizontal objects like cans or tubes, some of which are decorated with a variety of heraldic-looking devices. Some of the figures are nude, but others are partially or fully clothed; the clothing visible on some of the figures includes veils, hats, crowns, and draperies of considerable elaboration, which should be traceable to a particular place and time with a little research. A few of the figures, as noted by Petersen on his hand transcripts, may well be male rather than female. A careful study of the apparently intentionally distinctive designs on their "cans" may provide a clue to identification of the beings, or permit cross-matching some of them on different diagrams. Some of the "cans" have crenellations like castle battlements. Figure 11 shows an analysis of the numbers of figures on the different rows in each diagram; these arrangements may correspond to some classification of the days of the month important for medical practice: for example, the "Egyptian days" or "critical days".

The months of April and May with zodiac signs Aries and Taurus, stand out in contrast to the rest in that they each have two circular medallions (folios 70v1, 71r, 71v, and 72r1), and each has only fifteen figures, as if the two diagrams for the same month were intended somehow to complement each other, an idea supported by the fact that the bull or ram is light-colored in one case and dark-colored in the other. An amusing matter for special note is the fact that the animal in each case is enjoying a meal: Aries is dining with evident relish on the leaves of a small shrub, and Taurus is applying himself with equal determination to the contents of a sort of manger or feedbox carefully and realistically placed at his disposal. These details, in my view, support a horticultural, medical, or agricultural context rather than a magical or mystical one (although

16

this can be only an impression). At any rate. I find it a pleasing indication of the scribe's pragmatic and down-to-earth approach to his subject matter. whatever its meaning may one day prove to be.

A number of other drawings in which the sun. moon. and stars are prominently featured may be provisionally classified as astronomical. I will attempt to present. in the following paragraphs. a sketch of the principal structural elements in each of these. since it is impossible to reproduce most of them in this paper. Figure 12 provides a summary of the numbers of major elements in these diagrams along with the "cosmological" diagrams to be discussed in the next section.

Folio 67r1 shows a central face. probably representing the moon. surrounded by a twelve-pointed star; one side of each ray is decorated with stars. the other filled in with solid pigment. In the continuation of the pair of segments containing each ray. single words or phrases in the Voynich script alternate with groups of one or two small stars. Three concentric rings of text surround the whole. with a decorative marker indicating what may be a starting position. Folio 67v1 is based on a somewhat similar plan. showing a widely-smiling sun face in the center of a system of seventeen double rays. in which phrases of text alternate with groups of from one to four small stars. A single outer ring of text is interspersed with decorative separators.

Folio 67r2 is a complex circular design based on twelve-major-divisions. In its center is an eight-pointed star. surrounded by a ring of eight words. A dashed line indicates a starting point (?). Twelve moon faces. all facing to the right. occupy the next ring outside the central area; each is accompanied by a text string. Twelve pie-shaped segments extend outward. one from each of the twelve moon faces. Seven of these contain additional words. and all contain paragraphs of text. Each segment contains a phrase. apparently written in darker or heavier fashion. in its outer extremity. A paragraph consisting of three lines. (of which the middle one appears to be in heavier ink). is seen beneath the circular design.

Folio 68r1 shows a roughly circular field of stars. with words or phrases in the Voynich script written beside each. At the top is a larger circular medallion with a sun face. surrounded by a ring of text: a similar. balancing circle containing a moon face. also surrounded by text. appears at the bottom. There are at least twenty-eight stars with labels (some may have been cut off in the photocopy). Some of the stars also seem larger or differently-colored than others. a distinction which may have some significance in the doctrine of the scribe. Folio 68r2 appears to show a related or companion diagram. again on a circular field of stars; in this case. however. only the twenty-four stars in a central cluster are labelled. The sun face is at the bottom. the moon face at the top of the star field in this diagram. Attempts to cross-match the rings of text around sun and moon. or the labels of individual stars on the two folios have so far been fruitless. Folio 68v1 shows a central face. perhaps a sun. with a diadem or headband. surrounded by small flames or rays. A set of sixteen large double rays emerges from the central face. one side dark and the other filled with small stars. This seems similar in form to folio 67r1. and may be related to it in the sun-moon pairing that seems to form a basic theme in the cosmological or alchemical doctrine involved in the manuscript. The continuations of the thirty-two separate segments containing the rays contain alternate phrases of text and fields of small stars. Two outer rings of text surround the whole. with starting positions indicated by vertical lines.

Folio 68v2 shows an eight-pointed. sun-like center surrounded by eight petal-shaped rays; beyond this are four segments separated by four centrifugal lines of text. There is a further subdivision into eight segments. separated by four more centrifugal text lines emerging from the points of the central "petals." Four fields of small stars are interspersed among the segments. A single text ring surrounds the whole. its starting point shown by a vertical line.

Finally. folio 68r3 displays a moon face within a system of eight major pie-shaped radiating segments containing four alternating fields of small stars and centrifugal lines of text. separated by further subsidiary lines of text. in a plan similar to that of 68v2 just described. A single ring of text surrounds the periphery. in which no starting marker can be discerned.

It should be apparent that there is a systematic content of some sort in these diagrams. It may relate to contrasted hours of night and day. times or events governed by different classes of stars. or effects of the sun and moon on the humors. elements. seasons. ages of man. winds. directions. etc. (to name some of the entities that are grouped by "fours" in medieval cosmology and medicine). A group of seven small stars together in one segment of 68r3 (as noted also by other students). could well represent the Pleiades. Surely a careful and determined analysis of this wealth of structured content in conjunction with a study of medieval doctrines should turn up something of use to us in interpreting the meaning of the diagrams.

3.3.4 Cosmological or Meteorological Drawings.

There remain many diagrams based on a fundamentally circular plan which show radiating segments. pipe-like or cell-like elements. cloud and vapor clusters. and a central star-like or sun-like medallion. Text words and single letters are placed in or written along many of the cells and rays. and in concentric circular bands around them. with starting points indicated. in some cases. by vertical lines or decorative markers. Figure 12 shows a survey of the numbers of major elements in these and the astronomical diagrams. It seems likely that a systematic attempt to correlate numbers of related objects may turn up some

17

interesting parallels among known medieval cosmological systems. Number in itself had a magical significance in much medieval and Renaissance philosophy, probably originating in Pythagorean doctrines. Medieval magical books often showed elaborate parallel tables of "correspondences," comprising lists of like-numbered things that could be arranged in twos, threes, fours, up to elevens and twelves. In the Pythagorean philosophy of sacred or magical numerology, the numbers four, seven, nine, and twelve were considered especially important. Figure 14 shows some sets of elements extracted from tables in Agrippa (1970); figure 35 shows elements important in the Cabala (see Section 8.7), and figure 34 contains some parallel lists of elements from Galenic medicine.

One very curious, and also (to my eye) very attractive diagram on folios 85–86r2 (a portion of the recto of a large, multiply folded page) shows a central sun face surrounded by four major segments. A line of text with a pair of verticals indicating a starting place runs around the central sun. This is in turn surrounded by a sort of scalloped parapet, over which four human figures may be seen; these figures seem clearly to represent a child, a boy, a man, and an oldster bent forward over his cane. Over the head of each figure is a copious paragraph of text. The four main segments are separated by graceful spouts of vapor that emerge beyond an outer circular border containing a ring of text, and recurve gracefully back into the segment to the left of their point of emergence. This drawing seems likely to be related to the four seasons, the four ages of man, the four humors, etc., as shown in figure 34; it appears that these associations might provide a point of attack into the text within its four sections.

The general plan of the "four ages" diagram just described is highly reminiscent of a figure from an Anglo-Saxon medical manuscript (Caius College, Cambridge, MS. 428, fo. 50; Grattan 1952, p. 94). The Anglo-Saxon diagram shows four human figures holding jars from which four spouts fall toward the center of the circular medallion and divide it into four main segments. A small central circle shows another human figure receiving the effects of these outpourings, within a ring of text in very clumsy and illiterate Latin, illegible in the illustration. An outer ring of text surrounding the whole contains another laboriously copied Latin sentence, "Quattuor humores bisbina partes liquores effundunt teneri per corpora sic michrochosmi." On either side of the four large figures are more Latin words, some illegible, which seem to refer to the humors, properties, and elements ("colera rubia," "calidus," "sicca," "sanguis," "calidus," "humidus"; ??, "frigida," "humida"; "terra," "frigida," "sicca"). Figures of this sort are very common in medieval astrological and medical manuscripts, and refer to the central doctrine of the "microcosm" or "small world" of the human being, thought to reflect or recapitulate in miniature the elements and relations of the larger universe or "macrocosm." The usual form of such diagrams shows a human figure with lines connecting its parts with other words or pictures supposed to stand for forces affecting them in the stars, weather, etc. (cf Saxl 1915 and 1927; Bober 1948).

Another very remarkable diagram on folio 67v2 seems to stand in a class all by itself, unlike anything in other manuscripts. It suggests a meteorological theme, based on four major divisions that may be the seasons. Four puffs of vapor rush in from the four corners, half-concealing (or, perhaps, giving birth to or supporting?) two suns and two moons. (Newbold interpreted one or more of these features as a "solar eclipse.") A dotted line extends inward to the center from the sun on the upper left, perhaps indicating the starting point of the chronology or story. A sun with spiral rays inside a square occupies the center. More vapor puffs squirt out centrifugally between the four outer ones, and lines of text are written along bands leading to both sets. Strangest of all, the four outer corners are occupied by roughly circular arrangements of face-like, balloon-shaped objects strung along pipes or bands to form simple, angular, geometric figures (an "X", a "4", etc.). One of these forms, in the lower left corner of the page, shows four balloon-faces in a U-like arrangement opening at the top, superimposed on a circle with three segments colored blue, green, and red; as we will see below, this tripartite circular figure occurs elsewhere in the manuscript, and may represent a conventionalized map of the inhabited world ("T-map"). The only interpretation that suggests itself for these geometric figures is that of crucial conjunctions of planets, or magical "star-figures," associated with the four seasons, directions, winds, ages of man, or other important events in the unguessable doctrine being expounded in this enigmatic work. The stringing of circles or dots (although not faces) along lines in geometrical arrangements is seen in *Picatrix* (Ritter and Plessner 1962), where the intent is to show "star pictures" or constellations to be employed as magical characters (see 8.4). Somewhat similar characters made up of dots or circles strung on lines are seen in alchemical manuscripts as well as in some magical alphabets (see 8.8 and 9.4, and figures 41 and 42).

Another unique diagram, folio 57v, shows five concentric circles of text with a faintly-indicated common starting point at the upper left. In the center are four human figures, shown from the waist up; four bands of text radiate outward between the figures from a central scalloped medallion, and four more text lines are disposed between the figures in such a way that their raised hands seem to point at, grasp, or support these. The structure of eight bands of text in two groups of four each is similar to that of many other diagrams in the manuscript. This, too, is the diagram that contains a sequence of seventeen enigmatic symbols repeated four times around the second of its concentric text rings. It is one of very few cases of cyclically repeating lists anywhere in the text, and has been subjected to much attention by students as a possible "key" (see figure 24).

Folio 68v3 is the drawing referred to by Newbold as a "spiral nebula." A central circle is divided by a horizontal line through the center; the upper half is again bisected by a line from top to center. This plan resembles the scribbled geometric figure in the center of folio 85–86v3 (for which see below). A word or phrase is written in each of the upper halves, and a longer paragraph in the lower semicircle. A ring of text surrounds this figure, with a starting point shown by a marker. Four major outer segments are separated by gracefully-curving bands of text; within these are watery or wavy outlines, defining fields containing curving rows of stars on the same spiral plan. From the top center of each wavy outline, four smaller curved text bands spiral outward, in the same plan of two sets of four elements we have seen so frequently in other diagrams. An outer ring of text surrounds the whole, its start clearly marked by a decorative sign. This design, with its double-four structure, may also refer to the seasons, ages, humors, or the like. It may also have a geographical implication, since the ⊕ symbol occurs elsewhere in medieval iconography as a form of symbolic map of the inhabited world.

Folio 70r1 shows a six-pointed star with six words of text between its points. It is surrounded by a curious ring of fifty-eight carefully-drawn cell-like objects, alternately empty and occupied by pairs of dots, and a ring of text. Nine wave- or foam-like spouts emerge from a watery field surrounding the inner circle. Nine bands of text are written radially outward from the interstices of these waves. Three concentric rings of text surround the whole. There is little to aid us in understanding this drawing other than a possible focus on water as an element or moisture as a property, with their effects on health, and the numbers six, nine, and fifty-eight.

Folio 69r also shows a central six-pointed star; five single characters and one digraph are placed between the points. A ring of text surrounds this central medallion. Beyond are forty-five pipe-like, elongated rays closely packed together, with heavier lines separating them into irregular groups of one, two, and three rays. Text lines are written radially along twenty-one of these rays, and there is a ring of text surrounding all. Folio 69v is somewhat similar, with a central eight-pointed star having small stars between its points. Twenty-eight pipe-like things emerge radially from the center, with a text word or phrase written above the mouth of each as though issuing from it. Three rings of text run around the outer periphery.

A small moon face occupies the central field of folio 85–86v4; five frothy or bubbly concentric rings of cells, scallops, or waves run around the center. The heads, arms, and shoulders of four human figures rise from the middle ring as from a sea. Their arms are raised, and their hands are holding indistinguishable objects, one of which may be a cross. Four lines of text surround the whole, with a clearly-shown starting point on the left.

Folio 85–86v3 contains a very strange drawing dominated by four complex structures shaped roughly like inverted cones emerging from the corners of the page and extending inward toward the center. The upper left cone looks like a cluster of grapes, clouds, or cells; from its tip, directed toward the center, a spurt of some substance issues, with the head and hand of a human figure emerging from the cluster beside it. The upper right structure is like a broad tube made up of scales or scallops or waves in crosswise rows; from it a large gush of vapor or wind emerges toward the center, and within this a bird is flying vigorously. The two lower objects are more elongated in form and seem to be made up of layers of longitudinal fibers with intersecting crosswise rows of cells. One gives forth a large jet of specks like snow or rain aimed into the center of the page, with a human figure half revealed as if peering around one side of the jet and flinging out a smaller jet of droplets with his outstretched right hand. The remaining cone, in the lower right corner, emits no jets of vapor, but instead has a bird seated on its apex, as if on a nest; bending over the seated bird are three branch-like structures on stalks. Four text paragraphs occupy the four sides of the page between the large spouts, and a fifth paragraph is placed in the upper center.

It seems possible that the four jets may represent the Four Winds converging upon the earth, and that this diagram, like several others of this section, may be concerned with the seasons and the weather. The nesting bird, and the other, possibly migrating, bird would be explicable within this frame of reference. A scribbled diagram of a circle with three subsections ⊕, like that in folio 68v3, occupies the otherwise empty center of the page; next to it and scrawled across it is a disorderly scribbling that resembles carelessly-written Arabic script. This scribble is closely similar to another in the lower left center of folio 66v, where it also seems to be associated with a crudely-formed geometric figure. (See figure 21 for details of these scribbled phrases.)

Finally, folio 70r2 shows a central face, probably a sun, surrounded by eight large segments containing petal-like rays. A small ring of text runs around the center, and four more lines of text surround the whole. The outer lines appear to be in two pairs: the outer pair has a common starting point indicated by a double vertical, while the inner pair has a different common start shown by a single vertical. A paragraph of text accompanies the design on the upper right corner of the page.

The above lengthy, but still very incomplete discussion of these interesting cosmological diagrams can by no means do justice to the amount of information available in them for the student willing to accord to them the respect required for a careful and systematic examination. I believe it has been too readily assumed by most students that the drawings in the Voynich manuscript were too "weird" and nonsensical to warrant this attention. The research must await the efforts of someone who has access (as I do not have) to a large number of medieval manuscripts, or facsimile copies of these. A thorough investigation, pursuing some of the striking iconographical elements in the drawings, might turn up some useful parallels that could provide an understanding of the text.

3.3.5 Drawings Featuring Human Figures.

The drawings on folios 75r and v and 76v through 84v are probably the most mysterious and bizarre of all the many enigmas with which the Voynich manuscript confronts us. They show sequences of human figures, almost invariably nude and female, and (as has been very frequently and somewhat archly noted by other students) quite plump and matronly in form. Most of them have distended abdomens and bulging hips; they certainly do not present an appearance of voluptuous beauty to the modern American eye. The impression is rather one of agricultural fertility, maternal fecundity and nourishment, or something on a similar pragmatic plane. Many of the figures seem to have long hair, crowns, or elaborate veils in spite of their otherwise complete lack of clothing. Their poses are lively, expressive, and varied.

The female figures are shown variously sitting, standing, lying, or otherwise disposed in or on curious objects like tubs, tubes, pipes, coal-scuttles, pulpits, pods, or platforms. These objects are drawn in the same chunky, blocky style of architectonic solidity as was noted above in connection with the plants. In fact, some of them look quite a lot like the fruits, seed pods, and root or stem structures of these very plant drawings. Note, for example, the two striking spherical objects, somewhat resembling mines or bombs trailing fuses, crossed on folio 83v; to my eye, they closely resemble the twin fruits (?) on the plant in folio 90r1. A structure on folio 79v of three pipes surrounding a larger central tube resembles the root crown of the same plant on folio 90r1. Similarly, a tripartite structure on folio 77v made up of three nest- or pulpit-like swellings connected by pipes, with three tuber-like objects hanging from the central swelling, looks to me like the root crown of a plant with three main stems connected by underground roots or stolons (see figure 15 for examples).

Some of the female figures seem to be holding spindle-shaped objects that could be fruits or seed pods. The pipe-like structures that coil around the figures (and into which, or from which, they appear to be transmitting some mysterious vapor or liquid) could well represent plant parts such as roots or stems in schematic form. Also to be remarked upon are cloud-like clusters, puffs and sprays of vapor emerging from the numerous vents of these pipes, and the substantial-looking tubs of liquid in which groups of female figures seem to be sitting, standing, or moving about. Some form of humor, essence, moisture, or sap seems to be of primary importance in the doctrine expressed by these pictures. In some folios (e.g., 75r, to the left of a descending line of figures; 82v, at top right and also two more below, center), arc-like structures seem to span openings in some of the little scenes. These look a great deal like rainbows, although without seeing the original colors one can only guess; most of the arcs seem to have four or five separate concentric segments with a darker band at the top. (For a discussion of an alchemical drawing containing a pipe with multiple vents emitting vapor, in a style similar to the pipes on these folios, see Section 8.8).

Another important detail to be noted in several of the drawings of this section is a small cross with one long arm (for example, at the top of folio 75r, serving as a focus for diverging rays; on 75v to the right within a field of rays and clouds; on 78r at the focus of a grape- or cloud-like cluster at upper left; and on 79v, top, at the focus of a frilly canopy of rays over the head of a figure who also holds a cross in her hand). These symbols are quite small and unobtrusive, but usually seem to form a central focus or origin for rays descending upon the female figures. The obvious interpretation is one of Divine illumination or influence promoting the fecundating, nourishing, or healing virtues of the humors controlled by, or represented by the female figures. The crosses provide an unmistakably Christian frame of reference for the doctrine being expounded by the scribe of the manuscript—a point not specifically remarked upon by other students to my knowledge.

What are we to make of these strange drawings? A possibility that immediately occurs to me is that they may relate the doctrines of Galenic humoral medicine, with its four "digestions" and various byproducts at different stages, to the nourishing or curative properties of the plants or prescriptions of the herbal and pharmaceutical folios. Another possibility is a system of therapeutic baths; this was a common feature of medieval medicine; warmth and moisture were supposed to be, in themselves, healing forces. It is amusing to note in this connection that Roger Bacon, in his medical work *De Retardatione Accidentium Senectutis* (Bacon 1928a), recommends perfumed oils, warm effusions, and the application of precious "occulta" such as lign-aloes, "heart bone of a stag," and viper's flesh. (This medical work was a competent and complete compilation of earlier medical sources such as Galen, Pseudo-Aristotle, and numerous Arabic writers, and was plagiarized and exploited by later physicians; little in it, however, was original with Bacon.)

20

Brumbaugh (1975) has seen in these pictures a recipe for the "Elixir of Life." designed to look like Roger Bacon's work (Bacon's medical treatise, his work entitled *Epistola de Mirabili Potestate Artis et Naturae*, and some garbled or doubtful versions of his alchemical writings were the only fragments of his writings well-known in the sixteenth century). Panofsky (1954, p. l), suggests that the human figures may represent "astral spirits" transmitting the influences radiated from the stars into plants and other living things. Singer, in his letter to Tiltman, 12 November 1957, puts forward a different, though related, suggestion: "My own feeling—again very vague—about the little figures of nude men and women in the organs of the body is that they are somehow connected with the "archaei" of the Paracelsan or Spagyric School. This would fit in well with my suggestion about John Dee and Bohemia." Note that Singer sees the tubes, pulpits, and pipes in which the figures sit as "organs of the body," rather than as the plant parts they recall to me. Figure 13 shows an analysis of the numbers and grouping of female and male figures on the folios of this section.

3.3.6 *Network of Rosettes, Folios 85–86r3–4, v1–2.*

This elaborate array of circular medallions covers several segments of a large, multiply-folded page. It has received little or no study or mention by students; this may be partly because its complexity and bizarre character boggles the mind already overburdened by the "queerness" to the modern eye of so much else in the manuscript. The failure of some students to pay much attention to these designs is also probably due to the poor quality of the photocopy available to us for these pages. The photocopy made from Father Petersen's original copy is so dark, and the numerous scraps of text written here are there are so hard to read, that it is almost unusable.

A photostatic copy which I recently obtained from the Beinecke Library reveals the details of this remarkable drawing very clearly. There are nine elaborate circular designs, in three rows of three each. The central design in the middle row is larger than the others, and contains six pharmaceutical "jars" arranged in an oval pattern with stars in the center. Between the medallions are veils of cell-like or fibrous structures that link each circle to its immediate neighbors. One medallion shows a structure like a castle and other small buildings around its periphery; the castle has a high, crenellated wall and a tall central tower. The center of this figure contains a circular field of stars and a spiral arrangement of text. Nearby, in the outer corner of the page, is a small circle containing a ⊖ diagram with Voynich text "words" within its segments. In the opposite corner of the page is the small "clock-face" mentioned by Brumbaugh (about which more will be said below). In the other two corners are sun faces surrounded by wavy rays. Some of the medallions have petal-like arrangements of rays filled with stars, recalling features of the cosmological and astronomical folios discussed previously. Many medallions are provided with curious structures like bundles of pipes or gunbarrels clustered around the periphery of their outer circular outlines. This complex assemblage of symbols deserves far more attention than it has so far received, in my opinion, since it could provide some enlightening synthesis or frame of reference for individual diagrams elsewhere in the manuscript.

A mention should be made here of Brumbaugh's identification of a "clock face" among these diagrams. There is a tiny circle, surrounded by eight(?) designs vaguely resembling Roman numerals, and what may be a small ring of text, on the extreme left side of the structure. In the center of this circle is a triangular arrangement of two intersecting lines with three small spheres strung on them, at their free ends and at their intersection. While it is true that this circular design bears some superficial resemblance to a clock face, it seems possible to me that it may also represent a "star picture" like those of *Picatrix* and the similar alchemical characters mentioned above Section 3.3.4. The two "hands" look to me as if they are intended to be of equal length, and the "hands" are not centered on the "clock face" as one would expect, but rather arranged so that the entire triangular structure is centered in the circle. An exactly similar triangular symbol with three balls strung on it occurs frequently among the star spells of *Picatrix*, and was used by alchemists to mean arsenic, orpiment, or potash (Gessman 1922, Tables IV, XXXXIII, XXXXV).

3.3.7 *Small Marginal Designs.*

There are small drawings of people, animals, and other less easily-identifiable objects on some pages. Folio 66r, as has already been noted, contains a drawing of a man lying on his back clutching his stomach as if sick or dead, and surrounded by various indeterminate small objects. The last page, 116v, has several sketches of people, animals, and other mysterious shapes in its upper left corner. Most of the pages filled with text (folios 103 and following) have single stars, some provided with extensions like tails, to the left of each paragraph. These paragraphs, as has been pointed out by Tiltman (1975), probably comprised approximately 365 originally, thereby providing one "star recipe" for each day of the year, possibly a set of astrological predictions or prescriptions.

3.4 Meaning of the Collection of Drawings as a Whole

Voynich stated his impression on first seeing the manuscript, that "the drawings indicated it to be an encyclopedia work on natural philosophy" (1921, p. 1). Elizebeth Friedman says: "The 'botanical' and largest section of the manuscript (125 pages) is probably herbalistic in character, and the manuscript may constitute what is now called a pharmacopeia" (1962). Panofsky provides another clear summary: "So far as can be made out before the manuscript has been decoded, its content would comprise: first, a general cosmological philosophy explaining the medical properties of terrestrial objects, particularly plants, by celestial influences transmitted by astral radiation and those 'spirits' which were frequently believed to transmit the occult powers of the stars to the earth; second, a kind of herbal describing the individual plants used for medicinal and conceivably, magical purposes; third, a description of such compounds as may be produced by combining individual plants in various ways" (1954, p. 1). He confesses that he is unable to suggest any known medieval parallel synthesizing all of these doctrines into one compact book. (There were, in fact, a number of very large encyclopedic works of many volumes that covered a somewhat similar range of topics; an obvious example that comes to mind is the work of Albertus Magnus, a contemporary of Roger Bacon.)

Petersen provides a similar view of the manuscript as a whole: "The illustrations in the manuscript make it appear all but certain that the text deals with medicinal plants and their use in medieval remedies. The drawings of folios 67–86 seem to illustrate astrological matters, and possibly the medieval theory of vital spirits functioning as animate beings (represented by small nude figures)? .... Might not the 324 separate short paragraphs or sentences (folios 103–116) contain a sort of subject index or table of contents or list of recipes?" (1953, p. 1) Brumbaugh sees the manuscript as a treatise on the "Elixir of Life", designed to interest the Emperor Rudolph II by a forger who wished to make it appear to be the work of Roger Bacon. An "encyclopedic sequence of drugs", possibly compiled from a variety of earlier manuscripts, is followed by astrological lore; the folios featuring nude female figures may deal, Brumbaugh thinks, with "the biology of reproduction, the theology of psychic reincarnation, or the topical application of the elixir". (1975, pp. 348–349).

In studying the drawings in the different sections of the manuscript, I have come to feel strongly that they involve a highly symbolic, artificial, and conventionalized graphic or mnemonic "language" that uses the same representations or forms to call to mind particular key concepts on different folios and in various combinations with one another. This graphic "alphabet" or shorthand seems in many ways closely similar in its philosophy to the interesting structure of the Voynich script (to be dealt with in Chapter 4). For this reason, I believe that a careful, painstaking, and open-minded analysis of all the drawings and their component graphic elements, indexing and cross-matching all the forms, might repay the effort involved. An experiment using modern computer CRT terminals with graphics capabilities to perform such analysis would be worthwhile, if carried out within a carefully-reasoned theoretical framework (i.e., to pursue and investigate particular theories previously developed by the student concerning meaningful relations among the forms). More will be said in Section 6.9 regarding the use of computer techniques in studying the manuscript.

Chapter 4
Avenues of Attack: The Text

4.1 Nature and Characteristics of the Voynich Script

However complex and interesting the drawings are, the script in which the bulk of the manuscript is written is undoubtedly the most intriguing part of the elegant enigma. It has a deceptively flowing, rhythmic quality that suggests long practice and familiarity on the part of the scribe or scribes. The script seems like a reasonable, workable, well-constructed system of writing, with a look of ease and natural flow. On closer inspection, the surface appearance of simplicity vanishes, and a still more seductive and captivating character emerges, in the form of an intricate but structurally logical system of ligaturing or compounding of simple forms to build up more complex outlines. Whatever else may be alleged concerning the value of the manuscript as a whole to science, I am convinced that an understanding of the construction of this writing system cannot fail to be of great interest in the study of human thought. It appears to be a *tour de force* of artistry and ingenuity.

4.1.1 Provenience and Style.

Unfortunately, although many students mention the style, calligraphy, and appearance of the script as a factor in their judgements of the date and origin of the manuscript, they provide little real evidence or detail to back up their claims. Nowhere among the sources I have examined have I seen any really factual or complete discussion of the matter. Some sources mention, in passing, the possible derivation of the Voynich symbols from "Roman minuscule characters." McKaig (n.d.) states that "the text is written in a beautifully symmetrical script that slightly resembles writing used in Italy in the 1500's" (p. 48).

4.1.2 Relationships to Known Scripts and Character Sets.

Attempts to link the origin of the Voynich symbols to other systems of writing have been many and far-ranging. A diligent study of known alphabetic, syllabic, or ideographic scripts has turned up nothing remotely similar, though various individual symbols have distant parallels in some compendia. Several symbols resemble early forms of Arabic numerals; this has been pointed out by more than one student of the manuscript, for example, by A. W. Exell (of the Botanical Library, British Natural History Museum), in a letter to Tiltman, 30 August 1957, and by Robert Brumbaugh (1974, 1975). Figure 16 shows a comparison of some Voynich symbols and various forms of early Arabic numerals extracted from tables in Hill (1915) that look similar in my opinion. (See also Section 8.10 for a discussion of the history of Arabic numerals in Europe.) Some form of substitution cipher may be involved, of course; thus, the fact that a given Voynich symbol looks like an early form of "7" or "4", for example, need not imply that it actually stands for that number in the text. Early forms of Arabic numerals were often employed in a wide variety of codes and ciphers, as we will see in Chapter 9.

Similarities are also clearly apparent between some Voynich symbols and certain Latin abbreviations in use at various times during the Middle Ages. These relationships have been investigated and exploited by several students, notably Petersen and Feely. Figure 17 shows a selection of Latin abbreviations extracted from Cappelli (1949) and some Voynich symbols that resemble them in my opinion. A general similarity was apparent to me, and was also noted, independently and earlier, by Tiltman, between certain commonly-occurring looped symbols standing above the line and the decorative extensions of letters with tall stems in the top line of a manuscript illustrated in Cappelli (Table IV). Some artificial writing systems of various kinds that might throw some light on the Voynich script will be discussed in Chapter 9.

4.1.3 Attempts to Decompose the Symbols into Elements.

It has been concluded by most students that the Voynich script includes at least some compound symbols. Various attempts have been made to arrive at a rationale to explain the ligatures and resolve them consistently into component elements. Some students have proposed that the symbols may have been built up from elementary strokes in a manner similar to the method upon which they supposed that the Chinese writing system was based. Tiltman suggested that missionaries visiting the Far East, who had studied the Chinese system, might have brought back a description of it which then might have inspired some fifteenth- or sixteenth-century scholar to design the Voynich script (unpublished notes). A. W. Exell, in his letter to

Tiltman, 30 August 1957, refers to a theory (not further specified) that early Arabic numerals were built up from one, two, three, four or more strokes in a similar Oriental manner; he suggests a sketchy and incomplete correspondence between Voynich symbols and conventional numerals along these lines. No one has, to my knowledge, worked out a "stroke" theory of this kind in sufficient detail to test it out as a hypothesis.

In this connection, it is interesting to note that Roger Bacon provided extensive information concerning the Far East in a highly interesting section of the *Opus Majus* on geography and the customs of foreign peoples. He states there that he had closely questioned several missionaries and travellers recently returned from visits to these far-away places. His descriptions of many foreign peoples and customs are clearly recognizable, although some are fabulous and distorted, as might be expected. A clear description of Buddhist monks at worship, even including a garbled version of "Om mane padme hum", is particularly striking. The following is his description of writing in China: "The people in Cathay to the east write with the same instrument with which painters paint, forming in one character groups of letters, each group representing a sentence. By this method characters are formed with many letters together, whence reasonable and natural characters have been composed of letters, and have the meaning of sentences." (Bacon 1928b, p. 389.)

The compound Voynich symbols are not easy to "take apart" in any consistent and unambiguous way; they are too smoothly blended to form a single flowing outline. Figure 18 shows some examples of apparently compound forms, and some suggestions regarding their decomposition. Some symbols which appear to be simple at first sight may in fact also be compounds; for example, " ⊙ " may be made up of " ϲ " and " ↘ ", and " ♂ " may be a combination of " ϲ " and " ϒ ". My own feeling is that we need not go as far afield as the Orient to explain these complex outlines: the system of Latin abbreviations in common use throught the Middle Ages has the same character. An abbreviated form typically preserves one or two letters of a word and distorts or combines them to form a single sinuous, conventionalized character. Some of the parts of such a compound form may then be partially disconnected and used in abbreviations of other, partially similar words. The distorted and truncated scraps of words are usually combined with overlines, superfixed characters, loops, tails, and slant lines which mark the form as an abbreviation, or stand for a set of missing letters. Each of these structural features has a counterpart in the Voynich script: a horizontal stroke seems to connect many symbols; a comma- or hook-like mark often appears above certain symbols, and characters are frequently shown standing above or in the midst of others as infixes or superfixes; long tails curve up or slant down from letters at the ends of words and lines.

It is my feeling that we need not look beyond the system of Latin abbreviations, familiar to all learned men of the Middle Ages and Renaissance throughout Europe, combined with early forms of Arabic numerals and some common alchemical and astrological symbols, to find the inspiration for the design of the Voynich script. Unfortunately for the student, the designer has exhibited a truly remarkable ingenuity in blending and distorting these elements so as to make of them an entirely new writing system, fundamentally independent of and distinct from any of its sources, so that our recognition of similarities to known symbols has not helped us to unlock the secret of the script. It is interesting to note that the characters which occur as superfixes or infixes with other ligatured characters may also occur next to them in ordinary sequence: the explicit and carefully shown ligature must, therefore, provide some distinct element of meaning. (For example, is " ϹⲦ " the same as " ϲ ϲ "? How does " Ϥ " differ from " ϲ ϒ "? Is " ϤⲦ " equivalent to " ϒ ϲϲ " or " ϲϲ ϒ " or neither?)

Most cryptanalytically-oriented students of the manuscript have put considerable effort into analyzing the script and attempting to devise a working transcription alphabet for use in cryptanalytic and computer studies. Various researchers have adopted different theories regarding the decomposition of the symbols into elements, and the identification of variant forms of a single symbol. Some, like Tiltman and the First Voynich Study Group, arrived at a relatively small working alphabet of basic symbols, regarding all the rest as secondary compounds. At the other extreme, Currier, Krischer, and the Second Study Group included a number of obvious compounds in their working alphabet to produce a considerably longer list of symbols. Currier's alphabet and the others based on it embody a theory about the symbol " ↳ " and its occurrence in groupings of one, two, or three immediately preceding certain ending symbols (" ♀ ", " ⟩ ", and " ϟ "). My own transcription alphabet includes an attempt to allow for some relatively rare ligatured elements in addition to those in the commoner compounds. Figure 19 shows several different transcription alphabets.

4.1.4 *Variant and Embellished Forms of Symbols.*

While all have agreed that a relationship of some sort exists among certain families of similarly-shaped symbols, students have associated them differently depending on their theories regarding the exact nature of the kinships (see figure 19). Considerable interest has centered on the four looped symbols " ϒ ", " ϔ ", " ϒ ", " ϟ " that are all found as infixes or superfixes over the symbol " ϹⲦ " as well as alone. An interesting bit of evidence for the identity of " ϒ " and " ϟ " (and thus, by analogy, the other pair " ϒ " and " ϔ " as well), may be seen on folio 57r, where a sequence of seventeen symbols is

24

repeated four times around a circular band. It is so rare to find any sequence in the Voynich manuscript repeating all or some portion of itself that this example is almost unique. Figure 24 shows the four repeated segments arranged in parallel; in two instances. the symbol " 𝄞 ". with only one loop. occurs in the ninth place. while in the other two. we see " 𝄟 " with two clear loops in the corresponding position. Since all the other symbols appear identical. the conclusion seems inescapable that the single- and double-looped forms are functionally the same. Countervailing against this conclusion is the fact that the symbols are always made quite clearly and distinctly. with either one or two loops; there are rarely if ever any transitional or marginal forms with vestigial or carelessly-formed loops. In any case. there is an obvious family relationship of some kind among the four looped symbols. as shown by their similarity of form. their entering into similar constructions. and their assuming a similar function and positions in the structure of text words.

Embellishments are relatively few in the Voynich text. Figure 20 shows some variant and decorative forms of symbols as various students have tentatively identified them; many of the assumed identifications are my own opinions. Some of the decorative extensions and flourishes are quite attractive in a bizarre and idiosyncratic way. Small dots inside loops. parallel hatching along lines. dots arranged in rows. and exaggeration or prolongation of loops are frequent ornamental devices. The embellishments are. for the most part. highly restrained. and not at all the extravagant. disorderly overgrowth one might expect of a deranged mind. It should be noted also that the ornamental extensions rarely. if ever. impinge on or interfere with writing or drawings nearby. and that it is rare in general for writing or drawings to cross one another anywhere in the text. except in a controlled and orderly manner.

The curious embellishments appear to exhibit the same rhythmic. pragmatic. and compact character as is evident in other aspects of style throughout the manuscript. A particularly notable and amusing decorative flourish is the apparent disconnecting of the two loops of the character " 𝄟 ". so that one stem and loop is translated horizontally into a neighboring word. sometimes with several intervening curlicues; figure 20 provides a number of examples. It is possible that. in some cases. the intent may be to combine two separate occurrences of " 𝄟 " into one decorative flourish; there may also be some element of meaning in the practice. although it is scarcely frequent enough. especially in lines other than initial lines of paragraphs. to support such a conclusion.

4.2 Other Scripts and Hands

On certain pages of the manuscript are found isolated phrases and sentences in scripts and hands judged by most students to be different from. and probably later than. the bulk of the text (although none of the sources I have studied present any definitive evidence supporting a different date or authorship for these scattered text strings). Petersen reports that Miss Nill (a friend of Mrs. Voynich) had made a thorough examination of all the apparently extraneous passages in the manuscript: "Miss Nill . . . has listed all words or passages which appear to be written in different ink from that used uniformly for the text and the drawings throughout the manuscript. (She noted also that the original text seems to show not a single erasure and correction anywhere.) Miss Nill declares that the last page is written in the same ink as the bulk of the manuscript" (1953. p. 1). Unfortunately. no copy of Miss Nill's list has survived in the material to which I have access. I offer the following summary from my own examination of the photocopy available to me.

Folio 1r. There are very faint and barely legible traces of alphabetic sequences in the left and right margins. These are not visible at all in the photocopy I have studied. but Petersen shows them clearly in his hand transcript. The letters seem to be those of the ordinary "ABC". with some slightly distorted or odd forms. The two sequences appear to be parallel; in their fragmentary state. it is hard to tell whether they are consistently associated with the lines of Voynich text occupying the center of the page.

Folio 17r. A line of writing in a very small. crabbed hand crosses the top center of the page. It is very hard to make out; to my eye. the letters resemble Greek symbols. The writing becomes fainter and harder to read toward the right side and finally fades out completely. In the upper right corner. there is a faint. scribbled symbol like a shield or a crude *fleur de lys*. criss-crossed with lines. It is interesting to note that John Dee liked to use Greek letters to conceal comments in English in his personal diary; the symbols on this page. however. do not seem to spell anything that might be an English word.

Folio 66r. A small scattering of letters. which again look to me like Greek symbols. are to be found in the lower left corner of the page near a small picture of a man lying on his back. Above the "Greek" letters is a string of words in the Voynich script. Prof. Richard Salomon of Kenyon College has suggested a High German interpretation of the extraneous symbols. claiming that they stand for "der musz del". or "the mussteil". referring to an obligatory bequest of household goods from a man to his widow.

Folio 66v. In the lower half of this page (which shows a plant drawing accompanied by three text paragraphs) there is a scribble or doodle that slants downward toward the left. A rough oblong figure sits to the right and above the scrawl. The markings here resemble a similar scribble in the center of folio 85–86v3 (see below); some portions of the doodle have the appearance of Arabic script.

Folio 85–86v3. In the center of this cosmological diagram there is another doodle similar to that in folio 66v. A crude circle is bisected by a horizontal line, and the upper half bisected again by a perpendicular; a line of indecipherable scribbling something like Arabic script crosses part of this circle and extends to the left of it.

Folio 87r. To the left of the lower leaves of the plant drawing is a crude star-like doodle of intersecting lines.

Folio 116v. The several lines of text in a mixture of symbols on the last page of the manuscript have been extensively studied by many researchers as a possible "key" to the text. Figure 23 shows several transcriptions of this material made by different students along with a reproduction (admittedly poor) of the photocopy at my disposal. The symbols are very small, crabbed, and faint. It is interesting to note the differences among different students' interpretation of these enigmatic lines. The numerous ambiguities and obscurities have not prevented several students from basing extensive theories on their own rather arbitrary readings of the tiny, distorted letters.

Folio gatherings. In the lower corners of certain pages are numbers added in what appears to be a different ink and hand. These numbers correspond roughly to sets of eight pages. Those discernible in the photocopy I have studied are shown in figure 22, with the page number associated with each. The numerals are interesting in themselves, exhibiting some archaic forms; they are accompanied by symbols for Latin abbreviations, one of which, " **9** " for "-us", exactly resembles a common symbol in the Voynich script.

Folio numbering. At some point during the eventful history of this manuscript, someone added numbers in the upper right hand corner of the pages. These numbers agree with the present order of the pages, and show gaps where certain pages have apparently been lost since the numbering was done but before the finding of the manuscript by Voynich. Some students have dated the folio numbers to the sixteenth or seventeenth century; they may well have been added by someone at Rudolph's court. The forms of the numbers do not differ significantly from modern forms.

Month names in astrological diagrams. The name of a month has been written into the central medallion of each circular diagram associated with a recognizable zodiac sign. These month names are considered by most students to be written in a different ink and hand than that of the main text. Figure 10 shows details of these medallions and month names. A single word in the Voynich script is seen next to the two scaly fishes of the Pisces medallion (folio 70r2); attempts to identify this word with the month name or zodiac sign have so far been fruitless. No one has made any progress, or even, apparently, any determined attempt, to identify the language or provenience of the month names, despite the fact that they are among the few clearly recognizable and comprehensible bits of text in the entire manuscript.

4.3 Linear Sequences that Look Like "Keys"

Several pages of the manuscript are provided with columns or circles of single symbols or short words that seem to be arranged in some sequence that may be an index or key. Brumbaugh has exploited these sequences extensively in his theory of decipherment (see Section 5.4); according to him, the multiplicity of "keys", although associated with a deliberate attempt at mystification on the part of the scribe, still provide some valid and useful information about the cipher. Below is a list of these, insofar as I can identify them; some of the "key" sequences are also mentioned above under Section 4.2.

Folio 1r. The two parallel alphabetic sequences in the left and right margins, described above, have been thought to function as keys; a suspicion enters my mind, however, that they are the result of some later would-be decipherer's workings. It is surprising, considering the number of people who must have attempted to read the manuscript at Rudolph's court and elsewhere, that there are not far more doodled numbers, letters, and lines on its pages.

Folio 49v. A clearly discernible vertical list of twenty-six Voynich symbols runs down the left margin of the text accompanying a particularly decorative "herbal" folio showing a cyclamen-like plant. Figure 24 shows this sequence, which exhibits a partial repetition in three cycles.

Folio 57v. Seventeen symbols, some quite complex or unusual in form, are repeated four times around the second concentric circle from the outside in a cosmological diagram. The four sequences are shown in parallel in figure 24. This is a rare instance of sequences repeating almost exactly in the manuscript; in fact, I believe it is the only such instance.

Folio 66r. In the left margin is a rather complex sequence of single symbols associated with isolated short words and the lines of a text paragraph, all in the Voynich script. Brumbaugh employed these sequences as "equations" expressing a correspondence between the letters and the words (see 5.4 below). As is frequently the case in this manuscript, however, the horizontal association of the scattered letters and single words is not very accurate. and neither is clearly and consistently related to the lines of the paragraph.

Folio 69r. Between the points of a central star are six Voynich symbols.

Folio 76r. A string of nine Voynich symbols is seen in the upper left margin. spaced out vertically in rough association with certain lines of a text paragraph.

To my knowledge, no one other than Brumbaugh has directed much attention to these sequences. No consistent alphabetic or numeric order can be traced from one to the next. They may be conventional abbreviations standing for sequences of ideas or objects known to the scribe or scribes. Their presence as a salient feature of the text indicates that the writing system was capable of employing single symbols or pairs of symbols to stand for some sets of concepts. See figure 24 for examples of many of these "key" sequences.

4.4 Cryptanalytic and Stylistic Attacks on the Text

Students who have approached the Voynich text from the point of view of the professional cryptanalyst have been led on at first by a deceptive surface appearance of simplicity, only to bog down sooner or later in an exasperating quagmire of paradoxes and enigmas that reveal themselves one by one as analysis proceeds. Elizebeth Friedman has provided a clear. concise summary of the frustrations awaiting the cryptanalyst in the Voynich manuscript. I cannot improve on the clarity. completeness. and succinctness of her remarks. and so will quote them at length in the following paragraphs.

"What is generally the initial reaction of a professional cipher expert to the manuscript? At first glance. it looks as though it should be very easy to solve. because the 'text' seems to be in word lengths and word repetitions stand out clearly on practically every page.

"A single frequency table would be made at once of a portion of 'text'. just as Poe did in the 'Gold Bug'. But to do that necessitates deciding how many different symbols there are in the manuscript. and this is neither simple nor easy. For what seems at first glance to be a single symbol often appears to be a composite made up of perhaps two or three symbols.

"If a frequency table is made for a piece of text amounting to about 500 consecutive 'words' (which come to about 1500 characters). it presents the characteristic 'rough' appearance of a frequency table for a simple substitution cipher. A few symbols have a very high frequency; a few have a very low frequency; the rest are of varying but medium frequencies. Beside the many repetitions of single 'words'. there are also many repeated sequences of two. three. or more 'words'.

"The first impression. therefore. is that here is a simple substitution cipher. However. the decipherer is doomed to utter frustration when no solution based on such a theory is reached. Trials in Latin. Greek. German. Italian. etc.. yield nothing at all. So maybe it s not simple substitution.

"But then the possibility of transposition. of combined substitution-transposition. or of multiple-alphabet substitution are also ruled out for the reason that there is entirely too much repetition. We find thousands of repetitions of three-. four-. and five-letter words throughout the text.

"For example. in nineteen lines of text. a certain three-character group appears sixty-six times. And in regard to repetition of complete 'words'. the whole manuscript is quite homogeneous; the 'words' in all sections are very much alike.

"Indeed. sometimes. and not too rarely. one finds the same 'word' appearing three times in succession. producing something similar to Gertrude Stein's 'A rose is a rose is a rose...' Also. there are thousands of cases in which two 'words' of four. five. or more characters differ from each other by only one character. as in English. the words 'strike' and 'stroke'. 'store' and 'stork'" [1962.]

There have been several attempts to analyze the Voynich text using computers. Unfortunately. for a variety of reasons. little progress has resulted from these efforts. with the sole exception (to my knowledge) of the researches of Prescott Currier (see Section 6.8). Cryptanalytic studies have included monographic. digraphic. and trigraphic frequency counts throughout samples of various sizes. based on several different transcription alphabets. Reverse alphabetic sorts have been made to study "endings" of words. and word indexes have provided an analysis of different occurrences of the 'same' word and a comparison of their contexts. The difficulties of arriving at an alphabet. transcribing a sufficiently large sample of text. and gaining access to enough computer time have hampered students in their efforts over the years. Most of the proposed computer studies were never carried far enough to result in any solid gain in knowledge. More will be said in Chapter 6 regarding certain specific computer studies and some methodological considerations relating to the use of computers in general.

While relatively few have had access to computers. many students have made extensive hand studies of the text. Tiltman first described the apparent "precedence order" of characters within words. and demonstrated the preference of certain symbols. in certain combinations. for the beginning. middle. or ending portions of words. Petersen made an elaborate and complete manual concordance of the text. and studied occurrences of ligatured and compound forms of symbols.

4.4.1 *Phenomena in the Text Which Must be Accounted for by Any Theory.*

The following list of characteristics to be explained by any good cryptanalytic theory summarizes the findings of several researchers. notably the Friedmans and Tiltman; it includes also some observations which I have added from my own study of the text.

(1) The basic alphabet of frequently-occurring symbols is small (as few as fifteen according to some students. and probably no more than twenty-five).

(2) The basic forms are compounded or ligatured to create a large variety of complex symbols.

(3) The symbols are grouped into "words" separated by spaces (although some researchers have expressed doubts about the consistency of this spacing).

(4) The number of different "words" seems surprisingly limited.

(5) The "words" are short. averaging around four or five symbols in length; words over seven or eight symbols long are rare. as are also words consisting of a single symbol. Even two-letter words are relatively uncommon. (It should be pointed out that normal English text also presents an average word-length of about five characters; in English text. however. there are many one- and two-letter words. and a great many words of ten to fifteen characters in length. providing a very different pattern from that seen in the Voynich text.)

(6) The same "word" is frequently repeated two. three. or more times in immediate succession.

(7) Many "words" differ from each other by only one or two symbols. and such "words" often occur in immediate succession.[1]

(8) Certain symbols occur characteristically at the beginnings. middles. and ends of "words". and in certain preferred sequences.

(9) Certain symbols appear very rarely. and only on certain pages. indicating some special function or meaning.

(10) There are very few doublets (repetition of the same letter twice in succession). and these involve primarily the symbols "ɛ" and "ᾱ". ocasionally also "9". "ठ". and "O".

(11) Very few symbols occur singly (as one-letter "words") in running text; these are primarily "2" and "9".

(12) "Prefix"-like elements are tacked in front of certain "words" that also occur commonly without them: such prefixed elements are "40". "O". and "9".

(13) The symbol "4" occurs almost invariably followed by "O". and joined to it by an extension of the crossbar of the "4": the resulting compound symbol is rarely seen elsewhere than at the beginning of words.

(14) On most herbal folios. the first line of the first paragraph begins with a very small set of symbols. primarily "Ψ". "Ή". "Ψ". and "Ƌ"; these are usually immediately followed by "ɛτ". "ᾱ". "O". "9". "auɔ". or "89". No trace can be found of the alphabeticity that would be expected if the herbal paragraphs began with the names of plants in alphabetical order as was usual in many early herbals.

(15) Single "words" occurring as labels next to stars. "drug containers". plant sketches. or other pictorial elements in various drawings very *rarely* begin with the four looped symbols: instead. they often start with "O". "ठ". "9". and occasionally "2" and "ɛτ".

4.4.2 *Cryptanalytic Hypotheses.*

In the Voynich manuscript. we are confronted by a situation with many unknowns. In spite of the diligent and tireless efforts of many talented researchers over the half-century since its discovery. we still have very few definite facts to reduce the large area of uncertainty defined by these unknowns. We still are ignorant of the underlying language; we have little or no clue to the nature of the cipher. code. or writing system; we do not know when. where. or by whom the manuscript was written; we cannot even be certain of the subject matter. or the purpose for which it was compiled. In the following paragraphs. I will attempt to list. as completely as possible. the hypotheses that a conscientious cryptanalyst might entertain regarding the nature of the Voynich text. In some cases. information turned up by researchers can at least partly rule out some of these hypotheses. as Elizebeth Friedman has suggested in the passage quoted above. Some theories seem more capable than others of explaining the phenomena observed in the text. A systematic consideration of all the possibilities will

---

[1] On the matter of repeated words. a colleague has pointed out to me that two or three repetitions in sequence of the same syllable are not uncommon in Chinese. and in other. similar Eastern languages This is due in part to the lack of the "function words" such as modal auxiliaries. prepositions. articles. etc.. in these languages. and in part to methods of word building and compounding.

serve as a good foundation for the discussion of solution attempts in Chapters 5 and 6. Such a survey will also provide a vivid picture of the true magnitude of the problem which this enigmatic manuscript presents to the cryptanalyst.

The cryptanalytic possibilities to be dealt with are related to three principal factors, which I will designate by capital letters: P. the nature of the underlying plain text; E. the correspondence or substitution between elements of plain text and Voynich script elements; and T. other transformations that might have been carried out on the plain text in addition to substitution of Voynich symbols. In the following paragraphs, several possibilities will be listed under each of these basic factors; each such individual hypothesis will be designated by the letter (P. E. or T) followed by an Arabic numeral. I will assume that the reader is familiar with certain basic terminology and concepts of cryptology, such as the distinction between code and cipher, substitution and transposition. These concepts have been clearly defined and explained in many easily obtainable general works on cryptanalysis.

P. The Nature of the Plain Text.

P.1 Normal Latin text.

P.2 Normal text in some other natural language.

P.3 Code or synthetic language with a mixture of ideographic and natural language characteristics (e.g., grammatical endings added to code symbols).

P.4 A purely ideographic system like pictographs, with virtually no features of natural language preserved.

E. The Nature of the Substitution.

E.1 One plain text symbol is replaced by one Voynich symbol.

E.2 One plain text symbol is replaced by two (three) Voynich symbols, but always by the same number of symbols.

E.3 Two (three), but always the same number of plain text symbols are replaced by one Voynich symbol.

E.4 Two (three) plain text symbols are replaced by two (three) Voynich symbols.

E.5 Mixed length units (i.e., one, two, and three-letter strings) are involved in either or both plain text and Voynich script.

E.6 Each plain text unit has a set of variant or alternative Voynich symbol counterparts, from which the scribe could choose at will.

E.7 Whole words or concepts are represented by single Voynich symbols or by mixed-length Voynich strings (as in a shorthand).

E.8 Polyalphabetic substitution, or the cyclic use of a series of substitution alphabets according to some rule.

T. Transformations Other Than Substitution.

T.1 No plain text letters dropped, added, or moved.

T.2 Vowels dropped.

T.3 Words abbreviated arbitrarily, and represented only by certain letters.

T.4 "Dummy" characters, or "nulls" inserted into the text.[2]

T.5 Letters or syllables transposed within words (as in Pig Latin).

T.6 Letters anagrammed or transposed over longer stretches of text.

T.7 Plain text concealed in a much longer "dummy" or "cover" text, most of which is meaningless.

T.8 A Trithemian or Baconian system, involving the use of some binary or trinary characteristic (closed or open letters; tails up or tails down; ligaturing or lack of it; etc..) as the true message-carrying feature in a manner similar to the "dots" and "dashes" of Morse code, applied to a "cover" text or "carrier" text which is meaningless in itself.

As will be shown in Chapter 9, all of the above possibilities were known and used by early practitioners of secret writing, well within the fifteenth and sixteenth centuries. Roger Bacon mentions a number of them in an often-cited passage in his work entitled "De Mirabili Potestate Artis et Naturae" (Bacon 1859). The methods he lists include made-up alphabets, geometric figures combined with dots, shorthand ("ars notoria" or Tyronian Hand), and dropping vowels from the plaintext. In alchemy treatises attributed to him, Bacon is also thought by some to have employed anagramming, simple substitution (one plain text character to one cipher character), and concealment of a short message within a much longer meaningless "cover" text.

Using the scheme of individual hypotheses designated by letters and numbers presented above, we can set up a large number of compound hypotheses embodying various choices in various combinations. I will not attempt to list all of this very

---

[2] In notes made by Miss Nill, companion of Mrs. Voynich, she reports that John Manly had expressed his opinion in a letter to Mr. Voynich dated March 20, 1920, that the text of the manuscript represents a simple cipher disguised by the use of nulls. In another letter to William R. Newbold at about the same date. Manly stated (according to Miss Nill) that frequency counts he had made, based on eight pages of text, showed "a comparatively simple cipher disguised by extensive use of nulls".

large set of possibilities; instead. I will mention a few that seem to be ruled out by the evidence. or at least rendered relatively unlikely. and a few others that seem more consistent with what we know of the text and thus more worthy of further study.

Hypotheses Rendered Unlikely by the Evidence.

Simple Substitution on an Otherwise Unaltered Natural Language Text. As Elizebeth Friedman and others have observed. the text probably does not represent ordinary Latin or any other natural language enciphered by simple one-to-one substitution of Voynich symbols for single letters (that is. in terms of our scheme. P.1 or P.2 and E.1 and T.1). The short words. the many sequential repetitions. the rarity of one- or two-letter words. the rarity of doublets (doubled letters). all militate against simple substitution. So also does the strange lack of parallel context surrounding different occurrences of the "same" word as shown by word indexes. In the words of several researchers. "the text just doesn't act like natural language".

An Ideographic or Symbolic Representational Scheme. At the other extreme. a system involving our hypothesis P.4 (a purely ideographic or pictographic system, preserving no trace of endings, grammatical forms. or any of the structure of alphabetic strings) is equally unlikely. This possibility is ruled out by the salient beginning. middle. and ending structure demonstrated by Tiltman and since repeatedly confirmed. The prefix-like entities and the obvious similarities between words also indicate that there is some degree of language-like structure. involving units smaller than whole words or ideas. in the Voynich text.

Polyalphabetic Substitution. Hypotheses involving E.8 (the cyclic use of several different substitution alphabets according to some rule) is ruled out. as noted by Elizebeth Friedman. because there is far too much structured repetition in the text. Polyalphabetic systems. like the well-known Vigenère table. are explicitly designed to obscure the many patterns and repetitions in natural text which provide helpful break-in points for the would-be decipherer. The frequency counts of occurrences of Voynich characters throughout a sample of text are also too "rough"—that is. some characters are infrequent. while others are very common—for a polyalphabetic system. which obviously. with its many alphabets. tends to "flatten out" the frequency distribution for the text as a whole.

Transposition Systems. Systems involving anagramming or transposing letters over arbitrary sequences of text (T.6) are also unlikely for a number of reasons: first. the many repetitions of similar strings of characters in close proximity (e.g..

"　40ℓɾɛ9　40ℓ̃ɾɛ9　40x̃9　" and "　2o8g　ɾɛo8g　oℓɾo8g　"); second. the numerous short

words used as labels or captions; and third. the difficulty. ambiguity. and tedium of such methods for so large a volume of text. together with the difficulty of reading and deciphering what was probably a reference work to be consulted by more than one person.

Some Hypotheses Worthy of Further Consideration. Having narrowed the field somewhat by setting aside some of the possibilities as unlikely. we can concentrate our attention on certain others that seem more promising. I would like. first. to suggest certain general considerations that appear relevant to the nature of the writing system in the Voynich text. Whatever method of concealment was used would have had to be relatively easy to employ and to remember. The sheer volume of text (estimated at 250.000 characters) militates against any elaborate. multi-stage process such as that proposed by Newbold. The ease and naturalness and the cursive quality of the writing also argues against any tedious and involved sequence of enciphering operations (unless. of course. we assume that the entire manuscript had been copied from an earlier original).

The recent research of Prescott Currier (see Section 6.8 below) indicates quite clearly that there were at least two different scribes or scholars who worked on different folios of the manuscript. This implies that the system had to be such as to permit its joint use by several persons—a very important new bit of information. As has apparently been assumed without question by most students. the script was almost certainly written from left to right; this is shown by the clockwise progression of circular diagrams. the presence of starting markers on the left. the slant of the writing around circles. and the arrangement of lines on a page. Finally. it seems reasonable to me that there must have been other documents written in this script. and also one or more code books or dictionaries in use among the small secret society of scholars who employed the system. There is always a chance that such materials will turn up some day to throw some new light on the enigma. Considering these general factors and what is known about the behavior of characters in the text. the hypotheses below seem in my opinion. most likely to repay further investigation.

Latin Text With Vowels Dropped. Dropping vowels from Latin produces text having very different characteristics from those of normal Latin Text. Single Latin letters may be represented by single Voynich symbols. or. more likely. by mixed-length units; possibly variants (i.e.. a choice of more than one Voynich symbol to stand for a given Latin symbol) are also included. as well as nulls (dummy. meaningless letters chosen from a small set of alternatives and inserted irregularly throughout the text). Such a concealment system may be represented in our scheme of hypotheses as (P.1 and T.2 and (E.1 or E.5) and possibly also E.6 and T.4). These combined operations could all be carried out easily. naturally. and rapidly by a scribe after some practice and familiarity with the system. The resulting text would be very difficult to decipher for anyone unfamiliar with the method, and relatively easy for the initiate. A problem arises in dropping vowels from Latin, in that many important small words like "de" and "ad", "et" and "ut", "sit" and "est" become indistinguishable, and some words consisting only of a single vowel disappear entirely. This might not be a serious problem for readers and writers who knew what the text was about and were closely familiar with it.

Abbreviated Latin Words. Conventional Latin abbreviations, represented by mixed-length Voynich character strings or code-like entities, possibly with the added complications of variants and nulls, presents another likely possibility (P.1 and T.3 and E.5 or E.7; optionally also E.6 and T.4). This, too, would be easy to learn and to remember, and easy to read for the initiate within the secret circle, but highly difficult for anyone outside it to penetrate.

Latin Text, Enciphered by Simple Substitution, Concealed in a Longer Dummy Message. This hypothesis (P.1 and E.1 and T.7) would explain the many strange repetitions of highly similar words in close succession: one of the words represents a part of the actual message, while the rest are nonsense sequences made up, like meaningless babbling, and inserted to conceal the true cipher string. The scribe, faced with the task of thinking up a large number of such dummy sequences, would naturally tend to repeat parts of neighboring strings with various small changes and additions to fill out the line until the next message-bearing word or phrase. This theory would also explain the frequent illogicality and lack of consistent sequential structure in stretches of text which has so frustrated students.

A Synthetic Language or Code (P.3 and E.7; optionally also E.5 and E.6 and T.4). The most likely hypothesis in my opinion involves a simple code based on a small glossary of a few hundred Latin words related to plants, medicine, astronomy, weather, and other topics of interest to the scribes of the manuscript. The root or base forms would be represented by one, two, or three Voynich Symbols standing for a page number or column number on a page, or for a philosophical subject category as was usual in early universal or artificial languages. (See Section 9.3.) Endings or grammatical forms could then be represented by the strings of symbols in certain preferred orders noted by Tiltman and others at the ends of words. This, too, was a common feature of early synthetic languages. The addition of mixed-length variants for bases and affixes, and the insertion of nulls, all common practices in early codes used by the Catholic Church, would provide a complex concealment system exceedingly hard to penetrate for the outsider, while still very easy for the initiate to use. With some practice, it could be memorized almost like a natural language, especially if its basic vocabulary was as small as seems likely from the evidence.

A system of this kind would require one or more copies of a code book or dictionary to be consulted by users of the language. In Section 9.2, an early Vatican code (Silvester 1526) which exactly fits the above description will be discussed in some detail. Currier's findings concerning the differences in certain character frequencies and combinations between samples of text in two different "hands" are highly significant in this regard. A possible explanation is that one scribe used certain variants in preference to others, or employed the system of "endings" a little differently; in contrast to the practice of another scribe. These and other hypotheses will be discussed further from various points of view in Chapters 5, 6, and 9.

Chapter 5

Major Claims of Decipherment

The survey to be presented here will be quite brief. except in the case of the most recent claim. by Robert S. Brumbaugh of Yale University. The solutions put forward by Newbold. Feely. and Strong have been thoroughly dealt with by other writers. in treatments published in relatively accessible sources. I will provide only a rapid sketch of the main points regarding their work. for the sake of completeness. for students new to the problem. and for methodological reasons.

5.1 Newbold

Prof. William R. Newbold was among the first scholars to whom Wilfrid Voynich gave copies of the manuscript soon after its discovery. in the hope of getting it deciphered and translated. Newbold. a student of medieval philosophy and science. published his first presentation in 1921. He worked on the manuscript and on other alchemical texts attributed to Roger Bacon for several more years before his sudden death. Worksheets and notes of his research were edited and published by his friend and literary executor. Prof. Roland G. Kent (Newbold and Kent 1928). Newbold was familiar with the system of esoteric mystical philosophy developed by the medieval Jews in Spain and known as the Cabala (or Kabbalah). He studied the sentences in a mixture of scripts on folio 116v. and was immediately struck by a phrase "michi . . . dabas multas . . . portas" (as he read it). which he translated "Thou wast giving me many gates". (For several different readings of folio 116v. see figure 23). The word "gates" (Latin "portae" or "portas") was used in the Cabala. according to Newbold. to refer to all possible combinations of the letters of the Hebrew alphabet. taken two at a time. Assuming from the outset. following Voynich. that Roger Bacon was the manuscript's author. Newbold brought to bear evidence that Bacon was familiar with certain aspects of Cabalistic lore; he cites references in Bacon's Greek Grammar and his fragmentary writings on Hebrew (Bacon 1902). as well as his comments concerning concealed writing (for which see Section 4.4.2 above). as evidence of this familiarity.

Starting with this clue. Newbold examined some other works on the subject of alchemy attributed to Bacon. and claimed to have discovered a cipher used by Bacon for concealing messages within innocent-appearing Latin text (the method I have designated T.7 in Chapter 4). He maintained that a variant of this method had been employed in the Voynich manuscript as well. Thus. Newbold ascribes two different. but related. cipher systems to Bacon: first. a "Latin text" cipher from the alchemy treatises. and second. a more complex "shorthand cipher" used in the Voynich manuscript.

5.1.1 The Latin Text Cipher.

In the Latin alchemical manuscripts. a message was hidden. according to Newbold. within Latin words so chosen and arranged as to appear to be a treatise on alchemy or on a related topic. Alchemy texts were always expected to be mysterious and nonsensical to the uninitiated (and. one suspects. to many would-be initiates as well); such a work would thus provide an ideal "cover" for a secret message. Each pair of visible Latin letters in the cover text stood. in Newbold's view based on the Cabalistic "gates". for a single underlying plaintext letter. In this system. 484 letter-pairs (twenty-two letters taken two at a time) were generated. so that each of the twenty-two letters of the plaintext alphabet could be represented by any of twenty-two "variants". or alternative cipher pairs. A restriction was placed by Newbold on this large number of alternatives. such that pairs chosen to substitute for a plaintext letter in a word must have the first member of one pair the same as the last member of the preceding pair. For example. if "unius" were to be enciphered. it might be represented as "or-ri-it-tu-ur": the doubled letters would then be dropped. giving "oritur". a good Latin word (see Newbold and Kent 1928. p. 53 ff and Manly 1931. p. 34 ff for a fuller explanation). Added complexities were introduced to provide a cover text that appeared to be acceptable Latin and would not (at least in an alchemy text) arouse suspicion. These added steps involved a many-many substitution. and on top of that. a rearrangement or anagramming of letters within passages of fifty-five or one hundred and ten characters of text (our method T.6).

5.1.2 The Shorthand Cipher.

As described by Newbold (Newbold and Kent 1928, p. 106), there were six steps to be followed in deciphering the Voynich text:

1. Transliteration: identifying the shorthand characters, and transliterating them in order.

2. Syllabification: doubling all but the first and last characters and arranging the resulting string in pairs with the first member of each the same as the last member of the preceding pair.

3. Commutation: In any pair where the second member is one of the "commuting" set "C. O. N. M. U. T. A. Q", change the first member according to a "conversion alphabet" provided by Newbold; Where the first member is a commuting letter, change the second by a "reversion alphabet" provided; where both are commuting letters, change both, each by the indicated alphabet.

4. Translation: assigning to the commuted pairs their alphabetic values (by lookup in a table).

5. Reversion: Changing "alphabetic values" to "phonetic values" (the exact nature of this step is not clear).

6. Recomposition: Anagramming the letters to produce meaningful text.

The "shorthand" referred to in step 1 was supposedly based on an ancient Greek system of abbreviations, and was to be applied to each character of the Voynich script as inspected under a reading glass and broken up into many tiny component curves and lines. Extensive tables are provided in the back of the book to enable the student to carry out all the necessary reversions, conversions, translations, and so forth.

Newbold and Kent provide good illustrations of a number of folios from the manuscript, chosen from various classes of drawings; decipherments of the text on these folios are also presented, which bear little or no relation to the pictures. For example, a tale concerning two ancient Romans is read on a page with an astrological drawing (folio 72v). Human figure folios are read as describing procreative or gynecological matters, with at least some apparent justification (ova, fallopian tubes, spermatozoa, etc.) in the drawings. This seems to be a frequent reaction on the part of modern students to the naked female figures on folios 75 ff. Other drawings are taken as recording the appearance of a comet (folio 71v), an observation of a spiral nebula (folio 68v3), and an annular eclipse (folio 67v2).

The claims of Newbold were hailed with great enthusiasm by Voynich and many others, who wrote numerous reviews and commentaries (Bird 1921, Garland 1921, McKeon 1928). Roger Bacon enjoyed a spectacular, if brief, moment in the sun, while he was credited with the invention of the compound microscope and telescope, and the anticipation of many twentieth-century scientific discoveries. Catholic writers exulted in triumph on the one hand over what they saw as a vindication of medieval scholastic philosophy, and fell over one another on the other hand in their haste to apologize for, excuse, and minimize the persecution and neglect inflicted upon the thirteenth-century "forerunner of modern science" by his superiors in the Franciscan Order (Reville 1921, Walsh 1921). Even a number of prominent Baconian experts and specialists in medieval philosophy accepted Newbold's claims uncritically, and manfully strove to assimilate the indigestible anachronisms into their knowledge of Bacon's work and thought (Carton 1929, Gilson 1928). Some less credulous scholars were taking a harder look at Newbold's theories, and expressing their doubts (Steele 1928; Thorndike 1921, 1929; Salomon 1934).

At the same time another scholar, Prof. John M. Manly, a professor of English at the University of Chicago, had interested himself in the manuscript, and had been (according to his own words) "dabbling" with it for several years "at odd times". Manly was a friend of Newbold's, and had corresponded with him; Newbold had discussed his methods and findings with Manly over some time. In 1921, Manly published articles in *Harpers Monthly Magazine* (1921b) and in the *American Review of Reviews* (1921a), expressing a mildly favorable or neutral reaction, but also giving voice to some doubts and cautions. After Newbold's death in 1926, and the posthumous publication of his work in the book edited by Kent, Manly published another, much more outspoken article in *Speculum* (1931), emphatically disproving and rejecting Newbold's theories.

This is how Manly expresses his views in the *Speculum* article: "The more I studied the nature and operation of the cipher system attributed to Bacon, the more clearly did I see that it was incapable of being used as a medium of communication, and was indeed not Bacon's work but the subconscious creation of Professor Newbold's enthusiasm and ingenuity. I told Professor Newbold my conclusions and gave my reasons for them in several letters...." (1931, p. 347). Manly goes on to explain that, while he would not have chosen to make a point of attacking his late friend's work, he felt that it was necessary to set the record straight in view of the unquestioning acceptance accorded to the theory by so many prominent authorities. He says, "One of the most eminent philosophers of France, Professor Gilson, though bewildered by the method, has accepted the results; Professor Raoul Carton, the well-known Baconian specialist, in two long articles, accepts both method

34

and results with enthusiasm; and American chemists and biologists have been similarly impressed. The interests of scientific truth therefore demand a careful examination of the claims of the Newbold cipher" (p. 347). (See Carton 1929. Gilson 1928.)

Manly makes the following flat statement at the outset: "In my opinion, the Newbold claims are entirely baseless and should be definitely and absolutely rejected" (p. 347). He explains that the tiny lines and curves Newbold saw as microscopic Greek shorthand symbols were due simply to cracking of the ink on the rough surface of the parchment, thus vitiating step 1 of Newbold's method. A second telling attack is focussed by Manly on the sixth and final step, involving anagramming letters in stretches of fifty-five or one hundred and ten text characters. He demonstrates the amazing number of reasonable sentences, even including rhyming poetry, that can be generated from a single short passage by anagramming. For instance, he considers a sentence in one of the alchemy treatises attributed to Bacon: "incipiunt quaedam caret quaestiones Bernardi cum suis responsionibus et est. . . ." From this sentence, Newbold had obtained the following: "De via et terra et coelis despicit mixta principia lume[n]". Since each letter of the original sentence, in Newbold's "Latin cipher" system, can have a number of alternative equivalents, a huge number of possibilities present themselves for selection even before the anagramming begins. This is the sentence for which William F. Friedman, working in cooperation with Manly to test Newbold's theory, obtained the anagram "Paris is lured with loving Vestals. . . .", simply by choosing a different set of equivalents and a different arrangement among the many possibilities. For a full discussion of the problem of anagramming and the pitfalls of Newbold's theory, see Manly 1931, pp. 350 ff and Friedman and Friedman 1959.

Manly's article in *Speculum* succeeded in laying to rest Newbold's theories, and Friar Bacon returned again to his accustomed scholastic obscurity, consigned to even deeper darkness in an over-reaction on the part of some modern scholars against his illusory role as originator of twentieth-century scientific instruments, and observer of astronomical and gynecological secrets 600 years in advance of their appointed time. (Note, in particular, the savagely critical and "debunking" attitude toward Bacon expressed by Thorndike 1916 and 1923-1958.) It seems probable also that the controversy over Newbold's work, the amount of publicity it received, and its complete destruction so closely following upon its uncritical acceptance by many prominent experts who presumably should have known better, caused many scholars to wash their hands of the manuscript and to steer clear of any serious involvement with the problem it presents. If a scholar of Newbold's impressive reputation and knowledge of medieval philosophy could be made to appear so deluded and foolish after so many years of painstaking effort, it is easy to understand the reluctance of other scholars to risk their own reputations and peace of mind on the problem.

5.2 Feely

Elizebeth Friedman (1962) describes Feely and his claim to a solution of the manuscript as follows: "In 1943, a Rochester lawyer, Joseph Martin Feely, published a book entitled *Roger Bacon's Cipher: The Right Key Found.* Feely was the author of *Shakespeare's Maze, Deciphering Shakespeare,* and other items catalogued in the Friedman Collection under the heading 'Cryptologic Follies.' " However unacceptable his results may have been, he started his researches in a sensible manner, according to his description of them in his book: coming upon the manuscript through the pictures in the Newbold-Kent book, he did frequency counts on Roger Bacon's Latin in several works, including *De Perspectiva* (a work on optics) and *Communia Naturalium* (concerning natural science).

Feely noted that the "leaders" (by which he apparently meant the highest-frequency letters) in Bacon's Latin comprised the letters "E, I, T, A, N, U, S", and he attempted to make a parallel analysis of letter frequencies in the Voynich text, on an assumption of simple substitution (our hypothesis P.1 and E.1 and T.1). From these studies he moved quickly on to attempts at "cribbing" various words that might be related to the drawings and their accompanying text in the manuscript. He remarks with obvious exasperation that the Latin in Bacon's manuscripts was highly abbreviated; he estimates the text to have been reduced in length by thirty-five percent through this practice. He comments, also with evident annoyance, upon the differences between medieval and classical Latin. These difficulties apparently frustrated and hindered his statistical researchers to a considerable extent, and perhaps drove him to the much easier and less demanding approach of guessing at possible "cribs" in the text.

Feely's attempts at cribbing apparently met with some success. On folio 78r, shown in Newbold and Kent (1928, Plate V), Feely found his first break into the text. This page is one of those showing nude female figures bathing in pools or tubs of liquid. Feely assumed that two cloud- or grape-cluster objects at the top corners of the page (see figure 15 for a detail of one of these) were "ovaries" and that the channels leading down from them and joining in the middle of the page were transmitting "ova" into the two "sacks" below. In the "sacks," according to Feely, the "ova" were shown as female figures standing in the liquid. There are "labels" in the Voynich script next to each cluster, the sections of pipe conducting the stream of mysterious substances from them, and the pools into which they pour. Feely obtained his first "clews" (as he likes to call the results of his cribbing) by a study of these labels and an attempt to assume various Latin words they might represent. Figure 25 shows the results he obtained from these initial researches.

His initial "clews" provided Feely with a number of letter substitutions for common symbols in the Voynich script, which he then employed in an effort to puzzle out the remainder of the text on the same page. It should be noted that he at no time had access to a complete photocopy of the manuscript; he carried out all his work on the illustrations in Newbold and Kent 1928. The plaintext which he obtained was a crude, abbreviated pseudo-Latin, which he translated to produce English text on gynecological topics for folio 78r. On folio 68v3 (Newbold and Kent 1928, Plate XXII), he claimed to have found Greek words, and to have deciphered a mysterious reference to a statue of Memnon (Feely 1943, p. 37). On other folios, Feely claimed to have found the personal diary of a scientist observing living cells under magnification: the informal "jottings" of an early researcher, hidden in cipher from the hostile eyes of religious authorities.

Although he hedged a bit at coming out flatly in favor of Roger Bacon as author of this scientific diary, Feely maintained that his decipherment tended to support and confirm Bacon's authorship. Figure 25 shows the alphabets he developed as a result of his studies (probably by successively cribbing and then guessing at letters to fill in the gaps, forcing his assumptions until he produced something like Latin, etc., in a cut-and-try fashion). Like many other students, he saw the Voynich script as containing many compound symbols built up from simpler forms. Unfortunately for Feely, however, no other student has accepted his solution as valid. Tiltman, summing up the general opinion, dismisses Feely's efforts as follows: "His unmethodical method produced text in unacceptable medieval Latin, in unauthentic abbreviated forms" (1968, p.6).

5.3 Strong

Professor Leonell C. Strong, a highly respected medical scientist in the field of cancer research at Yale University, became interested in the Voynich manuscript when he saw O'Neill's article (1944) dating the manuscript after 1493. He took up the riddle of the enigmatic book in the context of a long-enduring interest in Renaissance literature. Over a five-year period, he attempted without success to obtain copies of the text for study. He was forced, finally, to carry out his analyses in the same way as Feely had, on the basis of illustrations of individual folios in published works concerning the manuscript. In due course, he published a brief article claiming a solution to the mystery (1945). His decipherment was based on what has since been termed a "peculiar double system of arithmetical progressions of a multiple alphabet, indicating that the Voynich manuscript author was familiar with ciphers described by Trithemius, Porta, and Seleni" (McKaig nd, p. 49).

Strong's decipherment resulted in what he claimed to be a form of medieval English; he attributed the manuscript to one Anthony Ascham, brother of the better-known Roger Ascham or Askham, a tutor to the children of the Royal House of Tudor in the sixteenth century. Anthony was a physician and astrologer; he published several almanacs, a treatise on astronomy, and an herbal (Askham 1548a, 1548b, 1550, 1552, 1553). As described by McKaig (n.d., p. 49), Strong's efforts produced text presenting "an extremely candid discussion of women's ailments and practical matters of the conjugal bed—you might call it a sixteenth-century equivalent of the Kinsey Report". He identified an herbal contraceptive among its recipes, and ran a laboratory experiment to test the effectiveness of the prescription for that purpose. The ingredients comprised pitch from the cut bark of pine trees, honey, and "oil of spindle." Strong claimed that the oil of spindle was found in his experiment to have caused spermatozoa to lose their motility, thereby verifying its effectiveness as the active ingredient of the contraceptive (Strong and McCauley 1947, p. 900). The details of his cryptanalytic work and his method of decipherment, however, have apparently never been explained, and remain problematical.

Strong's plaintext, of which he provides several examples in his articles (Strong 1945, Strong and McCauley 1947), has been rejected by other scholars as completely unacceptable for medieval English. The reader may arrive at his own conclusions from the following sample: "When skuge of tun'e-bag rip, seo uogon kum sli of se mosure-issue ped-stans skubent, stokked kimbo-elbow crawknot." This astonishing string of letters is translated by Strong thus: "When the contents of the veins rip (or tear the membranes), the child comes slyly from the mother issuing with the leg-stance skewed and bent while the arms, bent at the elbow, are knotted (above the head) like the legs of a crawfish." (Strong 1945, p. 608.) To my mind, at least, this seems a highly unlikely thing for any writer of any age to have said, whether in cipher or not. It seems strange to me, also, that so many students have become obsessively preoccupied with gynecological or sexual interpretations of the text. The presence of the scattering of quite unexceptionably matronly little nude figures on a small proportion of folios seems to me an entirely insufficient justification for this obsession.

Nothing further has been heard from Dr. Strong in support of his theories, to my knowledge, even though the Voynich manuscript has now been accessible to scholars at Strong's own University, Yale, for a number of years. According to Elizebeth Friedman, "experts said that what he produced was not medieval English. As for his cipher 'method', he said little about it, but what he did say made no sense to cryptologists" (1962).

5.4 Brumbaugh

Robert S. Brumbaugh, a professor of medieval philosophy at Yale University, became interested in the Voynich manuscript during the 'thirties, and when it was donated by H. P. Kraus to Yale, he "was drawn by an irresistible impulse to look at it" (Brumbaugh 1975, p. 348). He was also struck by O'Neill's identification of American plants in the drawings (1944). Brumbaugh published an article in *Speculum* (1974) announcing that he had solved the mystery, and had read some labels on plant pictures in the pharmaceutical folios as well as what he refers to as "star maps from folio 75 on" (1975, p. 348). He also states that he has deciphered the name of Roger Bacon in the "key" sentences on the last page. He regards the manuscript as a deliberate forgery for the purpose of fooling Emperor Rudloph II of Bohemia into parting with the large sum of money he paid for it.

Stating that the complete solution will take a lot more study, Brumbaugh still claims that "extensive work with a section on astrology, with some botany, and frequency studies of samples throughout the text show that my decipherment is correct" (1975, p. 348). He makes considerable use of the "key"-like sequences of symbols in the margins of folios 1r, 17r, 49v, 66r, and 76r, and in the second ring of 57v, as well as the sentences on 116v; these sequences, while to some extent deliberately misleading, still provide aid in penetrating the cipher, according to Brumbaugh. The text on folio 116v Brumbaugh finds to be enciphered using what he calls, without further explanation, a "standard thirteenth-century cipher" (1975, p. 350); he sees confirmation for this in the paired sequences in left and right margins of folio 1r, in which he finds a monoalphabetic substitution of two normal alphabets, with "a" of one set against "d" of the other. Using this cipher, and some rearrangement of syllables, Brumbaugh obtains "RODGD BACON" from a portion of folio 116v which he reads as "MICHI CON OLADA BA" (note that this is the beginning of the same text string that Newbold read as "MICHI DABAS MULTAS . . . PORTAS"). He suggests that the name was "planted" in such a manner as to be easily seen by Rudolph's experts and thus to attract and delude them into accepting the attribution of the manuscript to Bacon.

On folio 66r, Brumbaugh sees a set of "formulae" in the words and letters scattered down the right margin; these formulae, he suggests, serve to equate symbols to other symbols by a sort of "cryptarithmetic," of which he provides several examples (1975, pp. 350–351). I must confess that, while those he explains are convincing enough, the rest of the "formulae" remain somewhat mysterious to me in the absence of further clarification. Using these "equations" and the recoveries of labels for plants (which he "cribbed" by exploiting word patterns with repeating letters such as "p" and "e" in "pepper," "pa" in "papaver," etc.), he sets up a four-by-nine table of correspondences; he says that this table is similar to "a standard alchemist's or astrologer's cipher, well known in the trade" (1975, p. 351), and he finds among the text of 116v the words "quadrix nonix" which he sees as referring to this four-by-nine structure. Figure 26 shows the cipher box as Brumbaugh recovered it.

All the Voynich symbols, Brumbaugh suggests, stand for forms of the numerals zero through nine (or one through nine, the function of zero, if any, is not made clear in his presentation). The encipherment, as he sees it, is a two-step operation, which first replaced letters by numerals using the four-by-nine box, collapsing the letters of the alphabet onto the nine digits, and then substituted choices among several different fanciful designs for each numeral in order to conceal their identity, designs chosen from "modern and archaic numeral forms, Greek and Latin letters, and several cursive compendia" (1975, p. 353). It will be noted that this process involves multiple variants in both the Voynich script and the plaintext. Decipherment involves first recognizing the numeral underlying one of its variant forms in the Voynich script, then writing under it the two, three, or four possible choices of plaintext correspondences; when this has been done for a word, a pronounceable sequence of letters is selected from among the choices.

An example of the application of this method to a portion of folio 116v will serve as an illustration of the procedure. Brumbaugh singles out a sequence of eight Voynich symbols from the mixed text on this page, just preceding a phrase that he reads as High German: "valsch ubren so nim ga nicht o.", and translates as "the above is false so do not take it". Identifying the eight Voynich symbols with numerals according to the correspondences he has set up (which he does not explain anywhere in his papers except in very fragmentary form), he obtains the digits "0 2 0 2 7 3 3 9". Assigning to these their multiple plaintext equivalents from the nine-by-four box, he produces the following:

```
0 2 0 2      7 3 3 9

A B A B      G C C  I
J K J K      P L L
V R V R      Y W W  -US
```

He selects among the few pronounceable alternatives (AKABYLLUS, ARAKYLLUS, AKARYCCUS, URUBYLLUS, ARABYCCUS, etc.,) the word "ARABYCCUS", which he sees as a reference to the Arabic numerals underlying the cipher. In his first article (1974), he presents a number of other examples of his method drawn from plant labels on pharmaceutical folios. In most cases, the choice among pronounceable possibilities is quite limited, a phenomenon that lends credence to the theory.

The plaintext produced by Brumbaugh's decipherment is described by him as "an artificial language, based on Latin, but not very firmly based there; its spelling is phonetically impressionistic; some sample passages seem *solely* repetitive padding". To add to the decipherer's problems, "the upper cipher key changes slightly every eight pages" (1975, p. 354). Brumbaugh asserts, plausibly enough, that such ambiguities, while rendering a cipher system unsuitable for modern military use, were customary and expected in magical, astrological, and alchemical texts of the times in question.

Tiltman (1975) makes these critical comments regarding Brumbaugh's theories: "The idea that the manuscript is a forgery is not original to him. I suggested it as an uncomfortable possibility in 1951 . . . . He claims that all the symbols in the script are really digits in variant forms and that the key is a box providing single digit substitution for letters . . . i.e., each digit represents two or three letters . . . . All this is so ambiguous that it can only be justified by the production of a great deal of confirmatory evidence, but he supplies hardly any evidence at all and I remain quite unconvinced . . . . Brumbaugh is not alone in assuming the symbols to be numbers in various forms. This has been suggested several times."

My opinion on a careful study of Brumbaugh's two published papers is that his theories are quite plausible on the face of such evidence as he presents. His proposals are based in, and explain, more of the observed phenomena in the manuscript and what is known of its history than those of any other decipherer. I have made two painstaking attempts to reconstruct as many as possible of the variant forms for numerals he mentions in his articles, in so far as I can guess at them from his brief and frequently cryptic references. From the fragmentary set of correspondences I have thus obtained, I have attempted some decipherments of other plant labels and isolated text strings with mixed results. A lot of them are meaningless, so far as I can see, and some are suggestive of Latin or pseudo-Latin words; many are very similar (as would be expected from the known repetitiveness of the text). There is just enough plausibility in the process to lead one on, but not enough to leave one satisfied. Figure 26 shows my very conjectural attempt to reconstruct Brumbaugh's variants with their correspondence to the nine-by-four matrix, and a sample of his decipherments of plant labels.

A new article by Brumbaugh has recently appeared in the *Journal of the Warburg and Courtauld Institutes*, University of London (1976). In this article, Brumbaugh says that his recent research has convinced him even more firmly of the correctness of his decipherment.

Chapter 6

History of Other Substantial Analytic Efforts

6.1 The Forms in Which the Manuscript Has Been Studied

The Voynich manuscript was for a long time held in private hands, first by its discoverer, Wilfrid Voynich, then by his widow, and finally by H. P. Kraus. Because of its great financial value, its owners were understandably reluctant to allow unlimited access to it or reproduction of it, although they frequently cooperated with serious scholars seeking to unravel the mystery. In the first few years after his discovery of the manuscript, Voynich made vigorous and repeated attempts to interest students in it, and Newbold was introduced to the problem through his efforts. It is possible that the disastrous outcome of Newbold's researches, and the disappointment occasioned by their failure may have resulted in an atmosphere of caution and of greater restriction on the part of the owners in providing access to the manuscript in subsequent years.

As we have seen in the previous chapter, Feely and Strong were able to study the text only through illustrations in the published works of Newbold and others. The manuscript has come before the eyes of many other students, however, in the form of photostatic copies. The copies used by Friedman, Tiltman, Krischer, and Currier, and the copy available to me, all derive ultimately from a photocopy made by Father Petersen of Catholic University on April 29, 1931, from a set of photostats provided by Mrs. Voynich. Tiltman (in a report of Petersen's work made in conjunction with an inventory of his papers after his death in 1966), states that "virtually all copies of the manuscript in private hands are derived from Fr. Petersen's photostats." The pages I have studied are, in fact, copies of copies at four or five removes. Friedman (in a note accompanying the copy in the Friedman collection) provides this interesting account of the photocopies in private ownership at that time, and how they came into existence:

> "On 25 May 1944 W|illiam| F|.| F|riedman| wrote a letter to the widow of Dr. Wilfrid M. Voynich who was the discoverer of this famous manuscript, requesting a photostatic copy. The request was granted and a complete copy was made from a negative photostatic copy provided by Mrs. Voynich. In her letter dated 31 May 1944, she stated that photostatic copies were extremely rare, one is in the New York Public Library; another is in the British Museum[1]; another was given to Dr. Petersen of Catholic University; another was given to a scholar whom Mrs. Voynich did not identify; finally Mrs. Voynich herself had a copy. With the copy in the Friedman collection there now appear to be in all six copies in the world. . . ."

In general, the photocopies I have seen provide a degree of definition and clarity which is quite remarkable. Details of penstrokes, guidelines on diagrams, and other fine details show up very well, and the text is clearly distinguishable almost everywhere. Certain deficiencies should, however, be mentioned, since they may have had a definite limiting or distorting effect, however slight, on the research carried out by many students. First, the complete lack of color in the black and white copies inevitably results in a loss of some meaningful information. This may be important not only in identifying plants and in understanding the meaning of other drawings, but even in isolating some details against a dark background. When everything is seen only in shades of grey, writing or small designs within colored fields are sometimes indistinguishable. The same difficulty can arise in cases where the photocopy is very dark, so that the grey background obscures many details.

A second defect of the photocopies available to me applies primarily to the large, multiply-folded folios. Because the copies had to be made in pieces, their over-all relationship to form a whole is often very difficult to reconstruct; the student does not see the complete system of drawings as they appeared in the original form. Worse yet, in some cases material has evidently been obscured by being out of focus around the edges of a page, or has been partly cut off, so that we do not see everything that was on some pages in the original. This is notably the case for the large, intricately folded folio 85–86, containing a complex system of inter-related circular diagrams.

Another feature of the photostats I have studied, while not constituting as much of a hindrance to research as some of the problems already mentioned, is annoying and at times confusing to the student. There are numerous notes, circles, underlines, and other jottings and scribblings of modern researchers on many pages. Among these are copious and obtrusive

---

[1] I am informed by Mr. James Gillogly, who has studied this copy, that it is incomplete, comprising only about the first third of the manuscript made up primarily of plant folios.

remains of at least one previous computer processing project. including circled words and paragraphs. lines marking off parts of the text. and legends such as ''start here''. ''omit punch''. and ''punch just this.'' In some cases. these comments and marks cross the text and drawings in such a way as to obscure or confuse some features of the original. Generations of cryptanalysts have indulged their characteristic and apparently irresistible habit of underlining patterns and repetitions. and have otherwise triumphantly noted their guesses about the meaning of the diagrams (''the four ages of man.'' ''the four seasons.'' ''Sagittarius—archer''). While one can empathize with the momentary joys and sorrows of one's predecessors as they struggled with the enigma. most of these jottings are trivial at best. and at their worst serve only to further aggravate the difficulty of the task. I. for one. would prefer to see nothing more on the pages than what Wilfrid Voynich saw when he first viewed them in 1912.

A final unavoidable disadvantage of working with copies is the inability of the student to verify or reject hypotheses concerning the faint. partially-erased writing in other scripts and hands discussed in Section 4.2 above. Without a careful examination of the original. perhaps aided by special chemical or photographic techniques to reveal the faint fragments of writing more fully. we cannot make the most of the opportunity they provide for a crack in the smooth shell of the mystery. So little ''crib'' information is available; the scribe or scribes were so consistent in ''enciphering'' or ''encoding'' everything. leaving no clues ''in the clear''. that we need every precious bit of added information we can glean from these extraneous or atypical scribblings. whatever their source.

Such. then are the photocopies with which most of the students have worked whose researches will be described in this chapter. The first problem facing the analyst has been the attempt to arrive at a firm set of elementary symbols comprising an ''alphabet'' for the Voynich text. We have seen in Section 4.1 and figure 19 the wide differences between transcription alphabets adopted by different students. Armed with a list of symbols that satisfies him at least as a beginning. each student has then set about the task of making counts. indexes. concordances. and other analyses. either by hand. or if he is so fortunate as to have access to computers. by machine. Some students have copied or transcribed large quantities of text by hand; this is a good way to get the ''feel'' of the text. and to become familiar with the symbols and their variant forms. In the remainder of this chapter. several major analytic efforts will be reviewed. These studies. while not leading to a claim of a decisive break-in or decipherment. have in many cases added substantially to our knowledge about the manuscript; they are informative also from a methodological standpoint. and deserve the attention of any serious student who prefers to learn from the work of his predecessors rather than blindly repeating it.

6.2 First Voynich Manuscript Study Group, 1944–46

After the debunking and rejection by scholars of the three major solutions claimed by Newbold. Feely. and Strong. William F. Friedman decided to mount a large-scale effort against the manuscript with the aid of a uniquely (if accidentally) well-constituted team of researchers. This group. made up of scholars engaged in war-work in Washington. included (according to Elizebeth Friedman 1962) ''specialists in philology. paleography. ancient. classical. and medieval languages: Egyptologists. mathematicians. and authorities on other sciences depicted in the manuscript.'' Awaiting demobilization at the close of their service to the Government during World War II. they agreed to get together after working hours under Friedman's direction and focus their talents on the mysterious manuscript.

The group was called together by Friedman in May of 1944. On the twenth-sixth of May. sixteen people attended the first meeting of what was termed an ''extracurricular'' undertaking. Friedman provided an outline of the manuscript's history and previous solution attempts. and the attendees examined the photocopy lent to them by Dr. Petersen. Sample sheets of copy were distributed to those present. and plans were made to work up a standard list of the symbols and a transcription alphabet in Roman letters with some digits and special characters (punctuation. etc.) for processing on IBM punched-card accounting equipment. Figure 19 shows the list of symbols and English equivalents they arrived at. Meetings were held at approximately biweekly intervals through June; transcription of text and study of the script continued and various background topics (Athanasius Kircher's work. John Dee's activities. studies of medieval Latin. etc.) were investigated and discussed.

Meetings seem to have been somewhat less frequent and regular thereafter. or at least considerably less fully documented in the minutes I have seen. Nevertheless. in September 1944 an ''IBM run'' had been made (on tabulating and sorting machines. since no programmed computers were in general use at that time). In subsequent months. more text was transliterated and machined. In December 1944. meetings were ''resumed.'' implying that a hiatus of some duration had elapsed during which the group had not been meeting. A new enthusiasm was communicated to the attendees. and a new impetus provided to their efforts (according to the minutes) by William Friedman's presentation of his findings concerning a synthetic language developed by Wilkins (see 6.6 and 9.3 below for further details). Studies of this language indicated that word beginnings and endings, letter frequencies, number of different symbols, and word lengths seemed comparable to those found in the Voynich text.

During January and February, the group continued to work on IBM runs and frequency tabulations. There is, unfortunately, no record of their work after this time in the materials available to me, although there is evidence that work continued sporadically into 1945 and 1946. It is hard to tell, in the absence of any summary of their results, how much text they succeeded in processing by machine and what analyses they performed on it. Judging by the printouts of machined text that were preserved in our records, they transcribed and keypunched an impressive amount of text—at least 48,000 characters, or 1663 thirty-character lines. The tabulations of results and any report of the analytic studies have disappeared from the file, if they ever existed in final form. Subsequent students have had to repeat, over and over again, all the work of transcription and machine preparation, as if it had never been done by others.

Elizebeth Friedman presents the following perspective on the outcome of the First Voynich Manuscript Study Group: "Because the preliminary work of transcribing the text into machine-processable symbols could only be done after working hours, demobilization was practically complete before the manuscript was ready for final study. The scientists thereupon disbanded and returned to their universities or research projects. Their considered opinion as to the age, authorship and general nature of the manuscripts, based on their extracurricular work, are still valid today...." (1962).

6.3 Theodore C. Petersen

Father Petersen (1883–1966) was a teacher and priest at St. Paul's College and Catholic University. (The following details are largely drawn from unpublished biographical notes and a survey of Petersen's work on the manuscript compiled by Tiltman after Petersen's death in 1966.) He had one hundred and twenty-two sheets of photostats made on April 29, 1931 from Mrs. Voynich's copy at a cost of $25.00. Thereafter he spent considerable time, especially from 1952 until the time of his death, in a painstaking and thorough study of the manuscript. His work included a complete hand copy, carefully corrected by reference to the original, which he examined in the New York Guarantee Trust safe deposit vault where it was kept until Mrs. Voynich's death. A note on the front page of this transcript attests to the fact that he finished it July 19, 1944. Tiltman (1975) reports that the task of copying the approximately 250,000 characters of text occupied about four years.

Petersen was a scholar of wide learning in ancient languages and history, and compiled a quantity of valuable and interesting information about religious, astrological, and mystical manuscripts and other sources of possible relevance to the Voynich manuscript. He also directed considerable attention toward identifying the plants depicted in the herbal drawings. The pages of his transcript are copiously annotated with these gleanings and commentaries. In addition to the transcript, Petersen made (also by hand) a laborious and complete concordance of the entire manuscript, showing every word with reference to all the pages where it occurred and several words preceding and following each occurrence. As Tiltman suggests, in the absence of a complete computer index, this concordance can be of great value to students of the manuscript.

In his scholarly and wide-ranging background research, Petersen studied the works of Ramon Lull and St. Hildegard of Bingen, magical manuscripts such as *Picatrix*, astrological, alchemical, and herbal writings, and the works of Albertus Magnus and Roger Bacon. There is, unfortunately, nowhere in the material available to me any report of theories Petersen may have held, or conclusions he may have reached concerning the decipherment of the manuscript. At his death, his papers were given to William Friedman; they were inventoried at Friedman's request by Tiltman, and are now a part of the Friedman collection at the Marshall Library in Lexington, Virginia.

6.4 Second Voynich Manuscript Study Group, 1962–1963

In 1962, Friedman succeeded in interesting computer specialists at the Radio Corporation of America in an experimental effort to study the entire manuscript by computer. The first meeting of a new study group was held on 25 December, 1962. According to the minutes, Mrs. Friedman presented background data on the history of previous work and general information on the manuscript. Mr. Friedman then gave a presentation on the "Salient External Features and Cryptologic Characteristics of the Manuscript." The group worked together, again "extracurricularly" and with a minimum of publicity, over the next several months. A small team of "dedicated wives" (as they were described by a participant in the study group) were hard at work transcribing and keypunching a quantity of text, using facilities provided by RCA after working hours.

Ambitious plans were laid for an impressive set of computer runs, intended to involve, according to the records I have studied, at least 2000 thirty-three character records, or upward of 66,000 characters of text. There are flowcharts, program specifications, and all the other paraphernalia of a full-scale computer attack, which (had it been completed) would certainly have provided students with a powerful tool for research. The computer runs planned included studies of all character sequences ("n-graphs") from one to six letters in length; single words and sequences of words in their context; the occurrence of letters at different positions within words; words in different positions within sentences; and, finally, a study called "letter permutations" whose nature is not clear to me from the documentation. This plan would have resulted in a complete computational-linguistic analysis of the Voynich text.

I cannot determine how many characters of text were actually machined, and whether any processing was ever completed. There is clear evidence in the records that programs had been written to generate the computer files required to carry out the processing, and that detailed specifications had been set up for performing the sorts and tabulations. In September, 1963, plans were still being pursued to complete transcription and machining of text. Figure 19 shows the transcription alphabet used by the RCA group to represent the Voynich script characters. Unfortunately, the second study group suffered the same fate as the first; higher management at RCA decided to terminate even the minimal "extracurricular" involvement of their resources, and the group was forced to disband before any definitive results could be obtained.

6.5 William F. Friedman

A specialist in genetics and biology who became one of the world's foremost cryptologists, Friedman was also a devoted student of the Voynich manuscript from the early twenties on. He worked with John M. Manly in testing and disproving Newbold's claims. Elizebeth Friedman (1962) provides an amusing account of the sport she, her husband, and Manly had together in demonstrating other "decipherments" that could be had from Newbold's text using his methods but with different arbitrary and subjective choices and arrangements of letters at certain stages of the process (see Section 5.1 above).

In 1944, as we have seen earlier in this chapter, Friedman brought together the gathering of war-working scholars who formed the First Voynich Manuscript Study Group. Their work, unfortunately cut short before it could reach fruition, has already been described. Elizebeth Friedman has this to say concerning her husband's enduring interest in the problem, which never flagged up to the time of his death in November, 1969: "Through the years since 1921, Friedman has continued to interest scholars and cryptologic experts in the problem, besides giving it what spare time he could himself. In the opinion of this writer, Friedman's studies have produced a theory which constitutes a logical basis for an attack that may lead to a solution of this baffling manuscript" (1962).

Friedman published a statement of his theory, in the form of an anagram, in a footnote to an article on another cryptologic topic in the January 1959 issue of the *Philological Quarterly* (Friedman and Friedman 1959). At the same time, he deposited a statement in clear English in the archives of the Quarterly's editor. He did this in order to establish and date his claim to the idea, which he could not yet work out in detail and prove sufficiently to publish. This is the anagram, as it appeared in the footnote: "I PUT NO TRUST IN ANAGRAMMATIC ACROSTIC CYPHERS, FOR THEY ARE OF LITTLE REAL VALUE—A WASTE—AND MAY PROVE NOTHING.—FINIS." (Friedman and Friedman 1959, p. 19). In his article, he states that an anagram of this length is possible, though extremely difficult, to solve; in order to read it, one would have to know something of what it said. In this way, Friedman planned to have a cryptographer's last word, and thus triumph, even from the grave, over any later discoverer of the same idea.

The theory which Friedman concealed in the anagram has since become known to a number of students, and there seems to be no further real secrecy concerning its nature. Tiltman had later independently reached the same conclusion (see Section 6.6 below), namely that the text of the manuscript was written in a synthetic language built up on the basis of categories or classes of words with coded endings or other affixes. Friedman's and Tiltman's researches into known languages of this type have been mentioned above, and more will be said on the topic in 6.6 and in Chapter 9.

6.6 John H. Tiltman

Brigadier Tiltman, a professional cryptologist of long and distinguished experience, was introduced to the elegant puzzle of the Voynich manuscript in 1950 by William Friedman, who provided him with copies of several folios from the final section of the manuscript, consisting of text without drawings. Tiltman quickly carried out, by hand, a thorough set of statistical studies on the text, concentrating his efforts on the most frequent symbols and their combinations. His analysis, demonstrating a "precedence" structure of symbols within words and the orderly behavior of characters as "beginners," "middles," and "enders" of words, has remained one of the most solid and useful findings gleaned by students of the manuscript during many years of study. In 1951, Tiltman prepared an informal report in the form of a personal communication to his friend William Friedman, in which he summed up his work (Tiltman 1951). The next few paragraphs will briefly review some of the salient points in that report.

Tiltman directed his attention toward the behavior of the seventeen commonest symbols in the manuscript; figure 19 shows his transcription alphabet. He notes the ordering of characters within words in such a way that they seem to reflect entities like stems and affixes. Certain symbols most often begin words, and cluster there with certain other symbols; others exhibit a preference for the ends of words, where they cluster in certain arrangements with other symbols. There is a structure of repeated "ı" and "c" symbols after "a" and "o", and before "ɔ, ʔ, ɣ, ɤ". A table of these "a-endings", as found by Tiltman, is shown in figure 27. He mentions also the frequent sequential repetition of "aʔ" in phrases such as "aʔ aʔ", "aʔ aʔ aɣ", etc., repeating the suggestion of a friend of his that these and other similar short repeated groups might stand for Roman numerals (for example, "aɯɔ" might be "iij", and "aʔ aʔ aɣ" might be "xxv"). While mentioning this idea as an interesting possibility, Tiltman points out that it does not work out well in some cases, and it still leaves us with too many unsolved problems. In any case, the ordering of symbols within words clearly demonstrated by Tiltman, and since confirmed by others, presents us with a phenomenon which must be satisfactorily explained by any valid decipherment theory.

As he stated in his 1951 report to Friedman, Tiltman had independently arrived at the same theory about the plaintext underlying the Voynich script that Friedman himself had earlier developed. He states this theory thus: "As you know, I early formed the opinion, which you held much earlier than I, that there was no cipher involved at all (in the commonly accepted sense of the word) and that the basis was more likely to be a very primitive form of synthetic universal language such as was developed in the form of a philosophical classification of ideas by Bishop Wilkins in 1667" (1951, p. 1). Tiltman became convinced, from his study of the behavior of symbols within words and words within lines of text, that the phenomena could not be explained by any simple substitution system. In pursuit of confirmation for his theory, he undertook a determined search to trace back the concept of "universal" and "synthetic" languages to a time that might be consistent with the origin of the Voynich manuscript (1550 or earlier).

Friedman, as we have seen above, had turned up two interesting synthetic language systems: one developed by Bishop John Wilkins (1641, 1668a, 1668b), and another of somewhat later date devised by George Dalgarno (1661, 1680). Tiltman studied these two languages carefully, looking for stylistic and statistical similarities to the Voynich text. While both systems were probably of too late a date to have been used by the author of the manuscript, they might have arisen in, or been based upon, an earlier system that could have been so employed. Tiltman concluded that both Wilkins' and Dalgarno's languages were "much too systematic" to account for the phenomena in the Voynich text. He postulated, instead, a language that employed a "highly illogical mixture of different kinds of substitution" (1951, p. 2).

Looking back further in history for a still earlier form of "universal language", Tiltman discovered a system called the "Universal Character", devised by one Cave Beck (Beck 1657). This system looked somewhat promising, though it was still hardly early enough in date; it was certainly "illogical" and "mixed" in its methods. The words of a small English dictionary were assigned numbers from one to 3999, in rough alphabetical order, creating a crude four-digit code as a foundation for the language. A subset of about one hundred and seventy-five common words could also be represented by three-letter groups in addition to the basic four-digit code groups, constituting, in effect, a set of variants for these words; these special trigraphs all began with "s" or "t".

Code groups representing nouns in Beck's system were preceded by the letter "r", and adjectival groups by the letter "q". Synonyms (e.g., "to think" and "to cogitate") had the same four-digit group assigned to them. Plurals were shown by an "s", or sometimes, an "8", after the digit-group. Verbs might have up to three letters prefixed to their four-digit group for certain forms. The digit-groups themselves could be written also in letters, each digit being represented by a syllable (consonant-vowel, vowel-consonant, or consonant-vowel-consonant). This variation, intended by Beck to produce pronounceable forms for the code words, constitutes from a cryptographic point of view a substitution of digraphs or trigraphs for the digits, to provide a set of variants. Finally, because of the arbitrarily mixed letter-number makeup of words, a separator was required to show where one word ended and the next began. Tiltman points out that the common "ending" group "89" in the Voynich text could stand for a plural "s" followed by a word separator as in Beck's language.

Tiltman discovered another, still older "synthetic language" proposal by a man named Johnston, developed under the direction of a Bishop Bedell about 1641. No detailed description of this system has survived, unfortunately. In Chapter 9, more will be said about synthetic and universal languages in general. I will also present, in Section 6.10 below, my own findings in tracing the evidence for the existence of similar synthetic languages or codes back considerably earlier—perhaps well into the fifteenth or at least into the early sixteenth century.

In later reports (1967, 1968, 1975), Tiltman describes his other principal line of research on the Voynich manuscript. He spent some time in England in 1957 consulting experts on early herbals and medical manuscripts, and attempting to track down an origin for the plant illustrations. He presents an excellent overview of the history of early herbals and botanical illustrations (1967, 1968). Summing up his own and others' failure to discover any clear parallels to the Voynich manuscript, he says, "To the best of my knowledge no one has been able to find any point of connection with any other medical manuscript or early printed book. This is all the stranger because the range of writing and illustration on the subject of the plant world from the early Middle Ages right through into the sixteenth and even seventeenth centuries was very limited indeed. . . . In general, the illustrations in the early printed herbals are limited to two or three collections of stylized woodcuts copies over and over again in more and more degenerate form" (1968, p. 11).

Aside from the substantive contributions Tiltman's research has made to our knowledge of the manuscript, another important result of his work should be mentioned. Over the many years of his association with the problem, he has served as a coordinator and contact point for students interested in the manuscript and desiring information about the text or about studies carried out on it by others. His papers and presentations have provided many researchers with a full introduction to the subject, and have motivated a number of students to take up an interest in the manuscript. It should be evident to any reader who has persevered this far in reading this lengthy monograph that the puzzle of the Voynich manuscript presents a complex challenge, and can best be approached by cooperative research, building on the earlier findings of others as in any orderly scientific enterprise. Tiltman's publications and communications have provided such a foundation on the basis of which newer students can advance, without being forced to exhaust their resources needlessly repeating all the work that others have already accomplished.

6.7 Jeffrey Krischer

Krischer, a man of very broad interests and talents comprising mathematics, computer science, medicine, and cryptology, became interested in the manuscript and made a computer analysis of the text as a research project during his graduate study at Harvard University. This research was described in a paper which received a limited circulation at Harvard and among students of the manuscript (Krischer 1969). In Part I of his paper, Krischer provides a brief sketch of the earlier solution claims by Newbold, Feely, and Strong, and reviews some general information about the history and background of the manuscript. In Part II, "Statistical Analysis," he presents an interesting discussion of the problems involved in arriving at a transcription alphabet and a description of the alphabets used by Newbold, Currier, and Tiltman. He suggests and describes several stylostatistical techniques which might usefully be applied to the Voynich text.

Krischer's approach to the computer study of the manuscript is uniquely interesting because he employed a special package of programs developed for machine processing of Chinese characters on the Digital Equipment Corporation PDP-1 computer. As Krischer states, this set of programs was general enough to permit its application to the Voynich script symbols. The symbols (following Currier's alphabet) were drawn on a cathode ray tube "scope" display attached to the PDP-1 computer. The text "could then be transcribed by pointing with a light pen to the corresponding character on the scope for each character of the script" (Krischer 1969, p. 4). This method of transcription was more direct and convenient than the laborious hand copying and keypunching required by other computer studies. The PDP-1 system also permitted convenient editing and correction of the transcribed text from the scope. The output of computer runs could be processed on the Stromberg-Carlson 4020 equipment to produce a graphic reproduction of the Voynich characters, thus avoiding entirely the cumbersome and distorting artificial Romanizations that all other students have had to resort to. The Voynich text could be fed directly into the computer, where it could be subjected to any desired manipulation or statistical analysis. Approximately two percent, or 5500 out of the 250,000 characters in the manuscript, were machined by Krischer in this way, according to his own statement (p. 53). His frequency counts are shown in figure 28; it may be noted that they add up to about 6200, a discrepancy for which I can find no explanation.

In Section III of his monograph, Krischer discusses some statistical tools for comparing different samples of natural language text. He selects three such techniques as potentially useful in comparing the Voynich text to samples in known languages. These statistical tools are: 1) a statistic or "characteristic" "k", describing the degree of compactness or economy in the sequences of characters in the text; 2) a statistic representing the "entropy" or degree of "orderedness" in a body of text, having a characteristic value for each natural language; and 3) Markovian analysis, a way of studying the probability that any particular letter will be a successor to any other particular letter in a string of text. Krischer suggests that these measures, which have proven effective in other stylostatistical researches, may be useful in helping us to determine the underlying language of the Voynich text. (In this approach, he assumes first, that the method of concealment or encipherment has not obscured any of the characteristics of natural language plaintext, and, second, that a recognizable natural language does, in fact, underlie the text. As we have seen in Section 4.4 above, neither of these assumptions can be taken for granted, and in fact, they are both counter-indicated by much of the evidence, as noted by Tiltman, Elizebeth Friedman, and others.)

The "k" statistic and the "entropy" measure were computed by Krischer for characters and for words of the Voynich text sample he machined. He states, however, that these are of no use without parallel measures for Latin or other natural language text for comparison. He also considers his own text sample much too small for the useful application of the "Markovian Analysis" method, which would, he states, require at least five times as much text, or 25,000 characters. At the time of writing his paper, Krischer planned to carry out further studies; I cannot find any record of any subsequent results, however. This promising and interesting computer project, which pointed out a way of testing some important hypotheses about the text, seems to have been terminated, like so many of the others, before it came close to achieving any useful results.

6.8 Prescott Currier

Captain Currier, a prominent professional cryptologist and close associate of Friedman and Tiltman, participated in their researches and became an enthusiastic student of the puzzle. Tiltman (1975) sums up Currier's recent work on the manusc.ipt as follows: "Since his retirement... seven years ago Captain Currier has spent a great deal of time performing his own analyses of the manuscript. He holds the view that there are at least two different handwritings which he calls A and B. In every case the two sides of a leaf recto and verso are in one and the same hand. . . . Further his analysis shows that there are significant differences in their content, as in the frequency of symbols associated with one another in words. . . . When I came to prepare this lecture, I saw at once one difference between the content of the A and B pages which convinced me. In his account of suffixes following a number of the common roots the suffix 8G (or *89*) occurs eight times in twenty-five A pages and 554 times in twenty-five B pages. . . . My own feeling is that the two "languages" express different applications by two scribes of the same rather loose set of rules to similar text".

Currier was able, in 1973, to have computer studies made comparing two carefully-chosen matched samples of text, one in hand A and the other in hand B, both selected from the herbal folios. The results of the study clearly demonstrated significant differences between the samples. In the course of subsequent hand studies, Currier has arrived at a number of further conclusions regarding the contrast between material in hands A and B, and he is still pursuing this productive line of investigation. He has extended his studies to other sections of the manuscript in addition to the herbal folios. His work is documented in four unpublished papers (Currier 1970–1976, D'Imperio 1976).

6.9 Some Comments Regarding Computer Methods

The subject of computers as tools in humanistic research, and specifically in the attack on the Voynich manuscript, is one that holds a special interest for me since I am a computer programmer by profession and my academic background is in classical philology. There are several ways the computer can aid in the study of the Voynich manuscript, as in other, similar, text-processing undertakings. These are: 1) *a data processing function*, permitting the manipulation and organization of text in larger and more significant sample sizes than can be dealt with by hand; 2) *an exploratory data reduction function*, allowing us to apply various indexes, counts, and other selection, display, summarizing and tabulation techniques, in order to explore the data and show up any patterns or regularities it may contain as an aid to hypothesis searching; and 3) *a hypothesis-testing function*, for investigating various specific theories we may have developed as a result of "hunches" or from exploratory hand and machine studies.

Most of the use of computers by students of the manuscript falls in the first (data processing) and second (exploratory data reduction) categories. While these are both useful and necessary in their place, the third use of computers, in systematic hypothesis-testing, seems in my opinion to be the most powerful and the most likely to produce solid and meaningful contributions to our knowledge of the problem. A significant example of this effective use of computers is Prescott Currier's recent study of hands A and B, discussed in the previous section. Currier had developed his idea about "hands" by visual inspection of the manuscript before he came to the computer specialists to seek their aid. He had a definite hypothesis, which I will presume to paraphrase as follows: "If, in fact, there is a real and significant difference between the text in the two sets of pages that look different to me, then they will have different distributions and clusterings of characters." Accordingly, he requested only certain carefully-planned machine runs, to be made only on two matched samples of text chosen so as to keep other variables constant in so far as was possible. The computer runs clearly confirmed his theory, demonstrating the

45

differences he had postulated between the two samples: a result that might never have been obtained through any amount of machine processing applied indiscriminately to masses of unselected text.

In my opinion, this is the best way the computer can serve us at this stage in our research on the manuscript. All the more obvious and easier data processing and data reduction displays have been made again and again by various students, with disappointing results. It seems evident that, if anything new is to be learned from computer runs, we must perform some more carefully-planned selection of the data, or some more specific and sophisticated manipulations such as would show up concealed patterns in the internal structure of words and sentences, in response to a particular theory regarding the cryptologic nature of the text, or some theory about its possible content or provenience. It is all too easy to plug away at machining more and more data in very general ways, with no guiding principle for selection and interpretation. Our abilities to process data by machine today frequently far outrun our planning and imaginative capabilities. We are likely to end up too often with many feet of printouts that tell us little or nothing, since we still have no meaningful questions to ask. One of the most demanding aspects of scientific work is the framing of useful questions, and the design of experiments that will produce useful answers. We need to apply this scientific approach to our study of the manuscript, and especially in our use of computers. In hand studies, the limitations of patience and time on the part of the investigator effectively preclude many of the more wasteful activities, or at least prevent their assuming wasteful proportions, but the computer permits us to transcend these limitations and, alas, to carry out wasteful activities on a grand scale.

Chapter 7
Collateral Research: Roger Bacon (A.D. 1214?–1292?)

The necessarily brief and sketchy review in this chapter cannot approach an appropriate treatment of the remarkable thirteenth-century scholar whose name has so frequently been associated with the Voynich manuscript. As may be seen from the discussion of Bacon's possible authorship of the manuscript in Section 2.2.2 above. there is no solid evidence either supporting or denying his connection with the work. however indirect. Nevertheless. anyone interested in the manuscript. (and, indeed, anyone who cares about the history of Western thought) should learn as much as possible about Friar Bacon. if only because he was so evidently a man worthy of closer acquaintance. He is especially appealing to the modern reader (or would be. if his works were made more accessible) in that he has told us. in a forthright and ingenuous manner. so much about himself in his own writings; in fact. almost all that is known about him today originates in his own words. since his contemporaries rarely. if ever. mentioned him in surviving records. Bacon's own voluminous writings. and the many and varied specialized studies of his life and work made by scholars of the nineteenth and twentieth centuries. afford a wealth of insight into those problematical relationships between wisdom and science. God and Nature. human value and objective technology. which still confront us today. however we may attempt to disguise them by recasting them into modern jargon.

7.1 Works By and About Roger Bacon

Bacon's life and works have been described and analyzed in a number of major studies. though I believe it is still fair to say that, up to the present, no truly complete and definitive treatment has been attempted. Few of his writings have been translated into any modern language; much remains unedited and unpublished even in the original Latin. Bacon himself exacerbated the problem by reworking and re-using his writings over and over again. so that it is hard to tell which of the many fragmentary works that survive are copies or revisions of parts of other works. and which are separate compositions. The condemnation of his doctrines by the Franciscan Order. and the resulting suspicion and fear on the part of later writers. contributed to the confusion. since many scholars quoted or copied his works without daring to mention his name. As a consequence of these many obscurities and difficulties. Bacon's works are not all accessible to the modern reader. with the sole exception of a translation into English of the *Opus Majus* (Bacon 1928b).

Scholarly studies of Bacon's writings have been carried out primarily from very specialized and narrow points of view. At one extreme. historians of science have been interested in Bacon as a part of their search for precursors of modern objective experimental methods; at the other extreme. Catholic philosophers and scholars have examined his pronouncements on various technical points concerning medieval Scholastic philosophy. Émile Charles (1861). despite the early date of his work. provides a remarkably clear. fair. but sympathetic general presentation. expressed in elegant scholarly French and bolstered by a quality of learning formidable in its thoroughness and dedication. A careful reading of this enjoyable. humane book is recommended as a starting point for anyone interested in Bacon. Later writers are indebted to Charles for much of the information presented in their volumes and for much of its interpretation as well. A much more recent book by Stewart C. Easton (1952) is also to be recommended unreservedly; his approach is remarkable in its imaginative use of historical analysis and its creative extrapolation from the few available facts to develop a striking picture of Bacon's personality and a clear perspective on his thought. James Blish (the well-known Science Fiction writer prominent in connection with the Star Trek series) has written a very fine fictional biography (1971). based primarily on Easton's study of Bacon. which I also recommend to the interested reader.

I have attempted to obtain and read every serious work concerning Roger Bacon which I could find. in an effort to gain a fuller understanding of his contribution to knowledge and his possible association with the Voynich manuscript. The bibliography appended to this monograph. (while it cannot claim to be exhaustive. and does not even include all the works I have examined. since some appear likely to be of little value to the reader primarily interested in the Voynich manuscript). should provide access to most of the major works on Bacon in English as well as many in other Western European languages.

47

7.2 Bacon's Life and Works

Bacon spent most, if not all, of his adult life as a scholar or teacher. He studied and then, having completed a Master of Arts Degree, taught at the Universities of Oxford and Paris in the 1230's and 1240's. The newly rediscovered works on natural philosophy by Aristotle occupied a central focus of intellectual excitement at the time. Aristotle's works had been preserved among Mohammedans along with other sources of Greek learning, while they were forgotten by a Europe immersed in the barbarism of the Dark Ages and the obscurantism of the early Church; translated into Latin and accompanied by a wealth of commentary by Mohammedan and Jewish philosophers, these new wellsprings of early Greek science brought about an intellectual revolution in thirteenth-century Europe. The task of attempting to resolve the basic differences between the philosophy of Aristotle and his pagan commentators, on the one hand, and the anti-intellectual, other-worldly viewpoint of the Church Fathers forming an integral part of Christian doctrine, on the other hand, preoccupied the attention and strained the resources of thirteenth-century thinkers.

Bacon was one of the first scholars capable of lecturing on the newly-revealed Aristotelian Natural Philosophy and Arab commentaries. He was evidently a good teacher, and must have enjoyed his years at the Universities. A voluminous manuscript, apparently representing a student's long-term collection of notes or transcripts of Bacon's lectures on various works of Aristotle, covering several years, has been edited by Steele (Bacon 1909–1940). Another manuscript, also described by Steele (1933), represents notes by a student in other, much more elementary courses on geometry, arithmetic, and similar topics given by Bacon.

At some point in his University studies, Bacon suddenly seems to have changed the course of his thinking; turning away from the promising and rather successful career he had been making for himself as a teacher, he apparently took off on a course of self-study, seeking out obscure scholars interested in the "natural science" of the day: alchemy, astronomy, and astrology. He became particularly preoccupied with "experimentum": an approach to nature that involved the collection and systematic comparison and analysis of other's reports on natural phenomena, along with a sort of informal tinkering or trial-and-error investigation of phenomena in order to understand them better. The "scientia experimentalis" of Roger Bacon was not at all like our modern, controlled laboratory experimentation, with its vast armament of equipment, procedures, and models; nevertheless, it had the same fundamental orientation toward the external, objective world, and the same motivation in open-minded curiosity. Bacon also began to place great emphasis on knowledge of languages other than Latin, in particular Greek, Hebrew, Arabic, and other original languages of the Bible and the Greek and Arab philosophers, regarded by Bacon as the sources of wisdom revealed by God.

Bacon wrote extensively on a variety of topics, notably on optics and the transmission of light; geography; astronomy and astrology; language, translation, and Biblical criticism; the reform of the calendar and of education; medicine; and alchemy. A prominent feature of his works was an emphasis on the utility of these arts and sciences for the salvation of man and the good of the Church. He was, first and foremost, a "mission-oriented" thinker, and constantly reiterated the meaninglessness of any knowledge without a moral goal and frame of reference. For him, the motivation of science and learning was to be found in the mission of the Church. He asserted the methodological unity of science, philosophy, and religion, and was interested, to a degree unusual for his time, in methodology as such. It is interesting to note, also, that Bacon spoke as often and as insistently of the "beauty" of philosophy and science as of their utility (for example, in an appealing and characteristic phrase quoted by Frankowska (1971, p. 36), from Bacon's *Communia Naturalia*, he says he wishes to compose a treatise on Perspective "quia hec est pulchrior aliis....", because it is "more beautiful" than other sciences).

Some time in the 1240's Bacon decided to join the Franciscan Order, for reasons he never discusses in his works. Many scientifically-oriented modern writers have speculated about this course of action, which appears to many of us, from our distant (and often irreligious) viewpoint, to have been a fatal mistake on his part. He never seems to have gotten along very well with his superiors, and incurred some degree of discipline or confinement on at least two occasions (on the nature and severity of these punishments, see Feret 1891). In 1267, he was asked by Pope Clement IV to send copies of his philosophical writings to Rome, and in response, produced the *Opus Majus*, *Opus Minus*, and *Opus Tertium* (his three best-known works). Clement's death in 1268 destroyed any hopes Bacon might have had of achieving recognition and support for his educational and intellectual reforms, although he apparently made several subsequent attempts to write a *Scriptum Principale*, or encyclopedic work on human knowledge, that was probably never completed. Again imprisoned or severely restricted by his Order in 1278, he produced little further until his death in 1292 (or, some claim, 1294). Lists of Bacon's extant writings and fuller treatments of his biography may be found in Charles (1861), Easton (1952), and Little (1892, 1914).

7.3 Survival and Significance of Bacon's Work in Later Times

The thirteenth-century Friar Roger, as has been noted by several writers, has been overshadowed and submerged in the far greater acclaim accorded by our age to his namesake, Francis Bacon, who is credited with the invention of modern scientific method. Roger Bacon seems to have been regarded by many recent writers as a sort of exasperating enigma; he stubbornly refuses to be stuffed into any of their favorite pigeonholes. Scientific writers are impatient with his "experimental science" because he did not provide diagrams and specifications of his constructions and laboratory equipment as a present-day scientist would be expected to do. Students of Scholastic philosophy find him an indifferent philosopher, and his name is omitted entirely from a number of modern surveys; in others he is passed over with a few ambiguous sentences. Sharp (1930) provides a clear and not overly favorable examination of Bacon's positions on various typical Scholastic questions, in comparison with a number of his other, more conventional, contemporaries. Many writers seem unable to decide whether Bacon was a religious mystic on the one hand, or an iconoclastic positivist and empiricist on the other.

Roger Bacon's main difficulty was undoubtedly his inability to be a "team player"; he did not ally himself with any school of thought accepted in his time, and in fact launched violent and outspoken attacks upon most of his better-known contemporaries. He frequently referred to them as a "stupid crowd," and castigated them for their "stultitiam infinitum"; this uncompromising combativeness was probably the real cause of his condemnation, however it may have been rationalized. He was apparently trying to articulate ideas for which his own age had no words, no predilection, and no understanding; our age has clearly swung so far to the opposite, positivistic pole that we have even less real sympathy and comprehension for the synthesis he was trying to form. Bacon went his own way, building his own amalgam of faith, magic, philology, and natural philosophy based on Greek, Arabic, and Jewish writings and borrowing from a very small number of living colleagues (Robert Grosseteste, Adam de Marisco, Peter de Maricourt). He rejected the Scholastic Method developed by Peter Abaelard, in favor of his "scientia experimentalis", and he minimized the importance of logic and verbal disputation, so dearly loved by his contemporaries. On the other hand, Bacon's "experimentum" included the study of reported "experiences" of the Greek and Arab philosophers, comprising fables and superstitions concerning such things as the virtues of viper's flesh, the influences of the stars, and flying dragons; stranger still to the modern mind, his "experimentum" included Divine illumination and mystical insight from God. Thus, Bacon succeeded at the same time in alienating all of his colleagues in his own time, and in confounding all of his would-be admirers in our century as well.

Condemned by his Order and prevented from writing or teaching, Roger Bacon was marked out for oblivion by his superiors and fellow scholars. His voluminous works were apparently ignored, but exploited indirectly and in hidden ways by his immediate successors who feared to mentioned him by name. His name was apparently even erased from some copies of his works. By the end of the fourteenth century, however, Bacon began to enjoy a gradual revival or emergence of sorts. His work on medicine (Bacon 1928a) was transparently pirated and plagiarized to good effect by some later medical writers This, together with his *Epistola de Mirabili Potestate Artis et Naturae* (Bacon 1859), and several garbled and spurious alchemical works (Bacon 1603; Singer 1932) were quite popular, and served to provide the Franciscan Friar with a formidable reputation for vast occult powers. John Dee was a devoted disciple of Roger Bacon, and did much to bring about a new Renaissance of his reputation and writings. It has been suggested that Francis Bacon was introduced to Roger's works at Mortlake, Dee's home, through the extensive library of Bacon's writings Dee had lovingly and assiduously collected. Some have even gone so far as to suggest that Francis was far more indebted to "a certain monk in a cell" than he ever admitted.

From the late 1800's on into the early twentieth century, Bacon had another revival, being hailed as a martyred forerunner of modern experimental science and technology. Much was made of his predilection for "experimentum", and his emphatic rejection of the ideas and methods of his contemporaries. Newbold's claim to have deciphered the Voynich manuscript, and to have discovered evidence there of Bacon's invention of the telescope and microscope, came at the crest of this wave and added briefly to its momentum. Catholic writers hailed the Newbold theory as a "vindication of thirteenth-century science" (Reville 1921, Walsh 1921). Rudyard Kipling wrote an interesting short story called "The Eye of Allah" in which Roger Bacon was a central figure (Kipling 1926; I am indebted to Brigadier Tiltman for pointing out this story to me). Typical of the effusions of some considerably less gifted writers is an article by Grove Wilson in a popular survey called *Great Men of Science* (1942); overflowing with pathos for the persecutions visited upon Bacon's "scientific" genius by the witch-hunting Church, this embarrassingly dreadful dose of purple prose even credits Bacon with the invention of the steam engine in his "laboratory."

Predictably enough, the pendulum swung rapidly to the other extreme, aided considerably by the debunking of Newbold's theory by Manly and Friedman. Lynn Thorndike (1916, 1921, 1929, 1923-58) went further than most in attempting to divest Roger Bacon of any claim to respect as a philosopher or a scientist. In Thorndike's monumental work, *The History of*

49

Magic and Experimental Science (1923–58), he dismisses Bacon as a superstitious medieval monk, a believer in magic, completely devoid of any trace of the modern scientific outlook, and thus not worthy of the attention of modern thinkers. While he deals almost as harshly with all the medieval writers he discusses in his work, Thorndike's debunking of Bacon seems to be a shade more savage and thoroughgoing, undoubtedly in an over-reaction to the effusive and misplaced adulation of Bacon by some earlier writers.

Steele (1921) provides what seems to me to be a very fair estimate of Bacon's place in history; he is supremely well qualified to assess Bacon's works, having edited more of them than most other Baconian scholars. He offers the following perspective, based on Bacon's stated plans for his unfinished *Scriptum Principale*: "In estimating Bacon's position among the men of his own time it is important to remember, first of all, the complete originality of his scheme. His great work, unfinished though it most probably was ... was as distinct in kind as in form from the works of his great contemporaries.... Bacon's schematic arrangement was not only unparalleled among the writers of his time; it was absolutely new. Nothing like it had been devised since the time of Aristotle.... The whole system of human thought was recast.... It may be that the framework of his scheme owed something to Al Farabi's *De Scienciis*, or to Avicenna, but in its conception and execution its originality is manifest" (pp. 141–142).

A very interesting recent study by a Polish author, Malgorzata Frankowska (1971), presents a very favorable, yet fully documented and supported assessment of Roger Bacon's contributions to knowledge and his influence on the development of modern thought. She provides several detailed examples of Bacon's approach to empirical science; his treatment of the cause of rainbows in the *Opus Majus*, for example, clearly supports a conclusion that he fully shared many of the systematic and analytic mental habits of the modern scientist (Frankowska 1971, pp. 85–87; cf. Bacon 1928b, pp. 587–615). Though the equipment, the data, and the sources at his command were woefully deficient, he used the reports of others and his own carefully-planned observations in a closely-reasoned, orderly manner to eliminate various competing hypotheses and to build up confirmatory evidence for one particular explanation of the observed and reported rainbow phenomena.

It is interesting to note that, in spite of his later explicit rejection of the Scholastic Method, Bacon made extensive and expert use of it in his earlier lectures ("Quaestiones") on Aristotle, and he was evidently a skilled master of this highly-developed form of analytic disputation (see Steele 1933). At the heart of the Scholastic Method was an arrangement of data (consisting, typically, of quotations from Biblical and Patristic authorities and from Greek and Arab philosophers) so that all those sources favoring and those opposing a given point at issue were matched in an orderly way, followed by a "solution" or "resolution" attempting to reach a conclusion from all the evidence. This method, when skilfully applied to valid data, was and still is a powerful tool of analysis, and differed essentially from modern scientific thought only in its raw materials (quotations from "authorities" rather than empirical measurements) and its purpose (the resolution of religious and verbal, rather than technical and empirical questions). In his analysis of the rainbow, Bacon put to good use the best features of the Scholastic Method as applied to the strongest and best data he could obtain.

Roger Bacon's principal contribution to knowledge, according to Frankowska, involved the nature and methodology of science. Rejecting the presentations of other writers, which she regards as one-sided (even in the case of Easton, whose view of Bacon she sees as overemphasizing the religious and mystical side of his nature), she assesses Bacon's accomplishments in the following considered tribute: "Bacon was the first to consider in such a large way the theoretical problems connected with science, he was also the first who had the vision of the unity of science, based on the unity of method and purpose.... Moreover, he was the first to originate theoretical reflections concerning the nature of science and its aims—reflections which were to find mature expression much later, in the time of Francis Bacon and Descartes...." (p. 134). She concludes that "The thought of Roger Bacon lies at the source of both the empiricism of Francis Bacon and the mathematical method of Descartes" (p. 136), and recommends, as have other scholars before her, a systematic historical study to demonstrate and prove the influence of Roger Bacon's writings on the better-known later thinkers.

Until his works have been edited, translated, and systematically studied as a whole, on their own terms and against the background of his known sources and contemporary thought, no definitive evaluation of Bacon's contribution to human knowledge is possible. He remains, for most moderns as for his own contemporaries, an enigmatic and recalcitrant figure who determinedly refuses to be filed away in any convenient cubby-hole.

7.4 *Was Roger Bacon Associated With the Voynich Manuscript?*

Coming now to the question of Bacon's possible authorship of, or connection with, the Voynich manuscript, what, if anything, can we conclude? I feel, although I cannot support my view with any definite evidence, that his authorship is highly unlikely, not only because of the great disparity of dates between Bacon's life in the thirteenth century and the probable origin of the manuscript in the fifteenth or sixteenth century. I base my opinion also on the impression I have gained from a careful study of what is known about his life and his writings, including an attempt (necessarily rapid and inadequate) to sample his own published works in the original Latin. I feel, in sum, that Bacon was not a man who would have produced a work such as the Voynich manuscript, even during his periods of imprisonment or persecution.

Far from being a rebel or iconoclast in any modern sense. Bacon was clearly a deeply, even passionately religious man who accepted the beliefs of his Church. He chose to become a member of the Franciscan Order, and chose to remain within it for the rest of his life, in spite of repeated harassments and disappointments. He claimed repeatedly that the only purpose of human knowledge was to serve God, uphold the Catholic Faith, convert unbelievers, and defeat the evil power (and technology!) of Antichrist. He was also fascinated, as we have seen, by mathematics, methodology, and inductive reason, however inadequate the data and techniques available to him may have been.

Bacon, in short, does not seem to me to be the sort of man to have created a magical manuscript, so provincial in style, so ambiguous and curious as the puzzle before us. Almost all of his authentic writings that have come down to us are clear, scholarly treatises in medieval Latin, quite uncompromising in their forthright and rational quality. He was skilled in draftsmanship, and trained assistants in the computation and drawing up of tables and diagrams. In none of his extant works is there any indication of a real personal interest in biology or botany, although he praised, in passing, the usefulness of agriculture and husbandry. His medical work was a faithful and complete compilation of information about medicinal plants drawn from other authorities, and not original with him. His approach to astronomy, astrology, and alchemy was abstract and conventional, oriented toward methodology and terminology; it provides no frame of reference within which we might understand the Voynich manuscript's idiosyncratic Zodiac diagrams and other drawings decorated with female figures and symbolic pipes, "cans," and tubs.

It seems to me much more likely that the Voynich manuscript is a product of the sixteenth century, probably related to alchemy, and perhaps, as suggested by Brumbaugh, ascribed to Bacon because of his reputation for occult learnings. (Any otherwise unidentified, mysterious manuscript was apt, in the past, to be attributed to Bacon, especially if it concerned magic or alchemy and was provided with bizarre diagrams.) Rather than ascribing such a work as this to a fastidious, essentially conservative, and learned man such as Roger Bacon, I can far more easily imagine a small heretical society of Hermetic adepts and illuminati, perhaps in Germany or Eastern Europe, concealing their strange and probably dangerous doctrines in a secret book of the kind we see in the Voynich manuscript. I urge the interested reader to explore some of the works on Roger Bacon listed in the bibliography at the end of this monograph, and, especially, to read some of Bacon's own works (if only the *Opus Majus*, the sole work accessible in English), and thus reach his own conclusions.

Chapter 8
Collateral Research: Medieval and Renaissance Cosmology and Iconography

The remaining chapters in this monograph are intended to provide a very broad-brush survey of some background topics that may be relevant to the problem of the Voynich manuscript. As we have seen in Chapter 2, it seems probable in the eyes of many students that the manuscript can be dated to late medieval or early Renaissance times, and is of European provenience. It seems, therefore, that any serious student should gain some understanding of the sciences, philosophies, methods of representation, and other features of those periods that can put into proper context the phenomena in the manuscript itself, and perhaps give us some "leads" toward an interpretation of the drawings and the purpose and motivation of the work as a whole. I urge the reader to consider the present sketchy treatment as a mere appetizer, a sampler of some very beautiful and curious products of human art and wisdom that have survived the iconoclasm and neglect of religious reaction on the one hand, and scientific positivism on the other.

8.1 Ars Memorativa: The Art of Memory

Probably the best and most general treatment of the Art of Memory is that of Yates (1966). Much of the presentation below is taken from that excellent study, and I recommend the book to any reader who wishes to learn more. In the long ages before pencil and paper became the trusty and abundant companions of every scholar and bureaucrat, other means had to be found to organize and remember the details of complex presentations such as legal cases and public speeches. Orators, philosophers, lawyers, and statesmen of ancient Greece and Rome prided themselves on their highly developed visual memories, which were so cultivated and emphasized as to be virtually eidetic in character. An important Latin source in this tradition for the Middle Ages was the *Ad Herennium*, attributed by medieval writers to Cicero ("Tullius"); this work described a mnemonic system supposedly devised by Simonides of Ceos (556–468 BC), and regarded as a vital part of the "Art of Rhetoric," itself an essential feature of ancient and medieval education.

In the memory system ascribed to Simonides, the orator went to a quiet, well-lighted place such as a large building, a forum, or some other structure provided with a series of distinct niches, columns, stairs, or other orderly architectural and scenic elements. He walked about there, systematically rehearsing the ideas of his presentation, and focussing his attention upon the successive scenic units so as to associate with each a key word or sentence of his speech, in conjunction with some weird, striking, and colorful visual image that would serve to remind him of the ideas later in their proper sequence. The "memory images" were to be chosen from such sources as Greek and Roman mythology and legend.

This system of "place-memory" gave us our modern word "topic," from the "topoi" or "places" constituting its main feature. (The medieval Stations of the Cross which have survived into current Catholic usage today provide an example of a "place-memory" system associated with vivid visual imagery). Greek and Roman orators boasted of the capacity of their "artificial memories," and competed to see who could remember the longest series of words or ideas— well into the hundreds and thousands—by means of such mnemonic methods. In addition to the *Ad Herennium*, another work, also by Cicero, *De Oratore*, described a similar memory system. A work by Quintilian, dating from the first century AD, provided clear directions for choosing Memory "places" and constructing images to be stored in them and associated with the ideas one wished to memorize.

With the advent of Christianity, the Memory Art became a major resource for preachers and religious educators in their spreading of the Christian Faith. Of the two great mendicant Orders of the Middle Ages—the Dominicans and Franciscans—each had its own favored Memory Art for preachers. The Dominicans employed the classical art as described above, with colorful images drawn from pagan mythology and other barbaric foreign sources (in a manner which often seems to us startlingly and amusingly inappropriate) as mnemonic tags for Christian teachings.

The Franciscans followed a different tradition instituted by Ramon Lull (A.D. 1235–1315), a flamboyant and innovative personality whose life and works are well worth studying for their own intrinsic interest (see Peers 1929, Yates 1954, 1960, and 1966 pp. 173–198; Rossi 1961). Instead of using images, Lull's "art" employed a set of revolving circles or other simple geometric figures marked with letters of the alphabet. which were manipulated in a combinatorial fashion. The rings or other elements were rotated against each other to produce all possible combinations of the letters. which could be made to stand for ideas such as "God", "Evil", "Man", "the Soul"; for lists of sins and virtues; or for any set of concepts or elements one wished to remember and meditate upon in sequence. Lull. a native of Majorca. was probably influenced by the mystical Jewish tradition of the Cabala (see 8.7 below) and also by the Mohammedan mystical philosophy of Sufism. It is interesting to note that Lull's combinatorial method of systematically listing and considering all possible combinations of a few basic elements is a very powerful and valuable mental tool. Shorn of its medieval and religious purposes it survives into modern logic and science. and is useful to computer programmers. for example. in analyzing events in data or elements of a problem (I made use of it for the scheme of cryptanalytic hypotheses in Section 4.4.2). It also undoubtedly inspired a number of cryptographic devices involving rotating discs.

The great *Divina Commedia* of Dante, and the iconography of medieval cathedrals with their "sermons in stone" are two striking embodiments of the encyclopedic Memory Art. still valued by and familiar to educated people today. In the Renaissance there was a great efflorescence of richly-elaborated mnemonic systems. Giulio Camillo (A.D. 1480?-1544) built a wooden memory "theatre" embellished with colorful images and provided with drawers in which scripts of speeches and other papers could be filed. using a "place" system of memory; the images represented such things as the planets. the Cabalistic "Sephiroth." names of angels. and other magical and mythological elements. Giordano Bruno (A.D. 1548-1600) had entered the Dominican Order and studied their Memory Art; leaving the Order later and embarking upon a career as a Hermetic Magus (which led ultimately to his death at the stake). he continued to be deeply interested in mnemonics and taught his own elaborate mnemonic system to wealthy patrons as a way of earning a living. His system. as reconstructed by Yates (1966. pp. 199-230) from Bruno's work *De L'mbris Idearum* (Bruno 1582). involved a giant memory wheel which had thirty main segments. each subdivided into five smaller ones. the whole arranged on the plan of Lull's figures so that rings within it rotated independently.

The main segments of Bruno's wheel were labelled with twenty-three Roman. four Greek. and three Hebrew letters for a total of thirty. Each of these could be combined with. or subdivided among. segments for the five vowels to produce combinations Aa. Ae. Ai. Ao. Au. Ba. Be. etc. Images shown within the segments and associated with them on various rings of the wheel represented elements such as the thirty-six decans (see 8.3 below). the seven planets. twenty-eight mansions of the moon. plants. birds. animals. stones. metals. etc.. in a vast and all-embracing synthesis. This conception was not intended to be merely a memory device; it was basically a system to permit the operator to attain encyclopedic philosophical knowledge coupled with the magical powers of a Hermetic Demiurge. Bruno founded a mystical sect in Germany called the "Giordanisti"; their beliefs were probably akin to those of the later Rosicrucians and Freemasons. John Dee was an admirer of Bruno's philosophy. which was in many ways similar to his own. The mnemonic art had a last magnificent echo in the work of Leibniz. in his design of a set of "notae" for use in a "universal calculus." The medieval and Renaissance Memory Arts undoubtedly formed the conceptual foundation and precedent for the synthetic and artificial languages which became fashionable in Renaissance and later times (see 9.3).

An interesting detail concerning a lost Art of Memory attributed to Roger Bacon is mentioned by Yates (1966. p. 261 fn). and by Hajdu (1936. pp. 69-70). Yates says. "There is a rumour that Roger Bacon wrote an *ars memorativa* treatise. but this has not so far been traced." Hajdu refers to a work by C. O. Reventlow (1843. p. 41). which. again. quotes a still older work by Von Aretin (1806). which latter I have, unfortunately. been unable to track down. Reventlow's comments may be summarized as follows: Bacon had written a *Tractatus de Arte Memorativa*. to be found in a manuscript at Oxford; this manuscript. never printed. has not so far been discovered. While Bacon was not known as a teacher of mnemonics. he was reported by Aretin to have employed a method based on that of "the classical authors" (presumably Cicero and Quintilian).

Westacott (1953. p. 92) provides another very tantalizing reference to this lost mnemonic art of Roger Bacon. and a "magical" method employed by him to teach the elements of Greek and Hebrew grammar. Bacon claimed on several occasions that he could teach the essentials of Greek and Hebrew to the first comer within three days. sufficient to permit the student to read and understand foreign words in scriptural texts. Characteristically. Bacon backed up his claim with the forthright and combative statement. "Dabo caput meum si deficiam" ("I will forfeit my head if I fail"). I have. alas. been unable so far to discover the source to which Westacott refers: a work. supposedly in preparation in 1953 by Beryl Smalley and Evelyn Jaffe. to be published in the Medieval and Renaissance Studies of the Warburg Institute. which would explain the magical art of language teaching employed by the Admirable Doctor.

Encyclopedic mnemonic systems such as those described above constituted. in effect. a sort of universal code or synthetic language. associated with single letters and clusters of letters from a mixture of alphabets. and used more or less arbitrarily to represent a variety of subject categories. This is the primary source of their relevance to our present task, the study of the Voynich manuscript. Some such system might well underlie the code-like structure of words demonstrated by Tiltman in the Voynich text. Many of the circular diagrams in the manuscript, with their rows of cells in concentric circles containing pictures or labels or bits of text, are also reminiscent of the diagrams of Lull, Camillo, Bruno, and others.

8.2 The Hermetic Tradition

A set of philosophical and mystical doctrines of great conceptual richness and beauty, the Hermetic writings were of primary importance during the late Middle Ages and the Renaissance. The best single general treatment of the topic is, again, by Frances Yates (1964). Another good clear overview, from a less sympathetic but still fair point of view, is that of Shumaker (1972). The Hermetic writings, composed by various anonymous Hellenistic authors around A.D. 100–300, represented an eclectic amalgam of Platonism, Stoicism, Jewish and Persian philosophy, and a certain admixture of ancient Egyptian religious elements. The doctrines became known to the Middle Ages when a monk named Leonardo da Pistoria brought to Florence a Greek manuscript of what came to be called the *Corpus Hermeticum*. It was translated at the urgent command of Cosimo de' Medici during the years 1462–63 by Marsilio Ficino (who was himself to become a figure of considerable prominence through his magico-medical system of astrological images and doctrines). The newly-translated *Corpus Hermeticum*, published in 1471, was explosive in its popularity and influence, and founded an intellectual movement which was to be of central importance in European thought.

The *Hermetica* (as the entire collection of Hermetic writings is called) were attributed to "Hermes Trismegistus," a legendary ancient Egyptian seer or god (identical with the Egyptian god of wisdom, Thoth), regarded as a recipient and channel of Divine illumination, and a contemporary or predecessor of Moses. Festugière (1944–54) provides what is considered the most scholarly edition and commentary on the *Hermetica*; Scott (1924–36) gives an English translation, although Yates apparently does not consider it accurate (1964, p. 22 fn). The Hermetic Tradition provided a motivation and frame of reference for astrology, magic, alchemy, and all the occult sciences which held a predominant influence in Western thought for many centuries; this philosophy, as it was interpreted by Renaissance thinkers, probably set the stage for modern science and technology as well. The Hermetic doctrines frequently emphasized the almost limitless power of the human mind, as partaking of the Divine Mind or Nous. It seems probable that the present all-encompassing hybris of modern science may be traced in part to an origin in the Promethean doctrines of Hermeticism, regarding man as a potent creative Demiurge, capable of standing beside God as co-regent of the natural universe. John Dee, Cornelius Agrippa, Giordano Bruno, Marsilio Ficino, Giovanni Pico Della Mirandola, Giovanni Battista Porta, Trithemius—these and many other figures of late Medieval and Renaissance philosophy drew their inspiration from the springs of the Hermetic revelations.

What was the nature of these philosophical and mystical doctrines, that gave them their power over the mind of man during some of the most creative centuries of Western history? Modern scientifically-oriented writers like Shumaker (1972) find it hard to understand their appeal. It is amusing to note that Shumaker, in his Preface, frankly speaks of his shock and bewilderment at the enthusiasm of his young students, who rush up to the podium to question him eagerly after a lecture on Hermeticism. In a highly interesting personal confession, he discusses his own adverse reaction to the Hermetic doctrines, his difficulty in comprehending the "irrational" point of view on reality embodied in them, and his inability to reconcile them with the positivistic attitudes of modern science with which he is so much more comfortable.

So that the reader unfamiliar with them may gain an idea of the impact and beauty of these writings, I will quote two paragraphs of an excerpt translated by Yates (1964, pp. 23–24), drawn from an account of the creation of the universe and of man in the *Pimander* (one of the books of the *Corpus Hermeticum*).

[The will of God first brought forth a second creative power, or Nous-Demiurge, who in turn fashioned the Seven Governors (planets) to envelop the sensible world with their spheres.] "Now the Nous, Father of all beings, being life and light, brought forth a Man similar to himself, whom he loved as his own child. For the Man was beautiful, reproducing the image of his Father; for it was indeed with his own Form that God fell in love and gave over to him all his works. Now, when he saw the creation which the Demiurge had fashioned in the fire, the Man wished also to produce a work, and permission to do this was given him by the Father. Having thus entered into the demiurgic sphere, in which he had full power, the Man saw the works of his brother, and the Governors fell in love with him, and each gave to him a part in their own rule. Then, having learned their essence and having received participation in their nature, he wished to break through the periphery of the circles and to know the power of Him who reigns above the fire.

"Then Man, who had full power over the world of mortal beings and of animals, leant across the armature of the spheres, having broken through their envelopes, and showed to the Nature below the beautiful form of God. When she saw that he had in him the inexhaustible beauty and all the energy of the Governors, joined to the form of God, Nature smiled with love, for she had seen the features of that

55

marvelously beautiful form of Man. reflected on the water and his shadow on the earth. And he, having seen this form like to himself in Nature, reflected in the water, he loved her and wished to dwell with her. The moment he wished this he accomplished it and came to inhabit the irrational form. Then Nature having received her loved one, embraced him, and they were united, for they burned with love.''

8.3 Astrology and Astronomy

Such a vast and complex area of symbolism is covered by the medieval and Renaissance disciplines of astrology and astronomy that only the briefest possible summary can be presented in these paragraphs. I will concentrate here only on a few salient matters of possible relevance to the Voynich manuscript and in particular upon certain sets or series of names and symbols that might conceivably underlie some of the sequences of text strings in cells of the astrological and cosmological diagrams. Good general discussions of the subject may be found in Shumaker (1972), Wedel (1920), Graubard (1953), Boll and Bezold (1931), Allen (1941), and Duhem (1913–1959). A detailed catalogue (with numerous illustrations) of Latin astrological manuscripts of the Middle Ages may be found in Saxl (1915 and 1927).

The twelve months of the year, the ''houses'' of the zodiac signs, the association of these with Cabalistic names for the celestial spheres and the ''Sephiroth,'' names of angels and demons, etc., all form sequences of twelve important elements. Another set of astrological symbols is that of the fifteen major fixed stars that enter into the zodiac constellations or are in the path of the sun across the sky (see figure 29). The star names are of obviously Arabic origin (transmitted to the Middle Ages by the Arab commentators on Greek works such as the *Almagest* of Ptolemy). A twenty-eight element sequence which may be of relevance to the Voynich manuscript is that of the ''stations'' or ''mansions'' of the moon. Figure 30 shows some names of these stations taken from two major sources.

An important series of thirty-six symbols is that of the ''decans,'' ''prosopoi,'' or ''faces'' of the zodiac signs. These decans, of which each sign has three, had their origin in ancient Egyptian sidereal gods of time, associated with the daily and nightly route of the sun among certain constellations and stars. These beings were regarded as powerful demigods or demons who ruled over the celestial spheres; they were often called the ''horoscopes.'' Each exercised powers over a part of the human body in Egyptian medicine, and each was associated with one of the ''nomes'' or geopolitical divisions of ancient Egypt. Gundel (1936) and Seznec (1953) provide a detailed summary of the history of the names, images, and attributes of these thirty-six celestial beings, from Egyptian times through classical antiquity into the Middle Ages via such works as *Picatrix*, and ultimately into the Renaissance and into modern astrology. Each decan, following Egyptian practice, was associated with a vivid graphic image: these colorful symbols were often depicted in Renaissance mosaics and frescoes, and served frequently as memory images in the richly embellished ''artificial memories'' of Renaissance magi such as Giordano Bruno. Figure 31 shows some stages of the development of decan names from Egyptian through Coptic and later times. Father Petersen collected and studied the Coptic decan names with a view to their possible relevance to the zodiac diagrams in the Voynich manuscript. Unfortunately, there seem to be no cases of thirty-six elements in these diagrams, or even in the cosmological and astronomical diagrams (see figures 11 and 12), and the decan images bear little relation, either in their original Egyptian or later Renaissance forms, to the nude female figures in the manuscript.

8.4 Magical Systems

I have not found any single work that covers all of the systems in a scholarly manner, though separate treatments exist for a number of the major traditions. Shumaker (1972) provides a good survey of Renaissance systems under the chapter heading ''White Magic.'' Thorndike (1923–58) presents extremely detailed (if also rather brusque and unsympathetic) individual summaries of the magical philosophies of many ancient and medieval writers. Walker (1958) provides good coverage of some late medieval and Renaissance systems. Yates (1964) deals thoroughly with Giordano Bruno and some other philosophers of magic. Ritter and Plessner (1962) cover the *Picatrix* magical writings with great completeness. Seligmann (1948) and De Givry (1971) make available numerous illustrations of magic alphabets, diagrams, seals, talismans, etc. Mathers (1974) covers the Solomonian and Mathers (1975) the Abramelinian schools or traditions of ritual magic. It is amusing to note that many of these works have recently been reissued in paperback to satisfy the current enthusiastic surge of public interest in the occult. The following paragraphs will include only a few major or salient magical systems, with an indication of their character and possible relevance to the Voynich manuscript.

8.4.1 Picatrix.

A comprehensive compendium of astral and sympathetic magic. *Picatrix* was influential from the fifteenth century on in European thought. Probably of Hellenistic and Arabic origin, it was translated from Arabic into Spanish at the order of Alfonso the Wise, in 1256, but did not become available in a Latin version until the fifteenth century. It is a rich, eclectic conglomeration of images, seals, characters, and incantations based on astral and planetary demons and their powers. The name *Picatrix*, according to Ritter and Plessner (1962), is a medieval garbling of an Arabic name Buiqratis, which may in turn be derived from the Greek "Hippocrates." The work includes hymns, prayers, and incantations to the planets and other celestial bodies; charms for all manner of purposes (to chase away mice and flies, prevent a sweetheart from getting pregnant, find lost objects, discover hidden treasure, cause people to quarrel or to make up, etc.). Many of the names, charms, and "characters" are referred to as "Indian" or "Egyptian"; in fact, hieratic or hieroglyphic symbols that seem clearly Egyptian are recognizable in some cases, as are Egyptian elements in spells shown in Roman letters (see figure 41).

I have been unable to find, in a careful study of Ritter and Plessner's translation, anything that is directly similar to any diagram or symbol in the Voynich manuscript, with one interesting exception. The "astral" or "planetary" talismans in the form of geometric figures made up of line segments interspersed with circles or dots representing constellations are strongly reminiscent of the odd geometrical figures adorned with faces on folio 67v2. As we will see below, similar figures were common in alchemical works as well (and may have had a common origin in astral magic).

8.4.2 Solomonian Magical Tradition.

The Jewish historian Josephus, in the first century AD, mentioned a book of incantations for summoning spirits, ascribed to King Solomon. A book called the "Testament of Solomon" refers to a magic ring given to Solomon by angels, which conferred upon him power over various demons (whose names and functions are listed). Medieval writers speak of magical books of Solomon, and a *Clavicula Salomonis* and *Sigillum Salomonis* (Key and Seal of Solomon) are mentioned in a pamphlet written in 1456. The version translated by Mathers (1974) is said to date from the fifteenth century. The Solomonian magical tradition was the best known of all medieval magical systems. S. L. MacGregor Mathers, the translator of this and the Abramelinian writings as well (1975) was an interesting figure in his own right: a practicing ceremonial magician and head of the Rosicrucian Order of the Golden Dawn at the end of the nineteenth century. The Solomonian system depended heavily on Jewish Cabalistic sources; it features Hebrew characters and other symbols that look much like some of those in *Picatrix*, and arranged in similar circular "seals" or magical diagrams. Like most high ritual or "white" magic, it involved purifications, a devout religious frame of reference seeking power and guidance from God and from good angels, and elaborate ceremonials with incense, robes, a special room or "oratory" and special furnishings, etc. There seems to be little in this apparatus that even suggests any diagram or symbol in the Voynich manuscript.

8.4.3 Abramelinian Magical System.

The magical books of Abramelin were translated by Mathers (1975) from a French manuscript in the Bibliotheque de l'Arsenal dating from the seventeenth or eighteenth century. This, in turn, claims to have been translated from an original Hebrew manuscript dated 1458. One Abraham the Jew, born 1362, is supposed to have obtained the magic lore from an Egyptian magician named Abra-melin; the magical system presented is said to be based on, but not identical with, the Cabala. Abraham wrote the description of this philosophy for his younger son, having presented his elder son with a compendium of the loftier and more highly-regarded Cabalistic tradition. The Abramelinian system is similar in its ceremonials, purifications, incenses, draperies, etc., as well as in its general character, to the system of Solomon discussed briefly above. The seals and charms, however, are considerably more verbal and abstract, and more explicitly "Cabalistic" in appearance; instead of circles and pentacles, they consist entirely in "magic squares" containing Roman letters representing Hebrew-sounding words. Long lists of demons and their functions are provided, along with detailed instructions for using and working with these demonic powers.

The pragmatism of some of the advice is remarkable, even startling to the unsuspecting modern reader coming upon these writings for the first time. I cannot resist quoting some examples: "It is not necessary to observe any ceremonies in order to send away the Spirits, because they themselves are only too glad to be far away from you." (Mathers 1975, p. 97). "Communicate unto them [the evil spirits] also the Form in the which you wish them to appear. . . .You ought the evening before to have demanded this from your Guardian Angel, who knoweth better than you your nature and constitution, and who understandeth the forms which can terrify you, and those of which you can support the sight." (p. 90). "Let me here once again insist on the absolute necessity in occult working of being courteous. *even to the Evil Spirits*; for the Operator who is insolent and overbearing will speedily lay himself open to obsession by a Spirit of like nature. the which will bring about his ultimate downfall." (p. 102)

Four familiar spirits were assigned to each operator in constantly rotating six-hour shifts; he could lend them to others, and is advised to keep them busy and out of mischief. He can, however, also give them "time off" when he has nothing for them to do. "The familiar spirits are very prompt. and they are able to execute in most minute detail all matters of a mechanical nature, with the which therefore it is well to occupy them; as historical painting; in making statues; clocks; weapons; ..." (p. 362). There is an irresistible realism and psychological sophistication about all of this, which almost forces upon the reader the belief that the magical "operator" was interacting with an actual force of some kind, at least within his own mind. In fact, the accepted modern theory of magic, on which present-day magicians base their thriving operations, locates the powers being tapped by the magician in the depths of his own subconscious.

In spite of the great intrinsic interest possessed by this magical tradition, it too seems, unfortunately, to be minimally related to the drawings and general character of the Voynich manuscript.

8.4.4 John Dee's System of Spiritual Magic.

John Dee, with his "scryer" Edmund Kelley, developed an elaborate magical apparatus involving convocation of, and communication with, angels or good spirits. Since, as we have seen, some students feel that Dee may have had some connection with the origin of the manuscript. his magical philosophy should be of particular relevance to our task. Dee regarded his magic as a devout religious undertaking that would bring him into closer contact with God; Kelley was a much more equivocal personality, mentally unstable, of a violent and avaricious temperament, and avidly ready to employ any means to get wealth and power. His main interest seems to have been in alchemy, and in a life-long endeavor to penetrate to the secret of making gold. To what extent Kelley victimized and deceived Dee cannot be guessed, but it may have been considerable, since all of the "angelic" messages were received by, and transmitted by Kelley. Dee himself had, as he confessed, no ability whatever to see the visions in his crystal or hear the angel voices, and was apparently entirely dependent on Kelley. On the other hand, some writers have suggested that Dee was subtly exploiting Kelley for his own purposes, and tolerated his treachery and his ill-natured outbursts for this reason. It is hard to imagine, in any case, how either of the two men could have invented so elaborate and remarkable a system without the knowing cooperation of the other.

Dee's angel names are reminiscent of Cabala, and have a strong Hebrew flavor; his magical system as a whole, however, is said by Deacon (1968) to be quite distinct from any other well-known Cabalistic or Hermetic tradition. It included a synthetic language of great complexity, in which large volumes of text were communicated to Dee and Kelley by various angels, and which employed an invented alphabet; this language and alphabet may be of relevance to research on the Voynich manuscript. They will be described, along with the practices and circumstances accompanying their revelation to Dee and Kelley, in Section 9.4 below. Dee's connection with the Rosicrucian movement, his philosophy in general, and the nature of the "hieroglyphic" manuscript in his possession will be discussed in Section 8.9. For more information regarding Dee's angelic magic, see Casaubon (1659). Deacon (1968). Dee (1963, 1968). Fell-Smith (1904). French (1972). and Josten (1965).

8.5 The Galenic Medical Tradition

Galen, according to Thorndike (1923–58), wrote a voluminous medical encyclopedia (twenty books of about 1000 pages each) about A.D. 129. These works are not well known to modern readers, and are described by Thorndike as "relatively inaccessible". The humoral system of medicine, ascribed originally to Hippocrates, was elaborated by Galen and by medieval Arabic commentators such as Haly ben Rodwan, Rhazes, Haly Abbas, and Avicenna. The tradition was predominant in Europe over a long period of time, and survived in some form up until quite recently; it continues to thrive, in more or less concealed forms, in much modern "folk" medicine. Good general treatments of early medical history may be found in Singer and Underwood (1962). Singer (1928, 1959), and Taylor (1922).

In the Galenic system, food was processed by the human body through four stages or "digestions", each of which produced a nourishing product to be passed on to the next stage, and a waste product to be excreted. The "humors" — blood, yellow (or ruddy) bile, black bile, and phlegm—were the excreta of certain stages of digestion. The words "melancholic." "choleric." "phlegmatic." and "sanguine" which still survive in our language to describe temperament or personality, are survivals of the names of the four humors. Each of the humors had certain "natural qualities", which gave it its influence on the human body. temperament. and mind. These were combinations of cold. warm. wet. and dry. Depending upon the balance among the four humors in the constitution of a particular individual. he was said to have a particular "complexion". Disease arose. according to the Galenic theory. from a serious imbalance among the humors and their natural qualities. Similarly. changes in this balance accounted for the different constitutions of youth. maturity. and old age. The balance differed also with the seasons. and in the constitutions of the sexes: different foods. herbs. and other substances had important effects on the balance of the humors and their qualities. and were considered to have characteristic qualities of their own. The celestial bodies each had a crucial influence on the organs of the human body. the digestions. and all the other elements of the theory. The "microcosm" or "small world" of the human body was held to reflect in miniature all the relations and influences at work within the "macrocosm" or universe as a whole.

The medical treatments employed by the Galenic physician took careful cognizance of the positions of the heavenly bodies. and certain "critical days" were singled out. on which certain treatments could not safely be applied. Cathartic (purgative) expedients acting upon particular humors were an important part of therapy. For example. the herbs sage and betony were supposed to draw and purge phlegm and water; rhubarb acted on choler (yellow bile): and senna purged melancholy (black bile). Blood was purged by the obvious method of opening a vein and bleeding the patient ("phlebotomy"). Thus. the Galenic physician was a skilled practitioner of "cathartic and phlebotomy".

Heat and moisture were highly important in the Galenic therapies. Heat was the principle of life: greatest at birth and early youth. it was thought to become gradually exhausted and cooled with advancing age. Old age involved an excess of coldness and dryness. so that warm baths and applications of warm oils and unguents were recommended for the elderly. Another sovereign remedy for the bad effects of old age was the contact or embrace of a young person or animal. enabling the aged person to regain some of his lost heat and moisture by contagion from the superabundance in the younger creature. The royal road to health could lead. thus. to a warm puppy. or better still. a youthful maiden. Astrological and astronomical lore were obviously also of great importance in Galenic therapy: the physician almost had to be a practicing astrologer as well. The "medical month" consisted of twenty-eight days (a number which recurs in the diagrams of the Voynich manuscript). and the influence of the moon was of considerable importance through its effect on moisture and the tides.

Roger Bacon. in his medicinal work (Bacon 1928a). provides an extremely complete. clear. and detailed explanation of astrology as it related to medicine (and Withington. in his preface to the work. gives an excellent general summary of Galenic doctrines and Bacon's contributions and sources as well). Figure 34 shows some salient features of Galenic medicine. in "fours": some of the terms may well underlie the labels and text strings in certain cosmological and astronomical drawings in the manuscript. and possibly in the zodiac diagrams also. They may be involved in the "human figure" drawings as well: the omnipresent puffs of vapor or foam could well represent the humor or qualities. the digestions. etc. Terms referring to degrees of coldness. warmth. wetness. and dryness may even be concealed in the text of herbal folios. as they are frequently mentioned in ancient and medieval herbals as properties of medicinal plants.

8.6 Ars Notoria: Demonic and Angelic Magic

I have found relatively little material directly concerning this topic. although it is mentioned in passing in many of the works cited in Section 8.1 above. Yates (1966) describes it as a magical art of memory. using "shorthand notae" or symbols. and regarded as a very black kind of magic. Walker (1958) discusses certain systems of "spiritual magic" in considerable detail. Thorndike (1923–58) characterizes Ars Notoria as an art designed to gain knowledge of and to communicate with God by the invocation of angels. using mystical characters and prayers; he also dismisses all the material as "meaningless jumbles of diagrams and magic words" without telling us much more about it. The essence of the Ars Notoria seems to have been the use of angels' and demons' names. and an attempt to exploit these intermediaries as channels of illumination and power from God. Trithemius (Steganographia. 1606). Picatrix. the Solomonian and Abramelinian magical systems. and John Dee's magical practices all made heavy use of invocations directed to demons and spirits. Figure 33 shows some lists of names from various systems. and figure 32 provides some examples of the seals. talismans. and diagrams employed to invoke and control these beings. The spirits were intricately connected with the four directions. the elements. the celestial spheres and other cosmological entities. and so may have been named on some of the Voynich manuscript folios.

8.7 Cabala

The mystical Jewish philosophy known as Cabala (or Kabbalah) developed in Spain during the Middle Ages. A thirteenth-century book called the Zohar. originating in Spain. was an important source of Cabalistic lore for later writers. The Cabala depended heavily on manipulation of the letters of the Hebrew alphabet and lists of sacred words. and was in general highly "verbal" and abstract in character. in contrast to the iconic. visual quality of many other magical systems. The names of God and of angels and the Hebrew letters were employed in ways strongly suggesting to us. today. cryptologic techniques (and. in fact. the manipulations of the Cabala may have inspired at least some early cryptographic devices). "Magic squares" were a prominent feature of the system. Ten basic elements called the "Sephiroth" were essential to the doctrine: these were supposed to represent the powers or attributes of God. and were associated with other entities (ten spheres of the universe. etc..) in a typical medieval table of correspondences (see figure 35). The Hebrew letters were all associated with unique numerical values and a Cabalistic method called "gematria" permitted alternative words having the same numerical values to be substituted for sets of names such as the "Sephiroth". Another Cabalistic art called "temurah" involved anagramming sacred words.

Most of the major magical systems of later times made at least some use of Cabala. Hebrew lore and the Hebrew language and alphabet were regarded. because of their Biblical association. as especially holy. ancient. and magically potent. While the imagery and "feel" of the Voynich manuscript does not seem very closely akin to the dry. abstract. and ascetic atmosphere of Cabala. the importance of the doctrine and of the Hebrew words originating in it to medieval magic in general make it worthwhile for a student of the manuscript to be at least superficially familiar with it. We have seen above (5.1) that Newbold attempted to use a Cabalistic principle involving all combinations of the letters of the Hebrew alphabet taken two at a time as a part of his decipherment method. This. in itself. seems to have been an ingenious and rather reasonable hypothesis. however mistaken it has turned out to have been. General coverage of Cabala may be found in Blau (1944). Mathers (1951). and Waite (1929).

8.8 Alchemy

The topic of alchemy has been dealt with by many writers in many different ways. Shumaker (1972) and Graubard (1953) present good general treatments. and Thorndike (1923–58) discusses alchemy in passing as he describes the writings of various ancient and medieval practitioners. Singer (1928–31) provides a comprehensive catalogue of alchemical manuscripts. and an equally comprehensive listing of alchemical terms and symbols may be found in Gessman (1922). Ashmole (1652) presents a large and valuable collection of old manuscripts. permitting the reader to gain an excellent feeling for the nature and style of their texts and illustrations.

The origin of alchemy apparently cannot be traced back to any one source with any certainty. It was attributed to the Egyptians. Babylonians. Jews. and perhaps even to the Hindus and Chinese. Medieval writers ascribed its origin to Hermes Trismegistus. and much of the alchemical lore that came down to the Middle Ages probably had its source among the Alexandrian Greeks in the early Christian era. It was transmitted to Europe from the Arab world through a translation in 1144 of a work entitled "Book of the Composition of Alchemy." Interest in alchemy was long-lived. continuing into the seventeenth century when it began to decline: the eighteenth century is regarded as the end of its real influence. Elias Ashmole (A.D. 1617–1693. founder in 1683 of the Ashmolean Museum in Oxford. the first public museum in the British Isles). was perhaps the last prominent enthusiast for alchemy.

The doctrines of alchemy covered a very broad range of technical practices and natural phenomena: it is difficult indeed to disentangle its intimate intermingling of Galenic medicine. philosophical and religious mysticism (Christian and pagan). mythology. astrology. botany. zoology. mineralogy and primitive chemistry. It was an all-embracing magical or religious philosophy as well as a more or less operational set of techniques. There were two main forms of alchemy: practical alchemy was the actual attempt to create new compounds or substances by chemical operations. and prominently. of course. the attempt to produce or multiply gold. It arose. in all probability. from early metal-working and smelting lore passed down through the ages from early man in the Near East. Theoretical alchemy. on the other hand. was a philosophical doctrine about the nature of the universe and of matter: an eclectic amalgam of Gnosticism. Neo-Platonism. Christian mystical doctrines. and pagan mythology. There was no hard-and-fast line drawn between these two branches of the art: typically. each practitioner of alchemy struck his own preferred balance between the smoke. smells. and gadgetry of the laboratory and the quiet of the study or the oratory of the magus.

It was customary for an adept in alchemy. especially one who claimed to have attained some practical success. to adopt a "son" or heir to whom he would pass on his wisdom at his death. Elias Ashmole was "adopted" in this way by an older alchemist named William Backhouse: Ashmole himself apparently never attempted the laboratory operations of practical alchemy but contented himself with reading and collecting manuscripts and studying the symbols and concepts of theoretical alchemy. Almost all alchemical writings were routinely couched in a highly mysterious. deliberately misleading and metaphorical language: codes and ciphers were commonly employed in the manuscripts. and extreme secrecy was the rule.

In essence. (as far as modern writers have been able to guess from the convoluted secret writings that have come down to us) alchemy was based on a theory involving a fundamental constituent of all nature called the "first matter" or "hyle." Individual objects gained their characteristic identities that made them what they were instead of something else. through the addition of "qualities" such as the cold. moisture. dryness and heat of Galenic medicine. In order to transmute an object into another object. one must remove the "qualities" of one nature. get back to the neutral "first matter". then add or "cast on" the "qualities" of the desired nature (usually those of gold). This process involved elaborate sequences of manipulations in the alchemist's "laboratory" that might occupy months or years. employ the services of many helpers. and consume incredible amounts of money and effort. Practical alchemy was a feasible hobby for only the richest of men.

The laboratory operations included a long list of activities which are variously (and. needless to say. mysteriously) defined in the many alchemical treatises. They are described by terms such as calcination. solution. putrefaction. congelation. fermentation. exaltation. and projection. The products of these processes and their appearance and behavior in the laboratory "glassware" or vessels were described in wildly metaphorical ways (a black residue was "the raven" or "the crow's head"; a corrosive acid was "the green lion"; other substances were called "the snowy swan". "the toad that eats his fill". "the dragon". etc.). Substances were referred to as "medicine." "menstrual fluid." "blood." etc.. or labelled with the names of parts of the human body. Metaphors were taken from human social life ("marriage" or "wedding." "copulation." "death" and "burial"). and religion ("the passion of Christ." "resurrection." "purification." "redemption"). In fact. almost any name of any natural or artificial object or process could appear as a "cover-word" for some alchemical process or product.

It is my own opinion that the Voynich manuscript could well be. at least in part. an alchemical treatise. I feel that this hypothesis explains the secrecy and mysteriousness of its form; the difficulty of deciphering it or recognizing its drawings in any conventional herbal or astrological illustrations of the times. and the apparent encyclopedic character of its content. In fact. the only two drawings I have found that have any close kinship in style or treatment to those in the manuscript are two illustrations in Ashmole's *Theatrum Chemicum Britannicum* (1652). These are: a drawing of a plant. "lunaria". on p. 348. and a symbolic representation of an alchemical operation on p. 350. Both of these are in a group of manuscripts of Ashmole's collection which are identified. alas. only as "anonymi." The text. in paired lines of Old English verse. discusses herbs. Christian mystical platitudes. astrological matters. etc. in the usual wildly heterogeneous conglomeration. It is apparently much farther toward the "theoretical" or philosophical end of the spectrum than the practical.

The plant figure has many of the odd stylistic features of the Voynich manuscript's herbal folios: the rigidly symmetrical arrangements of leaves and flowers: the "molded plastic". blocky. or sculpturesque forms: the platform with abrupt edges having a "cut out" look on which the plant is sitting. very similar in style to some root forms on the Voynich manuscript plant folios.

The other figure has elements resembling some of those in the folios showing nude human figures in tubs of liquid. A cloud-like form at the top. from which conventionalized rays emanate. represents God: immediately below. the figure of a man or angel breathes into the mouth of a bulbous alchemical vessel: his breath is clearly indicated in exactly the way that the vapors or liquids are shown passing through the elaborate "plumbing" on the Voynich manuscript folios. On the vessel are a sun (with a face) above and within a crescent moon: from each of these. vapors or emanations are shown descending through the vessel. The round bottom of the vessel is provided with seven spouts. spaced around its curved circumference. and the vapor emerges from all of these and trickles down over two nude. plump human figures locking arms and holding hands: these figures. while better drawn than the Voynich manuscript nudes. are short-legged and "hippy". with fat tummies. in a very similar style. Two dragons standing on their heads and a toad complete the composition. The style of the seven spouts on the vessel is so close to that of similar spouts and vents on the pipe-like forms in the manuscript as to be almost indistinguishable. and the symbolic use of conventionalized forms to create a new synthetic whole with a complex meaning also seems closely akin to the methods of the Voynich manuscript's scribe or scribes. While these drawings are identified only as "anonymous" in Ashmole's collection. I have discovered some highly similar figures in other works where they are associated with the writings of George Ripley. a fifteenth-century alchemist who produced numerous treatises with a strong Christian flavor (Philalethes 1678. Ripley 1591. 1756). De Rola (1973. figure 64) shows a figure similar to the second described above. citing its source as *De Erroribus*. by John Dastin (British Museum. Egerton 845. folio 17v).

In any case. it seems likely that a thorough examination of alchemical manuscripts and their illustrations might amply repay the efforts of any student who could gain access to them.

8.9 *The Rosicrucian Movement and John Dee*

While Dr. John Dee has already been mentioned quite frequently in this monograph. it remains to provide a fuller discussion of his thought. his writings. and his connection with the Rosicrucian movement. a philosophical tradition which mav. itself. have some bearing on the Voynich manuscript. There are a number of good treatments of John Dee's life and thought. notably Deacon (1968). Fell-Smith (1904). and French (1972). Yates (1972) covers the early Rosicrucian movement very thoroughly. and deals with Dee in that context. Dee's private diary (Dee 1842) and a list of the manuscripts in his large collection (James 1921) are of considerable (though less general) interest.

The Rosicrucian movement. centering in the Palatinate region of Germany but having wide-ranging repercussions in other European countries. was essentially an attempt to liberalize religious and philosophical thinking: it combined the rich heritage of the Hermetic tradition with Christian mysticism and a generous admixture of alchemy. Cabala. magic. and medicine. The Rosicrucians were fanatically secretive. The authors of the original Rosicrucian "manifestoes" (the *Fama* and the *Confessio*. both reproduced in translation in Yates 1972) never revealed their identities. They claimed to have founded a "brotherhood." and appeared to invite new adherents; all attempts on the part of would-be recruits to get in touch with the founders seem to have been fruitless and certainly received no open response (although there may have been some well-concealed contacts and activities behind the scenes).

The Rosicrucian doctrines. like those of alchemy to which they are closely akin. manifested a highly devious and convoluted use of symbols and imagery. To the amalgam of devices familiar in alchemy. the Rosicrucians added political symbolism related to the prominent conflict between Protestant nations and leaders. organized around Frederick V (Elector Palatine of the Rhine. and married to Princess Elizabeth. daughter of James I of England) and the reactionary Catholic house of Habsburg. These quasi-political symbols with religious and mystical overtones included the Habsburg eagle. the Palatine lion. the red rose. images related to the "Order of the Garter." and symbols taken from or akin to those in John Dee's writings. especially his *Monas Hieroglyphica* (Dee 1564. 1964).

John Dee. according to Yates. "belonged emphatically to the Renaissance Hermetic tradition. brought up to date with new developments. and which he further expanded in original and important directions" (1972. p. xii). Later. on the same page. she describes Dee's contributions as follows: "In the lower elemental world he studied number as technology and applied sciences.... In the celestial world. his study of number was related to astrology and alchemy. and in his *Monas Hieroglyphica* he believed he had discovered a formula for a combined cabalist. alchemical and mathematical science which would enable its possessor to move up and down the scale of being from the lowest to the highest spheres. And in the supercelestial sphere. Dee believed that he had found the secret of conjuring angels by numerical computations in the cabalist tradition."

Dee's influence was carried to the European continent. where he made extensive visits from 1583 on. He was. according to Yates. very active in stirring up new movements in Central Europe. though his work there has been studied less thoroughly than his life in England. It would seem that Dee was somewhat of an intellectual leader in Bohemia. not only in alchemy. but in a religious reform movement. the nature of which has not yet been investigated and explained fully. Most of the events discussed in Yates' treatment of Dee and the Rosicrucians probably took place after the Voynich manuscript was already in existence. It seems to me very likely. however. that there is some kinship between the philosophy underlying the manuscript and the Rosicrucian tradition. Because of the known association of the manuscript with Rudolph's court and possibly also with Dee. and the obvious similarity of its secretive. synthetic symbolism to that of the Rosicrucians. a serious student can scarcely afford to ignore any of this highly interesting material.

A brief word should be said concerning the "hieroglyphic manuscript" which Dee was reputed to have had in his possession. and which some writers have identified with the Voynich manuscript. The letter written in 1675 by Sir Thomas Browne to Elias Ashmole. and reporting the words of Arthur Dee. John Dee's son. concerning this mysterious manuscript. is quoted by Fell-Smith (1904) as follows: "The transmutation [to gold] was made by a powder they had. which was found in some old place. and a book lying by it containing nothing but hieroglyphicks; which book his [Arthur's] father bestowed much time upon. but I could not hear that he could make it out." (p. 311). Arthur Dee. born 1579. was apparently eight years old at the time he saw the events he describes.

Another history related by Fell-Smith probably records the origin of the manuscript and the powder: "Kelley is reputed to have been wandering in Wales. . .when he stumbled upon an old alchemical manuscript and two caskets or phials containing a mysterious red and white powder." (p. 77). It was Kelley. in any case. who brought the powder and the manuscript to Dee when they first became acquainted. In fact. one gains the definite impression that Kelley's original purpose in seeking Dee out (under an assumed name at first) was to gain his assistance. and probably his monetary backing. for an attempt to puzzle out the meaning of the manuscript and to use the powders to make gold.

Dee's diary. as edited by Halliwell (Dee 1842) provides no further information concerning the manuscript or the powder. Josten. however. in a highly interesting recent article (1965). describes a portion of the diary that had been discovered in a source separate from the remainder: this excerpt does. indeed. contain considerable information on the matter. It records in great detail an incident during the time when Dee and Kelley were engaged in communication with the angels: the spirits instructed them, through Kelley, to destroy all their precious books and occulta, including the hieroglyphic manuscript and the powder. This sacrificial act, intended to be a test of their high purity of purpose and submission to God's will, required their placing the objects into a furnace (undoubtedly a part of the furnishings of their alchemical laboratory) and permitting them to be consumed by the fire.

This ceremony or bit of sleight of hand (for it was apparently an elaborate deception, either worked on Dee by Kelley for some purpose known only to his unbalanced and unscrupulous mind, or else perpetrated by both men for some unknown common purpose upon a third party) was duly accomplished: the next day, all the "destroyed" arcana miraculously reappeared, to be rediscovered whole and undamaged by Kelley in the ashes of the furnace. The description of the ceremonial burning includes a tantalizing glimpse of the hieroglyphic manuscript itself, which is described as being small but written in letters "larger" than those of usual writing, and to have been stored in a velvet bag or sack.

On his break with Dee in Prague, Kelley kept most of the magic powder; what ultimately became of the manuscript is not reported in any of the sources I have consulted. It seems likely that Kelley kept that also (since it had apparently been his from the beginning) and subsequently sold or relinquished it to Rudolph. Unfortunately, the mere characterization of this book as being "in hieroglyphics" is not enough to warrant a secure identification with the Voynich manuscript, since many, if not most, alchemical treatises were couched in secret characters. It was more usual, however, for the secret symbols to be intermixed with Latin or some other more familiar letters after the fashion of a rebus. It also seems likely that Dee would have been familiar with the alchemical symbols, and would have had no trouble in making some sense out of them, however little success he may have attained in making gold according to their instructions. Section 9.4 provides a somewhat fuller discussion of alchemical symbols, and figure 42 shows some examples.

8.10 The History of the Hindu-Arabic Numerals

In view of the strong possibility that some, at least, of the Voynich symbols may be early forms of numerals, something should be said about the origin and development of these numerals in Europe. Figure 16 shows a sample of some early numeral forms that bear a resemblance to some Voynich script characters. Two good general studies of the origin of Arabic numerals are Hill (1915) and Smith and Karpinski (1911). The original birthplace of the numerals is veiled in uncertainty: they could have come from Egypt, Persia, China, or Mesopotamia. Their history can, however, be clearly traced in India and then in their very gradual adoption in Europe. The Hindu system of numerals, including place value and a symbol for "zero", was transmitted to the Arabs at a relatively early date. Smith and Karpinski trace the first introduction of the Hindu numerals to a visit A.D. 773 by a Hindu astrologer to the court of the Caliph, where his astronomical tables were translated into Arabic. Other Arab mathematicians (among them Al-Khowarazmi, who gave his name, in the form "algorism" or "algorithmi," to arithmetical calculation using the new numerals, and ultimately to our modern "algorithm") based their tables and computations on that translated work.

Arab writers continued to use the new numbers, consistently referring to them, and the arithmetic based on them, as "Indian" well into the thirteenth century. The adoption of the numerals into Europe is hard to pin down exactly; Smith and Karpinski attribute it to the travels of merchants and traders in Spain, where Arab influence was strong, as early as the ninth or tenth century. Numerous visits to the Near and Far East were made by traders and missionaries throughout the Middle Ages; the travels of the Brothers Poli were unusual only in the thoroughness of their documentation and the interest they have aroused in modern times. These travelers brought back many bits and pieces of foreign lore, some of it remarkable in the wealth of its detail and vividness of description. The Hindu-Arabic numerals undoubtedly became known at least to some through these accounts. One form of the numerals, employed in conjunction with the abacus, became known to Europeans under the names "characteres" or "apices," and involved unusually bizarre and ornate varieties of the symbols.

The adoption of the new numbers in Europe was an extremely slow matter. They seem to have been known or mentioned by some writers for a considerable time before they came into anything like general use. They were not employed by merchants for the practical calculations of commerce until surprisingly late. Leonardo Fibonacci of Pisa, born about 1175, did much to introduce the numerals to Europeans. His *Liber Abaci*, written in 1202 and rewritten in 1228, explained the new numbers and used them as they would be employed in the usual computations of business. The methods he presented were rejected both by the conservative mercantile class and by university circles, according to Smith and Karpinski (p. 131). The bankers of Florence were forbidden to use the new numerals in 1299, and "the statutes of the University of Padua required stationers to keep the price lists of books 'non per cifras, sed per literas claras'". (p. 133).

63

Still. the new system made some headway from 1275 on. It is interesting to note that the common folk of Northern European nations like Germany rarely used Arabic numerals before the sixteenth century. The invention of cheap paper. lead pencils. and modern methods of multiplication and division did not come about until quite recently: these were the developments that. according to Smith and Karpinski, really made the new "algorism" attractive and practical for everyday use. Before that time. the Arabic numerals were employed primarily on coins. for numbering the pages of manuscripts. and for dates. They are often found intermingled in bizarre ways with Roman numerals: e.g.. "IVOjj" for "1502": "M°CCCC°50" for "1450": and "M.CCCC.8ii" for "1482". In the early and transitional phases of their adoption. the numerals or "ciphers" were regarded as incomprehensible. mysterious. strange. and well-suited for use as cryptic symbols in secret writing systems.

8.11 *Medieval and Renaissance Costume*

The clothing of some of the human figures on the pages of the Voynich manuscript should afford us some clue as to the date and provenience of the work. Unfortunately. the drawing is so sketchy. and the figures are so small and lacking in detail. that there is disappointingly little to go on. A wide variety of hats and headgear are in evidence. even on figures otherwise entirely nude: these include a variety of diadems. tiaras and crowns as well as wide-brimmed hats. floppy tam-o-shanters. and hats provided with ribbons. veils. or plumes falling over the wearer's shoulder or back. Dress of women and perhaps also men includes a sort of long pleated robe with wide sleeves (see Virgo and one of the Gemini twins. figure 10): Very common is a kind of knee-length. pleated tunic belted at the waist (see Sagittarius. figure 10). Costumes of this type were common during the fourteenth. fifteenth. and sixteenth centuries throughout Europe. There seem to be no examples of more extreme styles: the tall conical hats or two-horned headgear for women: the exaggeratedly puffed pantaloons and huge ruffled collars for men in style after about 1550: or the curly-toed shoes. very short tunics over skin-tight pants with codpieces that were the height of fashion somewhat earlier. The garments shown. however sketchily. on the Voynich manuscript folios seem quite simple and restrained on the whole. and provide relatively little decisive information. They seem to me. from an admittedly superficial study. to be consistent with a date between 1450 and 1550 (see Von Boehn 1964 for a well-illustrated treatment of sixteenth-century costume). Some typical hat and dress forms from the Voynich manuscript are shown in figures 10 and 37.

Chapter 9

Collateral Research: Artificial and Secret Languages

Late medieval and Renaissance philosophy included a vigorous interest in synthetic languages of many kinds: these were variously intended for concealment of secrets, expression of mystical religious ideas, abbreviated and compact transcription of text, interlingual communication, and an encyclopedic mnemonic representation of human knowledge. As has been the case throughout these chapters on collateral research, I can present here only the barest suggestion of the material available to the interested reader.

9.1 Brachygraphy: The History of Shorthand

The ancient Greeks employed a system of abbreviations called Tironian Hand or Notation, ascribed to Marcus Tullius Tiro in the first century before Christ (see Rose 1874, Allen 1889, Boge 1973). Newbold attempted to use early Greek abbreviations in his decipherment method, as we saw in Chapter 5. Many later systems of abbreviations in Roman and medieval times were inspired by, or based on, this early Greek system. Figure 38 shows an interesting example of a medieval shorthand system derived from the Greek methods; its strokes are made up of parts of the letters "a" through "k" and early forms of the Hindu-Arabic numerals. This system, called "Notaria Aristotelis" by its author, an English monk of the thirteenth century, is of interest because of the resemblance of some of its symbols to the Voynich characters (probably, in my opinion, due to the derivation of both from early numeral forms). These symbols acted as bases, to which dots, lines, etc., were added to form words. Roger Bacon was reported by Johnen (1940, p. 34) to have been familiar with the Tironian Notation, which he called "ars notatoria".

Cappelli (1949) provides a summary of the history of Latin abbreviation systems and their development from classical into medieval times. The Roman system made use of several devices: single letters could stand for entire words or syllables, words could also be truncated or contracted, usually being provided with a mark or symbol showing that something had been omitted (a tail or curlicue extending upward or downward, a line or curve above certain letters, a slant line, etc.). Figure 17 shows some Latin abbreviations used in the Middle Ages that resemble characters of the Voynich script. Among general works dealing with the history of shorthand and covering the earliest systems are Giulietti (1968) and Johnen (1940). Alston (1966) provides a bibliography of works on the subject.

Most early European or English shorthand systems I have examined are designed around simple lines and curves, to which dots, dashes, circles, hooks, etc., are attached at various positions to form compound symbols standing for whole words. Most of these early systems were not "phonetic," i.e., they made little or no attempt to show the sound of words independently of spelling conventions as modern systems do. In fact, the early systems tended more toward an ideographic or symbolic representation of ideas, although alphabetic elements were also involved. All of the systems were extremely elaborate, requiring the memorization of vast arrays of arbitrary symbols that were difficult to write accurately and quickly; the modern reader can only wonder how anyone ever managed to learn or remember their large numbers of rules and forms, or to record the tiny dots and hooks with sufficient precision to permit distinguishing them later in attempting to read back what they had written. These methods certainly seem to have required far more effort than ordinary writing.

Duthie (1970) provides an interesting comparison of three major systems in existence during Elizabethan times. At least one of them may have been employed to record some of the texts of Shakespeare's plays during actual performances, so they must have been usable to some extent. I will summarize below, in highly abbreviated form, Duthie's presentation; the three systems seem typical of the methods available in the sixteenth and early seventeenth centuries. Their authors intended them, apparently, not simply for transcription of speech as modern systems are employed, but also for rapid and condensed writing, as a concealment method, and as a sort of elegant, philosophical mode of representing "ideas".

9.1.1 Characterie (Thomas Bright, circa 1588).

Figure 38 shows the basic strokes and the subsidiary elements to be added to each in Bright's system. Each of the eighteen base symbols consisted of a vertical line with a distinguishing hook, curlicue, etc., on its top: these symbols could be written in four different positions (vertical, horizontal, slanted left, slanted right). In addition, to the foot of each base symbol one of twelve additional squiggles could be added, making 864 combined symbols for use to represent common words; these were called "characterall words". Other words not in this basic list were expressed by "associating" them as synonyms or antonyms to a "characterall word", and prefixing to it the first-letter base symbol of the actual word, to serve as a sort of determinant (see the examples in figure 38). As Duthie remarks, this system was primitive and cumbersome, placing a great burden on the memory of its user, and producing forms which were very easy to garble and confuse.

9.1.2 Brachygraphie (Peter Bales, circa 1590).

Bales' system employed ordinary Roman letters in combination with dots, commas, and accents (collectively called by Bales "tittles"), which had to be very carefully and accurately placed around the letters to avoid confusion. The combinations of letters and "tittles" produced symbols for a basic list of common words as in Bright's system, and similarly, synonyms and antonyms were shown by using the base-word symbol with an extra stroke on the right or left. This shorthand method required the memorizing of over 500 different symbols; great precision in the placement of the "tittles" was mandatory in order to avoid garbles. It does not seem to have been any more practical than Bright's system.

9.1.3 Stenographie (John Willis, 1602).

Duthie finds Stenographie the best of the three, and considers it to be the foundation of modern shorthand systems. Figure 38 shows the twenty-six basic strokes, called "unchangeable particles"; these were partly phonetic, and "silent" letters were largely suppressed in writing words. A circle added to the foot of a stroke provided an "h" sound, and dots arranged in five clockwise positions around the basic stroke stood for vowels. Abbreviated forms of words were built up by combining these elements in a manner somewhat like modern methods. Willis' system is, in fact, very much like the later Pittman system (which may well have been derived from it). Duthie judges that Stenographie could have been employed to record slow, careful speech in condensed form, but not for rapid verbatim reporting. It is interesting to note that Willis called his system "Steganographie" as well as Stenographie, and considered it appropriate for concealment of secrets.

In summary, it seems unlikely that any of these systems or others related to them are closely akin to the Voynich script. The only element among the Voynich symbols that bears any resemblance to the dots, dashes, hooks, and "tittles" of the early shorthand methods is the hook or curlicue that appears frequently over the "double-c" character " ᴄᴄ " to form " ᴄᴄ ". There seems to be no visible structure of auxiliary marks added to a recurrent set of base symbols. It seems considerably more reasonable, in my opinion, to look for relationships between the Voynich characters and medieval Latin abbreviations, with some early numeral forms (see Section 4.1.2 and figures 16, 17).

9.2 Steganography: The Early History of Cryptology

There are records of ciphers in ancient Egypt and Rome; substitution ciphers of various kinds, some employing invented alphabets or geometrical symbols, were known from the early Middle Ages. Roger Bacon was greatly interested in secret writing, and much has been made (by would-be decipherers of the Voynich manuscript) of Bacon's statements on this topic in his *Epistola de Secretis Operibus Artis et Naturae*. He recommends, for the concealment of great and potent secrets, and to prevent them from being abused by the common herd of mankind, the use of the following expedients: 1) characters and verses (or "incantations"); 2) fables and enigmas; 3) leaving out certain letters, especially vowels (as the Hebrews, Chaldeans, and Arabs do to make their secrets harder to read!); 4) mixing letters of different kinds (as, for example, the astronomer Ethicus hid his knowledge by a mixture of Hebrew, Greek, and Latin letters); 5) employing letters "strange to one's own culture"; 6) creating characters from one's own imagination (this last being, according to Bacon, an especially good method, used by Artephius in his *Book of the Secrets of Nature*); 7) using geometric figures combined with dots and signs instead of alphabetic characters; and finally 8) the "notory art," which Bacon thought was the best method of all: the art of writing "as briefly and rapidly as one desires." Bacon claimed to have used some, at least, of these methods in his own writings.

This highly interesting and rather complete compendium of early cryptographic devices from the potent pen of the Doctor Mirabilis has understandably inspired many students of the Voynich manuscript to seek some or all of these techniques in its pages, and to see in it a result of Bacon's practice of his own recommendations. A considerable literature exists, dealing with ciphers attributed to Bacon in alchemical works (Hime 1904, 1914, 1915; Steele 1928a, 1928b; Manly 1931). An anagram, in which Bacon is supposed to have hidden a formula for gunpowder, is explicated variously by some, but debunked by others (who dismiss it as a superstitious tale about a split willow branch that magically rejoins itself, or as a careless misreading by an early editor of a sentence in a manuscript).

A variety of cryptographic methods are described by other early writers; Ramon Lull (Yates 1960, Rossi 1961), Trithemius (1564, 1606), Porta (1563), Agrippa (1970), and Athanasius Kircher (Kircher 1631, McCracken 1948) are all credited with systems which are essentially forms of ciphers and codes or could be used as such. John Dee was interested in cryptography, and made use of it in his missions for his royal patron, Elizabeth of England, according to Deacon (1968). Many early systems involved substitution ciphers, using inverted or distorted characters, geometric figures, numerals, alchemical and astrological symbols, Latin abbreviations, etc., in hybrid conglomerations. There were, in addition, some more sophisticated techniques. Lists of apparently innocent words all starting with a given letter could be used as alternate codewords for that letter, so that an innocuous-appearing sentence consisting of five Latin words might conceal a five-letter word that carried the true message. Correspondents each having a copy of the "code book" containing the long lists of cover words (made-up words, names of angels and demons, stereotyped religious platitudes, etc.) could use them as an effective means for concealing simple messages in letters (see, for example, Trithemius 1564, pp. 48ff.). Ramon Lull's rotating geometric figures marked with letters could be employed to produce digraphs (Aa, Ab, Ac, ..., Az, Ba, Bb, etc.) which could be made to stand for words or concepts. A number of early cryptographic systems employed cipher wheels with one fixed and one rotating alphabet (e.g., Alberti, in the late fifteenth century, and Silvester and Porta in the sixteenth; see Silvester 1526, p. 7; Porta 1563, pp. 73, 79, 83; and Meister 1902, 1906).

Another early cryptographic device concealed a message within a much longer "dummy" text by some rule agreed upon by the correspondents. Alchemy treatises, which were expected to be enigmatic even at best, were ideal vehicles for hiding a brief message in this way. A related concealment system employed groups of two or three letters in various combinations, or the presence or absence of some apparently decorative or accidental characteristic (small and large letters, tiny dots, underlines, or strokes added to some letters and not to others, shading, etc.). These groups could be made to stand for letters of a message by a variety of conventions; for example, in a triliteral system described by Trithemius (A.D. 1462–1516) about 1500, a set of groups AAA, AAB, AAC, ABA, ABB, ABC, ..., CCA, CCB, CCC could provide twenty-seven values for the letters of the alphabet and a few additional characters. The twenty-seven distinctions could be represented more abstractly by any three states of three things, arranged in all unique combinations (three different fonts, levels of darkness in printing, etc.). The famous cipher of Francis Bacon (about 1600) is of this type, differing from Trithemius' system only in that it used groups of five elements, made up of two distinctions or choices, and employed more sophisticated means of concealing the distinctions in a cover text.

An impressive variety of cryptographic methods, exhibiting a surprising degree of complexity and sophistication, were in use at an early date in the service of the Papal court and the courts of Italian Princes. A number of these systems are described in Meister (1902, 1906), Pasini (1873), Sacco (1947), and Alberti (1568). Meister (1902) provides a detailed history of early Italian ciphers, the earliest dating to 1226 from the Venetian Republic and others from many Italian cities during the fourteenth and the fifteenth centuries. Meister (1906) traces to the year 1326 or 1327 the earliest example of a device called a "nomenclator," consisting of a small list of code words or syllables standing for words and phrases commonly employed in Church or State correspondence ("Pope", "horses", "soldiers", stereotyped honorific phrases, place names, titles, etc.). Meister describes a number of remarkably complex and advanced systems in use for Papal correspondence during the fourteenth and fifteenth centuries. These employed variant substitution elements (many alternative cipher elements all standing for the same plaintext element), often drawn from fanciful, foreign, or invented alphabets. Many such systems also made use of "nulls" (a list of alternative dummy symbols having no meaning in themselves but thrown in to pad out the text, conceal patterns, and further confuse the would-be decipherer). All these devices could be employed in concert: a "nomenclator," really a primitive small code, plus an elaborate system of monographic, digraphic, and trigraphic variants, with a correspondingly varied set of nulls as well. Figure 39 shows a sampling of some early Italian cryptographic systems.

Of particular interest because of its relatively early date is a system described by Jakob Silvester (1526). This system was based on a Latin dictionary: a code consisting of Roman numerals was assigned to the columns of words on each page of the dictionary. As an alternative, to further confuse the decipherer, a set of digraphs in random order (AF, DC, BN, etc.) could be used instead of, or intermixed with, the Roman numerals to designate the column. Within each column, the individual words, arranged in roughly alphabetical order, were indicated by Arabic numerals. Latin endings were shown by single letters or digraphs. The alphabet employed is made up of invented and foreign symbols of great variety. Nulls drawn from a large set of choices could be scattered through the text. Figure 40 shows a sketch of the main features of Silvester's system, and two short samples of text enciphered in it. Unfortunately, Silvester's book does not provide enough detail regarding the

67

dictionary or other aspects of the system to support a complete investigation of its relationship to the phenomena of the Voynich text, nor does it provide any long samples of enciphered text that might be studied statistically.

The reader who remembers the remarks of Tiltman concerning the "beginning-middle-end" structure of words in the Voynich text, and the comments of Tiltman and Friedman regarding universal and synthetic languages, will recognize the possibilities of this early code system in accounting for the phenomena they had in mind (see also Sections 5.6.5 and 6.6 above, as well as 9.3 and the Appendix below). Friedman and Tiltman made strenuous attempts to trace the history of synthetic languages back to a date sufficiently early to be contemporary with the Voynich manuscript (i.e., before 1550). It is my opinion that the earliest history of such languages can indeed be found by searching in two areas: first, among early cryptographic systems, and second, in the medieval and Renaissance Ars Memorativa. Yates (1966, p. 378) mentions the work of Francis Bacon, Comenius, Bisterfeld, Dalgarno, and Wilkins directed toward the development of a "real character" (i.e., a system of signs like Chinese characters, supposed to be "directly" related to their referents as are ideographs or hieroglyphs, and independent of the spelling or sound of words). She traces this undertaking back to a foundation in an earlier tradition of memory art, citing the work of Rossi (1960). A complex cryptographic system such as that of Jakob Silvester could well form the basis of the Voynich text. It is interesting to note that a copy of Silvester's work in the British Museum Library, dated 1616, is autographed by, and had presumably been in the possession of John Dee (Shulman 1976, p. 2).

9.3 Pasigraphy: Universal and Synthetic Languages

At the time during the late Middle Ages and early Renaissance when Latin was no longer functioning as a Lingua Franca for learned internal communication and the vernacular languages were beginning to be employed more and more, many scholars began to be concerned about finding a substitute to fill the need for a universal language. At the same time, travellers, whether merchants or missionaries, were bringing news from the Far East of writing systems that apparently employed ideographs and characters that could stand for ideas as wholes, rather than representing the sounds of words through an alphabet. Thus there arose a number of efforts directed toward the development of a "universal character" or "real character" which would in some manner bypass the multiplicity of vernacular tongues and represent ideas directly in the same way for all nations.

This undertaking was not really a wholly new idea; in fact, it was solidly based in the encyclopedic mnemonic systems of the Middle Ages. Yates (1966) examines the work of Francis Bacon and others in the seventeenth century engaged in the search for a universal language. Leibnitz, as Yates shows, was a last great exponent of the ancient tradition, weaving the Art of Memory into the creation of the infinitesimal calculus (Yates 1966, pp. 378 ff.).

The early synthetic languages had much in common with cryptographic codes. As a foundation, a classification scheme was set up for words or ideas to form a framework of what were called "syncategoremata." The word-classes were chosen by each author according to his own philosophical bent and purposes; while intended to be independent of any one language, the scheme often involved numbers or codes assigned to the words of a Latin dictionary. Some of the categories are concrete and straightforward, but many others seem forbiddingly abstruse and philosophical to the modern reader. In a system devised by an anonymous Spanish Jesuit in 1653 called an "arithmeticus nomenclator," a class was set up for all words relating to "the elements"; this class was assigned Roman numeral I. Arabic numerals were used to select individual words within the class, e.g., 1. Fire. 2. Flame. 3. Smoke. . . . . 6. Wind. 7. Breeze. . . . . 12. Water, etc., (see Groves 1846, p. 55 ff.). Dalgarno's system involved twenty classes of words or ideas, represented by capital letters: A, for example, stood for the class "Ens. Res"; H for "Spiritus," U for "Homo," etc. (Dalgarno, 1661).

John Wilkins, inventor of a system of "real character" around the year 1668, set up forty classes including such things as: 1. "Transcendental, General"; 2. "Transcendental, Mixed"; . . . . 5. "God, the Creator"; 6. "The World, Creation"; 7. "The Elements"; etc. These philosophical classes embodied the concepts about the nature of the universe current in those times, and deriving from medieval foundations. Under each such class, subcategories were set up for "differences" and "species". "Differences" were shown by vertical and oblique lines attached on the left of the basic symbol for the class; "species" by an adjunct symbol attached on the right. Grammatical information (endings, etc.) was shown by dots or lines attached to the compound symbol. Wilkins' system had a spoken as well as a written form.

Groves (1846) and Kircher (1663) provide summaries of a number of early synthetic language systems. Bausani (1970) gives a very complete treatment of synthetic languages of all types, including religious, cryptographic, and mystical languages as well. Dalgarno's system is described in Dalgarno (1661), Comenius in Geissler (1959). Other systems are presented in Wilkins (1641, 1668a, 1668b) and Top (1603). These invented languages are of interest to students of the Voynich manuscript for several reasons. First, two dedicated and expert cryptologists who devoted years of study to the

68

manuscript—Friedman and Tiltman—arrived independently at the hypothesis that a synthetic language of this type might underlie the Voynich text. Second, the structure of the early universal languages (a base or root for the class, followed by one or more characters to single out the "species" or individual word, and finally characters standing for grammatical forms agrees very well with the "beginning-middle-ending" structure found by Tiltman in the words of the Voynich text. Finally, as we have seen in the previous section, the methods employed in some early codes used by the Papal Court were highly similar, and date to a time sufficiently early to be contemporaneous with the origin of the manuscript.

9.4 *Magical and Religious Languages and Alphabets*

There remains for discussion another large group of synthetic languages which may have a bearing on the problem of the Voynich manuscript. Under this heading I have lumped together a number of different secret or mystical languages of various types: alchemical or philosophical systems; languages purporting to be revealed by, or used in communication with, God, angels or demons; systems of symbols used in magical incantations, prayers, and spells. Bausani (1970) provides an excellent overview of all these made-up languages, including universal languages and the neologisms ("glossolalia") of schizophrenics and other mentally disturbed persons or persons in temporarily abnormal mental states (such as mystical ecstasy or inspiration). Gessmann (1922) lists a large number of the words and symbols employed by medieval alchemists, physicians, and astrologers.

9.4.1 *Magical Languages.*

We have already taken some glimpses of magical symbols and writing in the discussion of magical systems in Section 8.1. Most such systems included talismans, seals, diagrams, and devices (daggers, swords, candlesticks, etc.) liberally decorated with letters in a variety of bizarre alphabets. De Givry (1971) and Seligman (1948) provide copious illustrations of magical figures drawn from a wide range of sources and dates. Many of the alphabets appear to be based on Hebrew characters in more or less garbled and distorted forms; Mathers (1974, pl. XV) shows several of these Hebrew writing systems ("Alphabet of the Magi," "Celestial Writing," "Malachim" or "Writing of the Angels," and "Passing of the River"). Some symbols in *Picatrix* are called "Indian," and may be distortions of Devanagari or some other Indian writing system. Other *Picatrix* characters are clearly Arabic, and others still are similar to Egyptian Hieroglyphic or Hieratic characters. Egyptian words seem discernible in some of the incantations of the Hermetic writings (Festugière 1944-54) (for example, "osergariach," in a "true name of Hermes Trismegistus" may contain the words "wsr ka re", "strong is the Ka of Re". *Picatrix* also employs the "star picture" writing made up of circles strung on lines and curves mentioned earlier in Sections 3.3.3 and 8.4. It is interesting to note that two of the mystical Hebrew alphabets, the "Writing of the Angels" and "Passing of the River" also consist of small circles strung on lines in this fashion. Figure 41 shows some samples of magical alphabets from various sources.

While interesting and suggestive, few of the magical symbols discussed above seem to bear any direct resemblance to anything in the Voynich script or drawings, with perhaps one exception. The *Picatrix* "star pictures," some of the Hebrew alphabets, and certain alchemy symbols all are strikingly similar to the strange geometric figures decorated with faces in the four corners of folio 67v2. It is also possible that the small design which Brumbaugh sees as a "clock face" may contain the character " 🜨 ", which is quite common in the *Picatrix* spells and also in the other writing systems mentioned above.

9.4.2 *Alchemical, Medical, and Astrological Symbols.*

Gessmann (1922) presents a large collection of the symbols and code words used by medieval alchemists and other scholars and philosophers. Figure 42 shows a selection of these sufficient to indicate their general appearance and nature, and includes some that appear similar to certain Voynich script characters. It was apparently a common practice for alchemists to employ these symbols, interspersed in Latin text, as a sort of secret shorthand for alchemical products and processes. While a few of these signs are somewhat similar to Voynich symbols, most of them are not, and they offer disappointingly little help in our task. Of course, if a clear relationship were evident between alchemical symbols and the Voynich script, alchemists at Rudolph's court would have had little trouble in deciphering it, and the mystery would not have persisted to our day unsolved.

The use of prayers and incantations in medical manuscripts is interesting in that many of the spells were in languages foreign to the compilers and users of the recipes; their very foreignness increased the potency of their supposed effect. Another feature of these spells which may be relevant to our purpose is their repetitiveness: one, two, or three words are often repeated several times in a row, either exactly or with minor differences, in a manner reminiscent of the repetitions in many stretches of Voynich text. The oldest surviving Anglo-Saxon medical manuscripts exhibit numerous examples of these practices (see Grattan and Singer 1952. Storms 1948). Some of the spells are distortions of Old Irish prayers brought in by Irish missionaries (e.g.. "Gonomil orgomil marbumil marbsai ramun....." a spell against "black blains." Grattan and Singer 1952. p. 64). Some are garbled bits of Greek liturgy (e.g.. "Stomen calcos. Stomen meta fofu." and "Eulogomen patera cae vo cae agion pneuma....." Grattan and Singer 1952. pp. 49–50).

There are some interesting survivals in the Anglo-Saxon manuscripts of pagan Roman prayers. for example a beautiful hymn to the Earth Mother. "Dea Sancta Tellus. Rerum Naturae Parens ...." (Grattan and Singer 1952. pp. 45–46). Numerous relics of pre-Christian Anglo-Saxon religious rites and beliefs are discernible. Names of saints and apostles and snatches of Biblical texts were employed as charms. Some spells combined garbled Greek. Hebrew. and Latin words in an impressive-sounding conglomeration that must have had a strong psychological impact on the patient ("Ranmigan adonai eltheos mur O ineffabile Omiginan... sother sother miserere mei deus mini deus mi Amen Alleluiah." a spell for "loose bowels". Grattan and Singer 1952. p. 189). Even the word "Abracadabra." which has come down to modern times as a symbol for magical mumbo-jumbo. had a place in Anglo-Saxon medicine (the word "ABRACADABRA" was "to be written repeatedly on a parchment and applied to the patient". Grattan and Singer 1952. p. 10).

9.4.3 *Mystical and Religious Languages.*

St. Hildegarde of Bingen (A.D. 1048–1179). whose visions have already been examined briefly for possible parallels to the Voynich manuscript (see Section 3.2.3). was also gifted with the mystical ability of "speaking in tongues." Manuscripts have been found preserving a series of "carmina" (songs or hymns) by Hildegarde in an "ignota lingua"; she apparently sang or recited such compositions while under the sway of her mystic visions. An invented alphabet also formed a part of Hildegarde's language; the letters are obviously distortions of Latin letters for the most part. Bausani (1970) provides a number of examples of words from Hildegarde's language. preserved in a sort of glossary written down by her contemporaries. In many cases. associations with German and Latin are apparent. as is the use of inflections similar to Latin endings. Figure 43 shows the alphabet and some samples of transliterated words.

Bausani (1970) mentions other. similar mystical languages employed by Elizabeth von Schönau (a contemporary of Hildegarde. also in religious life. and a frequent correspondent with her). and Christiana von Trond. The latter was in the habit of uttering melodious and incomprehensible words from "between her chest and her throat" when in a state of religious ecstasy. The mystical Sufi sect within Mohammedanism also developed a highly complex synthetic language called "Balaibalan." provided with an extensive set of grammatical and syntactical rules and a large lexicon. Bausani (1970) gives some examples of this language. The possibility cannot be ruled out that a made-up language of this type underlies the Voynich script. devised by an exceptional individual under the power of religious inspiration.

9.4.4 *The Enochian Language of John Dee.*

Deacon (1968) presents a clear and detailed description of the secret language which Dee and Kelley claimed to have received as a revelation from the angels through the "scrying glass." He also provides a highly interesting discussion of the "angelic conversations" carried out by Dee and Kelley during the early 1580's (Deacon 1968. pp. 138–156). Casaubon (1659) describes these conversations in great detail. in a work based on Dee's diaries and manuscripts. previously transcribed by Elias Ashmole. The following account is drawn from these two sources. I strongly urge any interested reader to obtain access to Casaubon's work and read it in full (there is a copy in the Fabyan Collection. Library of Congress). It is a fascinating and remarkable account. and the present brief summary can by no means do it justice.

As we have seen above (Sections 8.4.4 and 8.9). John Dee was never able to perceive the visions in his crystal or hear the angels' voices. For these offices he relied entirely on Kelley. who was evidently a highly unstable and unscrupulous personality. How much of what went on in the amazing "seances" reported in the diaries was invented by Kelley in order to make himself indispensible to Dee or to gain a decisive influence over him. is a matter open to question. Deacon's view is that Dee was using Kelley rather than the other way around. and that both were engaged in cryptographic and espionage missions for the English Crown under cover of Dee's astrological and demonological activities. In any case. the manner in which the spirit communications were received and recorded seems so complex and demanding as to be almost unbelievable. Kelley evidently often became impatient with the effort involved. and Dee had to plead with him and importune him to get him to continue; one gains the impression that Kelley was never nearly as interested in the angelic communications as was Dee. and would much have preferred to focus his energies on the making of gold.

During the seances (many of which took place during a visit to the court of the Polish Count Lasky in Cracow and at Rudolph's court in Prague), Kelley sat before the crystal and reported what he saw and heard to Dee, who wrote it down, occasionally putting questions to the spirits through Kelley. Kelley often saw the angels themselves, and other persons and beings as well, often moving through elaborate scenes and actions as on a stage (walking along a road, climbing mountains, crossing streams, etc.). He describes their faces, gestures, manner, clothing, and activities in remarkably vivid detail. Casaubon's account provides extensive information concerning the setting, preparations, apparatus, and method of operation during these sessions, as well as a verbatim account of the visions themselves. From p. 75 on, he reports the communication of a set of cipher matrices or "tables" to Dee and Kelley by the angels. Kelley saw the matrix in the crystal with an angel standing nearby, pointing to its squares with a wand; Kelley then read them off to Dee, who made a copy of the matrix for their own later use. Many such "tables" were transmitted by the angels; the set called the "Book of Enoch," for example, comprised forty-nine tables, each having forty-nine rows and forty-nine columns. Ultimately, at least twenty-six complete books of tables and text were dictated to Dee and Kelley by the spirits.

Along with the tables, the angels dictated long lists of vocabulary words, each list followed by a passage of running text that used the words, much like an every-day elementary language lesson. During this process, Dee often asked some penetrating questions concerning affixes, structure, similarities he noted between words or parts of words, etc.; he also asked for and obtained repetitions of things he had not heard right or questioned for some reason. Casaubon gives page after page recounting this amazing linguistic research, for all the world like a series of sessions between a field linguist and his native informants.

Deacon (1968) provides the following description of the way running text was dictated: "Each of the tables which Kelley had in front of him consisted of a large square subdivided into forty-nine by forty-nine small squares, each containing a letter of the Enochian alphabet. These letters were in apparently random order. Kelley would look into the crystal and see the angel pointing to one these small squares in a replica of the table in the crystal and would call out—say 4D (as in map reading). Dee would find the square in his table and write down the relevant letter. . . . The result was a sentence in Enochian written backwards. It is almost impossible to believe that this could be faked, especially when one remembers that there were ninety-eight tables to choose from for memorizing, if one was faking it." (pp. 150–151). In Casaubon's account, individual words are clearly shown written backwards (with the last letter first), and the order of words in each sentence or paragraph sent as a unit is also backwards, so that the last word sent is the first word of the passage as it is to be read. Figures 43, 44, and 45 show the alphabet and some examples of Enochian text; (it may be noted that certain letters that appear in the text are not represented in the alphabet, a fact which is nowhere explained in the sources).

Enochian, according to Deacon, is unique and different from any other Cabalistic language or magical system, so it is hard to see how it could have been plagiarized from any other secret writings. Robert Hooke, a prominent seventeenth-century scientist and a member of the Royal Society, held the view that Enochian was essentially a cryptographic and espionage device, like a code. Deacon claims that Enochian is a bona fide language, and can be learned with some difficulty from Dee's unpublished manuscripts (e.g., *Libri Mysteriorum*, Sloane ms. 3188, British Museum), and from Casaubon's book (1659). The Rosicrucian Order of the Golden Dawn (England, 1875) adopted Enochian and employed it in their rites. The reader may verify for himself in the samples shown in figures 44 and 45 that words having a constant meaning are repeated with or without additions: "OD", "and"; "CHIS", "are"; and "ICHISGE", "are not"; "CAUSG(A)", "the earth"; "CHRISTGOS", "let there be"; etc. Whatever its relevance to the Voynich manuscript, this amazing account of research in field linguistics among the denizens of the spirit world deserves a careful study by modern psycholinguists and historians.

Chapter 10
Collateral Research: Early Herbals and Materia Medica

The history of herbals, botany, and materia medica is a major area of study which no student of the Voynich manuscript can afford to ignore. As we have seen in Sections 3.3.1 and 3.3.2 above, many researchers have made vigorous attempts to link the herbal and pharmaceutical drawings to those in other medieval and Renaissance medical works, with little success. A number of good general works on early herbals are available to the student: Arber (1953), Rohde (1922), and Singer (1927) cover the history of early herbals in general, with a strong emphasis on Old English herbals; Biedermann (1972) provides a large collection of beautiful illustrations of early botanical, magical, and medical drawings as well as a general treatment of these topics. Cockayne (1866) and Grattan (1952) cover the Anglo-Saxon herbals very completely, and also trace their history and sources. Excellent treatments of the history of medicine may be found in Singer (1928, 1962), Taylor (1922), and Thorndike (1963), while Thorndike (1923–58) provides extensive detail on the work of individual physicians among other scientists. Tiltman (1968, pp. 11–13) gives a brief but very useful sketch of the early history of herbals and botanical illustration in relation to the study of the Voynich manuscript. The following survey, drawn from these sources, while highly abbreviated, may serve to introduce the reader to the subject and its literature.

The earliest beginnings of botanical drawing and description are to be found in Greece, as is true of so much of Western learning and philosophy. Aristotle was said to have written a treatise on plants; this work was apparently lost at a relatively early date, and was not among the works of Greek learning preserved by the Mohammedans and transmitted to medieval scholars through them. Aristotle's pupil Theophrastus of Eresus, however, produced a work which served as a source for the Greek "rhizotomists" ("root-diggers", frequently ignorant and superstitious gatherers of medicinal plants who were the pharmacists, physicians, and medical suppliers of their day). In the first century B.C., a highly talented and unusually learned member of this class of rhizotomists named Crateuas compiled an herbal containing the first known set of plant drawings. Crateuas (132–63 B.C.) was physician to Mithridates VI Eupator, King of Pontus in Asia Minor. His herbal was illustrated with pictures apparently drawn with great care and artistry from life, each accompanied by a brief description of the medicinal effects and uses of the plant.

While no manuscripts of Crateuas' work have survived, a revision or extract of it has been preserved, with some of the original drawings, in the *Materia Medica Libri Quinque* of Dioscorides Anazarbeus, a physician attached to the Roman Army in Asia during the first century A.D. (Dioscorides 1959). Dioscorides' text and many of the drawings were reproduced in a beautiful manuscript herbal presented in A.D. 512 to Juliana Anicia, daughter of a Roman Emperor; this manuscript, called the Juliana Anicia Codex, is preserved in Vienna, and a part of a facsimile may be seen, according to Tiltman (1968), in the Garden Library of Dumbarton Oaks. Biedermann (1972) and Singer (1927, 1928) provide a number of illustrations of these exquisite drawings, whose lifelike and artistic quality are judged by experts to far exceed that of many, if not most, subsequent herbals well into the Middle Ages. In spite of its early date, the Juliana Anicia Codex thus constitutes a major high point in the history of early herbals, reached by few others for many centuries thereafter.

The first known herbal in which plants were described in alphabetical order was that of Pamphilius, compiled around A.D. 100. Many early herbals also employed an alternative arrangement dealing with plants in an order dictated by the body part to which their medicinal effects pertained, usually starting at the head and finishing at the feet. Pliny the Elder, in his *Naturalis Historia* (A.D. 77) compiled a massive encyclopedia comprising thirty-seven books covering all the natural sciences of the day. This collection of magical and superstitious beliefs, Old Wives' tales, myths, and observations concerning birds, beasts, plants, medicines, metals, minerals, and a host of other topics was greatly influential in the Middle Ages. An herbal based on Dioscorides' long-lived work was compiled by Apuleius (or "Pseudo-Apuleius", as he is frequently called to distinguish him from the author of *The Golden Ass*) about A.D. 400. This work, *The Herbarium of Apuleius Platonicus*, became one of the most widely known and copied of the early herbals; it survived in some form into the late Middle Ages and Renaissance, and was among the first illustrated printed herbals.

Aside from the above-mentioned "high-spots" and a few other influential works, there was little original research on plants, and almost no attempt to study or draw plant life from nature, or to make any objective, empirical trial of medicinal effects after the fashion of the modern scientist. The Greek herbals and their Latin translations were copied over and over again, their drawings becoming more and more debased and distorted in the process. The names of the plants, and the species originally illustrated, were of course those of the Mediterranean region or of Asia Minor; ancient and medieval herbalists seem never to have realized or understood that very different plants grew in different places. The names, often drawn from dead or moribund ancient languages, and couched in ancient forms that were no longer understood, were carefully copied along with the drawings.

The monks in English and Continental monasteries did the best they could to match the garbled pictures of foreign plants and their exotic names against the flora of their own monastery gardens and countryside. As a result of their efforts, long lists of synonyms for plant names in various languages were compiled and attached to the herbals to serve as glossaries. One cannot help wondering how many hapless patients lost their lives through the inevitable misidentification of poisonous plants as medicinal species. Singer (1928, p. 185) sums up the state of affairs in his discussion of the *Herbarium* of Apuleius: with the impatient hindsight of the modern scientist, he points to it as an instance of over a thousand years of slavish copying applied to "a futile work with its unrecognizable figures and its incomprehensible vocabulary".

The Latin and vernacular herbals of the West were thus, for the most part, simply translations or compilations of the Greek works. A Latin translation of Dioscorides' herbal became the basis for many later medieval herbals. The Old English herbals have been intensively studied by scholars, and are of particular interest because of the many primitive pagan survivals they preserve, in more or less superficially Christianized form. *The Leech Book of Bald* (Royal 12D, British Museum), is one of the earliest and most interesting of the Old English herbals, dating from the tenth century; it presents many examples of pagan magical spells and practices. Another early herbal preserving pagan survivals is *The Lacnunga*, also dating from the tenth century (Harleian 585, British Museum). A Saxon translation of the *Herbarium* of Apuleius extant in many copies, and another Saxon translation of a work of the Salernitan medical tradition in Italy, called *Peri Didaxeon*, both dating from the eleventh century, were also highly influential among early English herbals: see Grattan and Singer (1952), Cockayne (1866), and Storms (1948), and see also the brief discussion in Section 9.4.2 of pagan charms from the earliest herbals.

Singer (1928) traces the history of botanical illustration in some detail. During the Middle Ages, a relatively small number of schools or traditions of plant illustration came into existence. Most of the drawings were highly stylized and diagrammatic, produced with little or no thought of observing nature at first hand or even of revising details from personal knowledge which must often have contradicted what the compiler saw in the sources he was copying. A few notable exceptions provide some relief from the stereotyped rigidity of most plant drawings in medieval herbals. A Latin manuscript from Bury St. Edmunds in the twelfth century included some naturalistic drawings among a majority of traditional copies. The compiler apparently did his best to identify the ancient and garbled figures of foreign plants in his sources with the plants in his garden; where he succeeded, he attached the local plant name to a copied drawing. Where he could find no match for an English plant among the drawings, he made a new one to fill the gap. The stylization of plant drawings reached an extreme in the thirteenth century, according to Singer, when they deteriorated into geometrical forms rigidly enclosed within a gold frame. Albertus Magnus (A.D. 1206–1280?) included in his encyclopedic works a section called "On Plants", compiled from a Pseudo-Aristotelian work, and Albertus is credited with some first-hand observation of the natural objects with which he dealt.

In preparing herbal as well as other manuscripts, it was the practice of the medieval scribe or copyist to leave a space in the text of each paragraph for a drawing, usually of a shape and size matching the corresponding picture in the source he was copying. The illuminator then supplied the pictures, if the patron or owner of the manuscript had the money to afford them. Singer ascribes a major "advantage" (from our modern point of view) to the illuminator over the scribe, in that the former was relatively unlearned, and thus freer from the stifling rigidities of tradition binding the scribe to the past. For this reason, Singer judges the figures in some medieval herbals to be in advance of the text in naturalism and accuracy, and sees in them a fresher and livelier spirit. The illuminators made some attempt to show local plants rather than copying the meaningless exotic originals in the ancient sources. In some cases, the holes left by the scribe were never filled (presumably because the owner ran out of money before he could hire the services of an illuminator); sometimes they were filled much later with pictures of a different size or shape that did not fit into the spaces very well. It is interesting to contrast this common medieval practice, whereby a scribe left spaces to be filled later and separately by an illuminator, with the integral composition of drawings and text in the Voynich manuscript.

After the low point reached during the thirteenth century, herbal illustration increased in naturalism and beauty throughout the fourteenth and fifteenth centuries (at least as judged by the modern observer). Some late medieval herbals are remarkable for the life-like and artistic quality of their illustrations; reproduced by Singer (1928) are several examples in which insects (a dragonfly, beetles, caterpillars, etc.) are shown sitting on the plants, all represented in a style almost indistinguishable to the casual eye from a good modern drawing. Among the better illustrations are the beautiful woodcuts (made by Hans Weiditz) in Otto Brunfels' *Herbarium Vivae Eicones*, compiled in 1530. The text, unfortunately, is far below the standard set by the pictures; copied from the durable herbal of Dioscorides, it describes mediterranean plants completely inconsistent with the local plants in the drawings, from the Rhine region in Germany. A widely copied work produced in 1542 by Leonhard Fuchs (A.D. 1501–1566) called *De Historia Stirpium* presents a set of relatively accurate plant identifications and an outstanding series of woodcuts by Albrecht Meyer based on a study of nature. The first truly modern herbal is judged by Singer to be that of William Turner in 1551; it is described as the first scientific work on plants in our modern sense. Rembert Dodoens of Holland also produced a fine herbal in 1554; the famous *Herball* of John Gerard (1633) was based on Dodoens work. but employed for its illustrations a magnificent set of 1800 woodcuts made in Europe in 1590.

As Tiltman and other students of the Voynich manuscript have noted. they have had little success in relating its plant drawings to any of the limited traditions of plant illustration touched upon above. or indeed to any other herbal drawing or manuscript. There is a very general similarity of feeling or design in some Voynich manuscript drawings and a scattering of pictures in this herbal or that one. There is also a superficial similarity of style between some Voynich manuscript drawings and some of the very debased. distorted products of successive recopying in early herbals (although the stylization of the Voynich manuscript plants may well be deliberate rather than a result of degradation through copying; we have in any case been notably unsuccessful in discovering any source from which such copies might have come). There is nothing in these comparisons to convince any student that he has found a counterpart or original for a Voynich manuscript drawing in any other herbal manuscript. There is always a possibility. of course. that some manuscript or early printed work with drawings closely akin to those in the Voynich manuscript may yet be turned up by some diligent researcher. The alchemical drawings shown in figure 36 seem. at least to my eye. considerably closer in style and feeling to the plant drawings of the Voynich manuscript than most. if not all. of the herbal illustrations I have seen in my own admittedly limited search for parallels. It is my feeling that we should certainly include alchemy works in our investigations. even though they might not be expected to deal with plants as such. but rather as symbols for alchemical entities (the sun. moon. metals. chemicals. etc.).

Chapter 11

Concluding Remarks: Some Suggestions for Further Research

In closing this monograph on the Voynich manuscript. I would like to suggest some lines along which future work on the problem might profitably be directed. These suggestions include efforts aimed at gathering more data to resolve some of the many unknowns in the problem: and efforts designed to achieve a more rigorous. complete. and scientific analysis of the data we now have.

11.1 Paleographic and Other Scientific Studies of the Manuscript

In my opinion. it is of primary importance that the inks. pigments. and vellum of the manuscript be tested and examined scientifically and compared to those of other manuscripts by paleographers and art historians: and that the pages of the manuscript be studied under special lighting and otherwise treated to bring up traces of erased. faded. or illegible writing. As far as I have been able to discover. no such research has ever been carried out. Further. there are no current plans on the part of the present owner of the manuscript (the Beinecke Library at Yale) to make any such studies in the near future Nevertheless. only studies such as these can offer any hope of satisfactory answers to many of our questions. They could turn up crucial new information that might completely alter the complexion of the problem. I hope that some present or future student will be able to arouse interest in a scientific physical study of the manuscript. obtain funding for it. and set the necessary wheels in motion to accomplish the research and make its results known to other students. If any reader of this monograph knows of any such scientific studies already carried out on the manuscript. I hope he will inform me of them.

11.2 Uncovering More of the Manuscript's History

As we saw in Chapters 1 and 2. Wilfrid M. Voynich succeeded in ferreting out a considerable quantity of useful and interesting information about the history and previous ownership of the manuscript. In his historical sketch (Voynich 1921). he indicated many promising leads for others to pursue. Every known or suspected owner of the manuscript should be researched in depth: renewed attempts should be made to locate correspondence. libraries. and other collections of papers pertaining to or belonging to these people. and to track down any references to the manuscript and attempts to decipher it. Someone should certainly try to locate the Villa Mondragone or other places where papers and manuscripts once stored there might now be preserved. in the hope of finding additional records relating to the manuscript (for example. notes made by Athanasius Kircher or by the unknown previous owner who wrote to Kircher about the manuscript). The archives of Rudolph's Court at Prague should also be a promising source of correspondence or notes concerning the manuscript. Background sleuthing of this nature is certain to provide us with at least a few new nuggets of information that could transform the problem or. at least. reduce the discouraging number of unknowns that now confront us.

11.3 Collateral Research

While all the most obvious sources have apparently been examined. as well as some more obscure ones. in search of possible parallels to the Voynich text and drawings. it still seems worthwhile to keep up the hunt among less well-known and less accessible sources. I believe that alchemy writings. in particular. deserve closer attention. since they may not have been so thoroughly studied by Voynich manuscript researchers as have herbal. medical. and astrological sources. More attention to early cryptographic writings of the fourteenth through the sixteenth centuries might also richly repay our efforts. In fact. a determined. thorough. and painstaking attempt to search through manuscript collections and early printed books on almost any of the topics sketched in Chapters 8 and 9 of this monograph could still turn up a new and illuminating bit of evidence for a student specifically searching for a parallel to the Voynich manuscript. It seems to me highly unlikely that the Voynich manuscript scribe(s) and illuminator(s) never wrote or drew any other work in their lives: there is always a hope of finding somewhere a drawing of similar style that might give us a clue to their identity or place of origin. or another scrap of text in the Voynich script among someone's papers.

11.4 A Comprehensive Machine File of the Text

In Chapter 6. we saw that several abortive attempts were made to carry out computer studies of the entire corpus of Voynich text. Out of the approximately 250.000 characters of text in the manuscript. most students have studied only small samples ranging from 5000 to 25.000 characters in length. Currier has probably dealt with the largest machine samples of any student. and his transcription alphabet appears to be the most practical choice for machine processing. (I have discarded my own transcription in favor of Currier's. in spite of the fact that I had already placed some 19.000 characters of text on magnetic tape using my own alphabet before I came upon detailed descriptions of his research.) Father Petersen's concordance of the entire manuscript. made by hand. is preserved in the Friedman Collection at the Marshall Library in Lexington. Virginia. where it is not easily accessible to most students.

It would be of great value. in my opinion. to have a complete machine file of the corpus. in Currier's transcription. and including identification of "hand." "language." and the apparent subject matter (herbal. pharmaceutical. astrological. etc.) as well as any other property which students have found to be statistically significant. This file could be used as a basis for a wide variety of studies. to help in forming and testing hypotheses concerning the text. and exploring further the important "hand" and "language" phenomena discovered by Currier as well as other matters. Smaller. carefully selected samples could be formed from the entire corpus for any specific purpose.

11.5 Scientific Hypothesis Formation and Testing

Hypotheses about the nature of the text should be based on all the known phenomena. and on a careful study of the entire corpus of text (not just one section or a few pages here and there). The hypotheses should also take into account and attempt to explain all the phenomena clearly demonstrated by other researchers (Tiltman's "beginning-middle-ending" structure: Currier's "languages" and "hands": the repetitive patterning of "words." etc.). Finally. the hypotheses should be consistent with. and bear some relation to. what is known of the nature. background. and history of the manuscript itself. In addition. I think we should entertain not just one hypothesis. but a set of alternative theories that seem capable of explaining all or a large part of the data. Having set up such a body of reasonable hypotheses. we should design "experiments" based on samples selectively drawn from the entire corpus (all made accessible to computer processing in one format and transcription. as suggested above): samples such that we can attempt to confirm or disconfirm each of our theories in an orderly manner. This research will. of necessity. also involve parallel studies of text in Latin. in certain other natural languages. or in synthetic languages of various types.

In the absence of any cribs. parallel texts. or other breaks into the text via external or collateral data. our only hope of success lies in an orderly and cooperative scientific approach to the entire body of text and all the other data we have. In this way. perhaps we can some day achieve a solution whose satisfying completeness and appropriateness will do full justice to the elegant enigma of the Voynich manuscript.

"THE MOST MYSTERIOUS MANUSCRIPT IN THE WORLD"

THE ROGER BACON CIPHER MANUSCRIPT

(BACON, ROGER ?.) Cipher manuscript on vellum. Text written in a secret script, apparently based on Roman minuscule characters, irregularly disposed on the pages. 102 leaves (of 116; lacks 14 leaves), including 7 double-folio folding leaves; 3 triple folio folding leaves; and one quadruple folio folding leaf. With added signature marks (of the XVth or XVIth century), and foliation (of the XVIth or XVIIth century) 1-11, 15-58, 65-73, 75-90, 93-96, 99-108, 111-116. With about 400 drawings of botanical subjects, including many of full-page size; 33 drawings of astrological or astronomical subjects, plus about 350 single star-figures; and 42 (biological?) drawings, most of which include human figures. The drawings colored in several shades of green, brown, light yellow, blue, and dark red. Large 8vo (c. 250 × c. 160 mm.). Old limp vellum covers (now detached). From the libraries of John Dee (?), the Emperor Rudolph II (reigned 1576-1611); Jacobus Horcicky (Sinapius) de Tepenecz; Joannes Marcus Marci of Cronland (1666); Athanasius Kircher, S.J.; and Wilfrid M. Voynich. Accompanied by an Autograph Letter signed by Joannes Marcus, presenting the book to Athanasius Kircher.

No place or date, (XVth century, or earlier?).

An enigmatic mediaeval manuscript, which for over forty years has baffled the scholars and cryptographers who have attempted to wrest its secrets from it. It has been termed by Professor John M. Manly, who made a detailed study of it, "the most mysterious manuscript in the world."

Fig. 1.—Entry for the Voynich Manuscript from H. P. Kraus Catalog
(Reproduced from Tiltman 1968)

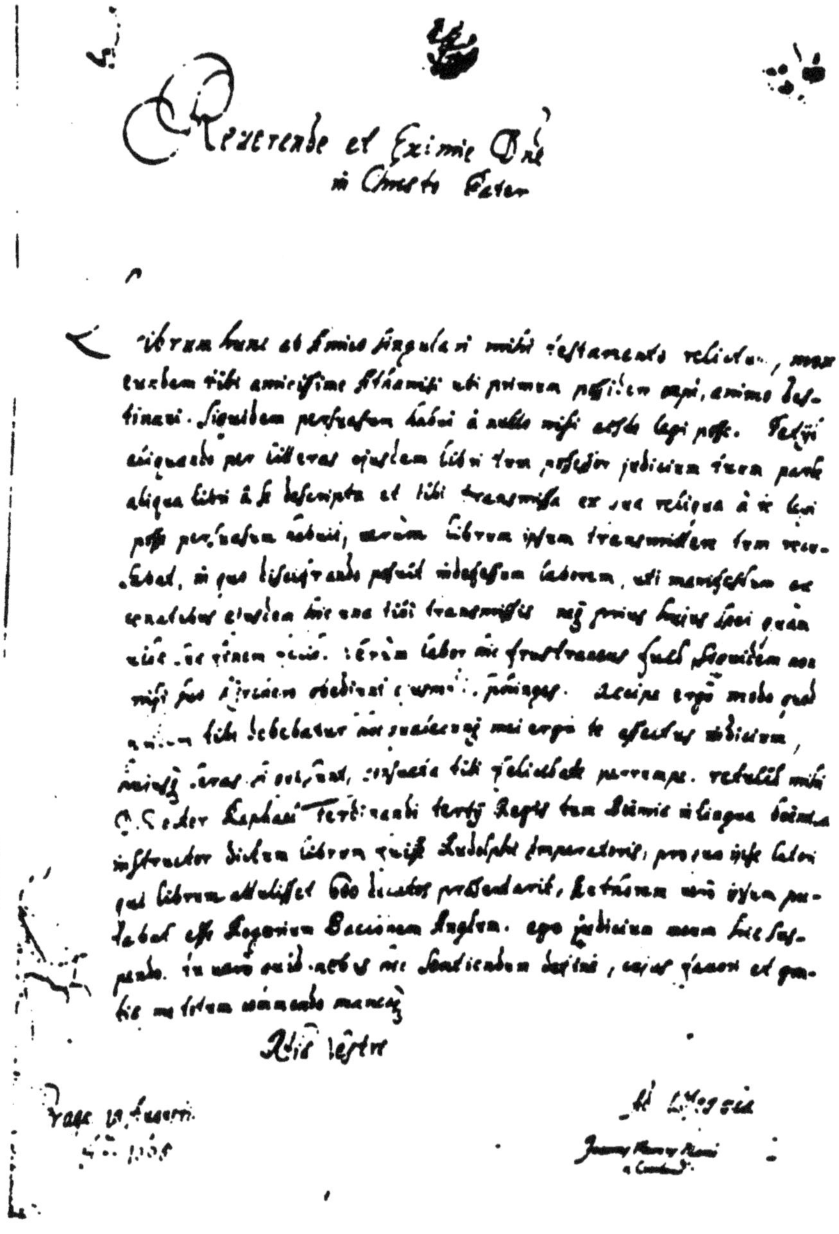
Reverende et Eximie Dne
in Christo Pater

Librum hunc ab amico singulari mihi testamento relictum, mox eundem tibi amicissime Athanasi ubi primum possidere coepi, animo destinavi. Siquidem persuasum habui a nullo nisi abs te legi posse. Petijt aliquando per litteras ejusdem libri tum possessor judicium tuum parte aliqua libri a se descripta et tibi transmissa ex qua reliqua a te legi posse persuasum habuit, verum librum ipsum transmittere tum recusabat, in quo desciferando posuit indefessum laborem, uti manifestum ex conatibus ejusdem hic una tibi transmissis, nec prius huius spei quam vitae finem fecit. Verum labor hic frustraneus fuit siquidem non nisi suo Oedipo obediunt huiusmodi Sphinges. Accipe ergo modo quod jamdudum tibi debebatur hoc qualecunque mei erga te affectus indicium, huiusque claustra, si quae sunt, consueta tibi felicitate perrumpe. Retulit mihi D. Doctor Raphael Ferdinandi tertij Regis tum Boëmiae in lingua Boëmica instructor dictum librum fuisse Rudolphi Imperatoris, pro quo ipse latori qui librum attulisset 600 ducatos praesentaverit. Authorem vero ipsum putabat esse Rogerium Bacconem Anglum. Ego judicium meum hic suspendo, tu vero quid nobis hic sentiendum definias, cuius favori et gratiae me totum commendo maneoque

Rdae Vestrae

ad obsequia
Joannes Marcus Marci
a Cronland

Pragae 19 Augusti
[illegible]

No. [illegible] BACON, ROGER (?) Cipher ms. on vellum. N. pl., n.d. (XVth century, or earlier?).
Autograph letter signed by Joannes Marcus of Cronland, presenting the book to Athanasius Kircher. (Original size)

Fig. 2.—Letter Found with the Manuscript

(Tiltman 1968)

REVEREND AND DISTINGUISHED SIR:
   FATHER IN CHRIST:
   This book, bequeathed to me by an intimate friend, I destined for
you, my very dear Athanasius, as soon as it came into my posession,
for I was convinced it could be read by no one except yourself.

   The former owner of this book once asked your opinion by letter,
copying and sending you a portion of the book from which he believed
you would be able to read the remainder, but he at that time refused
to send the book itself. To its deciphering he devoted unflagging toil,
as is apparent from attempts of his which I send you herewith, and he
relinquished hope only with his life. But his toil was in vain, for such
Sphinxes as these obey no one but their master, Kircher. Accept now
this token, such as it is and long overdue though it be, of my affection
for you, and burst through its bars, if there are any, with your wonted
success.

   Dr. Raphael, tutor in the Bohemian language to Ferdinand III,
then King of Bohemia, told me the said book had belonged to the
Emperor Rudolph and that he presented the bearer who brought him
the book 600 ducats. He believed the author was Roger Bacon, the
Englishman. On this point I suspend judgement; it is your place to
define for us what view we should take thereon, to whose favor and
kindness I unreservedly commit myself and remain

                    At the command of your Reverence.

                              JOANNES MARCUS MARCI.
                                    of Cronland

PRAGUE, 19th August, 1665:
                6:

Fig. 3—Translation of Letter
(Tiltman 1968)

81

Folio No.	Description	Folio No.	Description
1r	text only; (1) (2)	(74)	(missing)
1v–11v	herbal	75r.v	human figures
(12)	(missing)	76r	text only (1)
13r–57r	herbal	76v–84v	human figures
17r	(2)	85/86r1	text only
49r	(1)	85/86r2	cosmological
57v	cosmological; (1)	85/86r3	net of rosettes
58r.v	text only	85/86r4	net of rosettes
(59–64)	(missing)	85/86v1	net of rosettes
65r.v	herbal	85/86v2	net of rosettes
66r	text only; (1) (2)	85/86v3	cosmological
66v	herbal	85/86v4	cosmological
67r1.v1	astronomical	85/86v5.v6	text only
67r2	astronomical	87r.v	herbal
67v2	cosmological	88r.v	pharmaceutical
68r1.v1	astronomical	89r1.v1	pharmaceutical
68r2.v2	astronomical	89r2.v2	pharmaceutical
68r3	astronomical	90r1.v1	herbal
68v3	cosmological	90r2.v2	herbal
69r.v	cosmological	(91–92)	(missing)
70r1	cosmological	93r–96v	herbal
70v1	astrol.: Aries (dark)	99r–102v2	pharmaceutical
70r2	astrol.: Pisces	103–116r	text only, stars
71r	astrol.: Aries (light)	116v	(1) (2)
71v	astrol.: Taurus (light)		
72r1	astrol.: Taurus (dark)		
72v1	astrol.: Libra	(1) Key-like sequences	
72r2	astrol.: Gemini		
72v2	astrol.: Virgo	(2) Text in extraneous scripts	
72r3	astrol.: Cancer		
72v3	astrol.: Leo		
73r3	astrol.: Scorpio		
73v3	astrol.: Sagittarius		

Fig. 4.—List of Folio Numbers and Apparent Subject Matter
(Foliation of Petersen Photocopy)

82

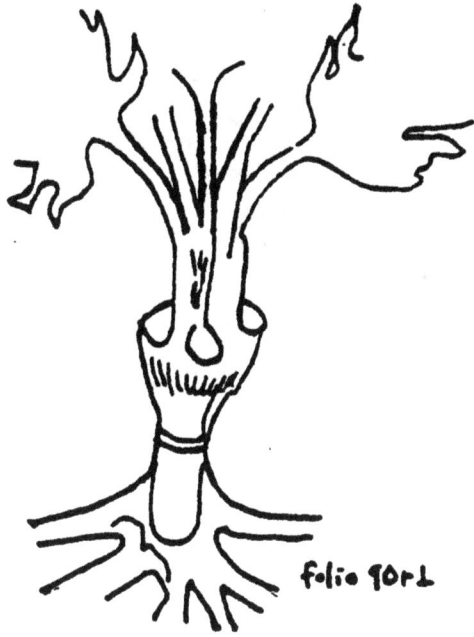

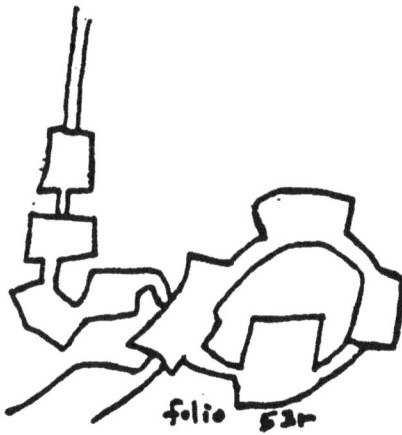

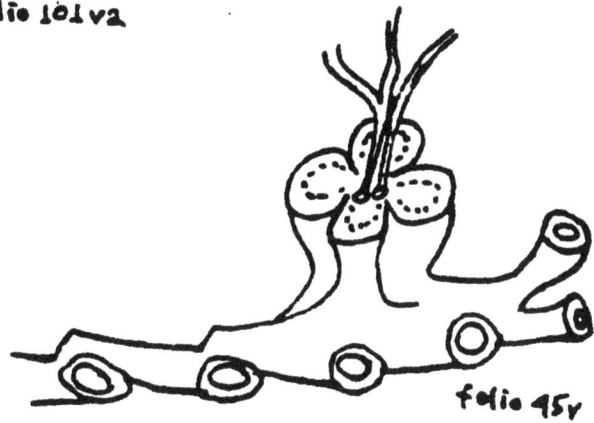

Fig. 5.—Some Details from Herbal and Pharmaceutical Folios
(Redrawn from a photocopy)

folio 93r

folio 88r

folio 15r

folio 99r

folio 86r

folio 45r

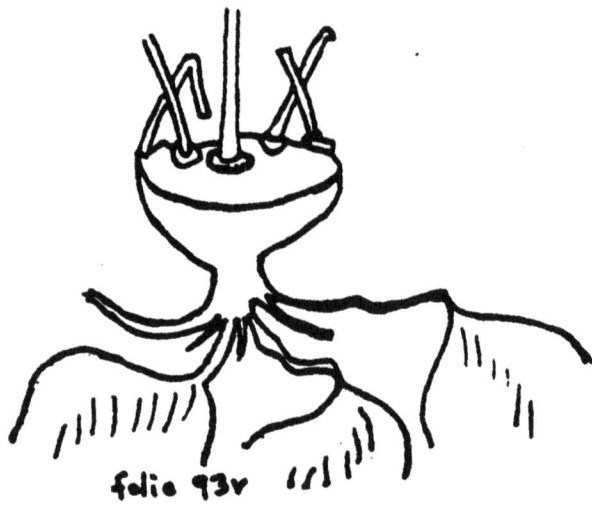

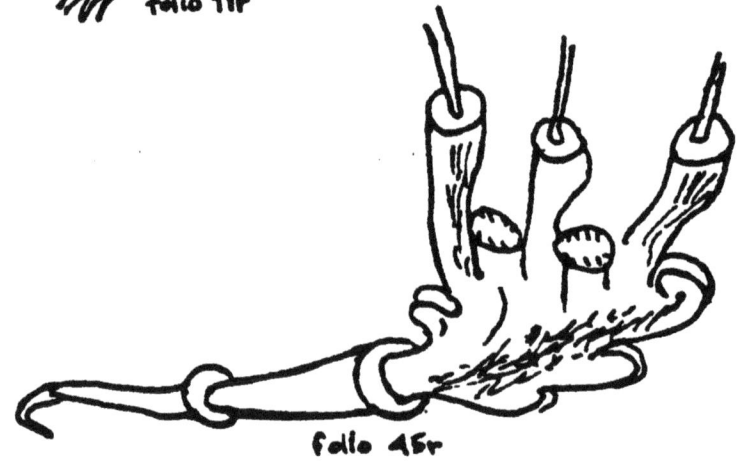

Fig. 6.—More Details from Herbal and Pharmaceutical Folios

(Redrawn from a photocopy)

84

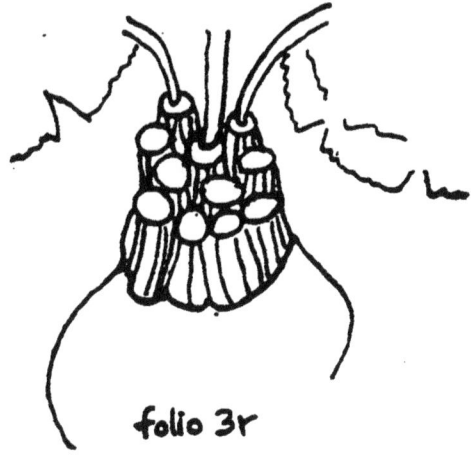

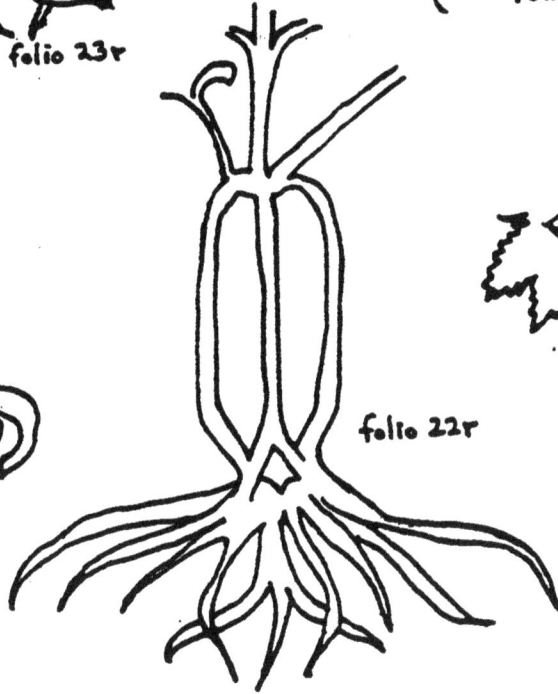

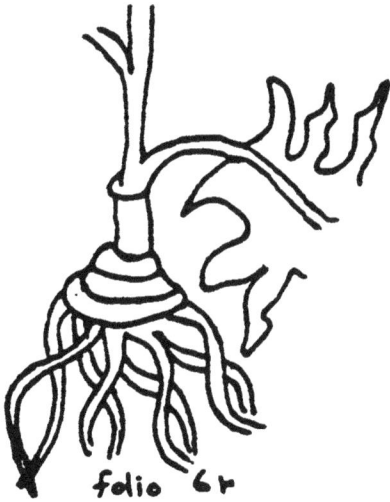

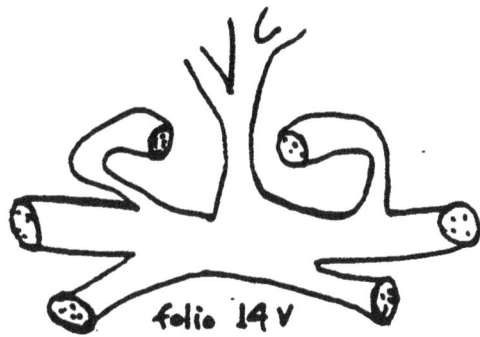

folio 23r

folio 3r

folio 2r

folio 22r

folio 5r

folio 6r

folio 14v

Fig. 7.—Details from Herbal Folios

(Redrawn from a photocopy)

85

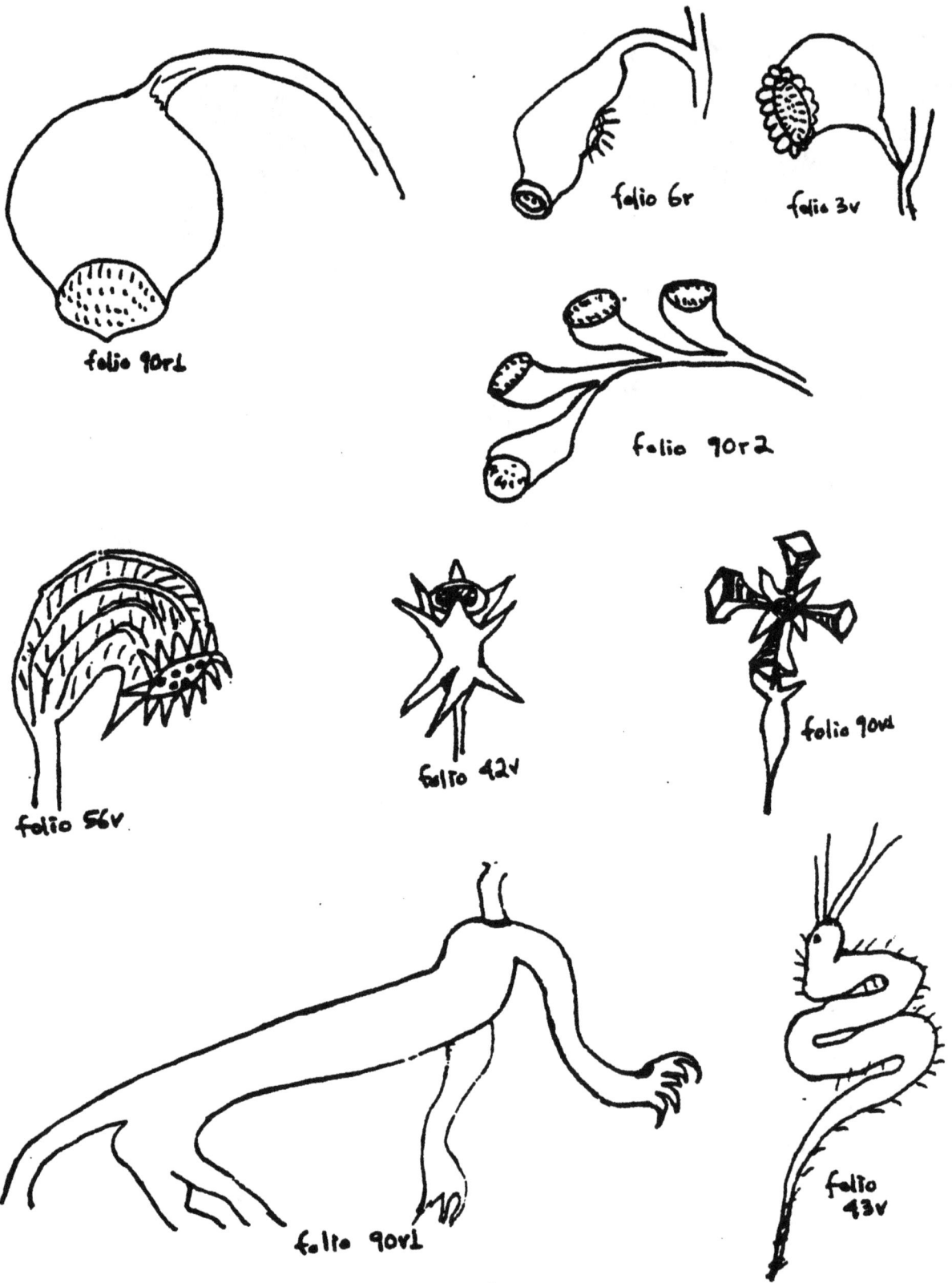

folio 90r1

folio 6r

folio 3v

folio 90r2

folio 56v

folio 42v

folio 90vd

folio 90vl

folio 43v

Fig. 8.—More Details from Herbal Folios
(Redrawn from a photocopy)

86

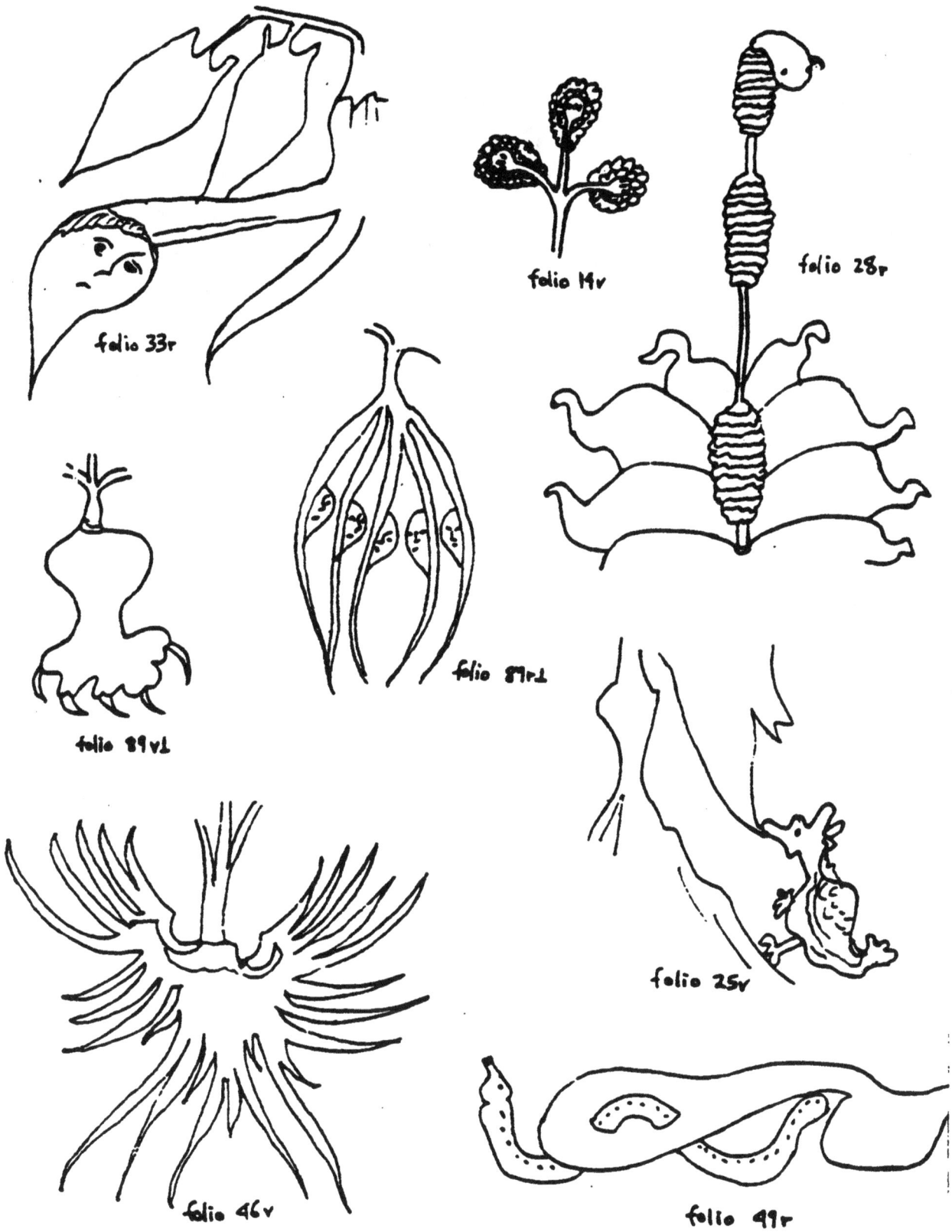

folio 33r

folio 14r

folio 28r

folio 89v1

folio 89r1

folio 46v

folio 25v

folio 49r

Fig. 9.—Details from Herbal and Pharmaceutical Folios

(Redrawn from a photocopy)

87

folio 70v2

folio 71r

folio 72r1

folio 72r3

folio 72v1

folio 72r2

folio 73v

folio 72v2

Fig. 10.—Some Zodiac Medallions and Month Names

(Redrawn from a photocopy)

88

Folio	Sign	Month	Rings of Figures (From Center)			Sum
			First	Second	Third	
71r	Aries (light)	April	5 (1) all c	10 (1) all c		15
70v1	Aries (dark)	April	5 (1) n and c	10 (1) n and c		15
71v	Taurus (light)	May	5 (1) n and c	10 (1) n and c		15
72r1	Taurus (dark)	May	5 (1) all c	10 (3) n. hats		15
72r2	Gemini	June	9 (3) all n	16 (3) 4 c. rest n	5 (3) n. hats	30
72r3	Cancer	July	7 (3) n. hats	11 (3) n. hats	12 (3) n. hats	30
72v3	Leo	August	12 (3) all n	18 (3) all n		30
72v2	Virgo	September	12 (3) all n	18 (3) all n		30
72v1	Libra	October	10 (3) n. hats	20 (3) n. hats		30
73r	Scorpio	November	10 (3) all n	16 (3) all n	4 (3) all n	30
73v	Sagittarius	December	10 (3) all n	16 (3) all n	4 (3) all n	30
74 ?	Capricorn	January	missing	n = naked		
74 ?	Aquarius	February	missing	c = clothed		
70v2	Pisces	March	10 (2) n. hats	19 (1) n. hats		29
(1) vertical "cans" (2) horizontal "cans" (3) no "cans"						

Fig. 11.—Groupings of Human Figures in Astrological Drawings

89

Folio	Elements in Rings (Inside Outward)				
	Central	First	Second	Third	Outermost
57v	8 (2 sets of 4 phrases)	4 phrases	4 paragraphs	68 (4 times 17 symbols)	4 paragraphs
67r1	moon	24 (12 double rays)	24 (12 double rays)		
67v1	sun	34 (17 double rays)	12 phrases		
67r2	8-pointed star	8 words	12 moons and phrases	7 words	12 paragraphs 12 phrases
67v2	sun in square	4 centripetal spouts	4 centrifugal spouts		
68r1	none	star field 29 words	sun at top moon below		
68v1	moon	16 (8 double rays)	16 (two sets of 8)		
68r2	none	star field 24 words	moon at top sun below		
68v2	sun	8 (4 double rays)	4 radial phrases	8 phrases	
68r3	moon	8 (4 phrases 4 star sets)	4 radial word pairs		
69r	6-pointed star	6 letters	45 pipes 21 phrases		
69v	8-pointed star	28 pipes and words			
70r1	6-pointed star	6 words	58 cells	9 waves	9 radial words
70r2	sun(?)	8 segments	8 subdivisions		
85/86r2	sun	4 quadrants	4 spouts		
85/86v3		4 cones from corners	4 paragraphs		
85/86v4	moon	5 frothy rings	4 human figures		

Fig. 12.—Groupings of Elements in Astronomical and Cosmological Folios

Folio	All Figures	Female	Male	Subgroupings
75r	14	14	—	2 tubs: top, 8 bottom 6
75v	29	29	—	2 tubs: top 10, bottom 19
76v	5	4	1?	scattered
77r	4	3	1?	scattered
77v	7	7	—	scattered
78r	15	15	—	2 pools: top 7, bottom 8
78v	9	9	—	one big tub with 7 "windows"
79r	7	7	—	scattered
79v	4	4	—	scattered; 5 animals also
80r	16	15	1?	3 rows: 10, 4, 2
80v	12	12	—	scattered
81r	13	13	—	2 tubs: top 7, bottom 6
81v	16	16	—	one big tub
82r	15	15	—	4 scattered; 11 in large pool
82v	7	7	—	scattered
83r	5	5	—	scattered
83v	4	4	—	scattered
84r	33	33	—	3 tubs: 12, 10, 11
84v	15	15	—	2 tubs: top 7, bottom 8
total	230	227	3?	

Fig. 13.—Groupings of Elements in Human Figure Folios

	Single	Dual	Ternary
Archetypical World	IOD	IAH EL	PATER SADAI FILIUS SPIRITUS SANCTUS
Intellectual World	ANIMA MUNDI	ANGELUS ANIMA	INNOCENTES MARTYRES CONFESSORES
Celestial World	SOL	SOL LUNA	MOBILIA FIXA COMMUNIA
Elemental World	LAPIS PHILOSO- PHORUM	TERRA AQUA	SIMPLICIA COMPOSITA DECOMPOSITA
The Minor World (Man)	COR	COR CEREBRUM	CAPUT PECTUS VENTER
Infernal World	LUCIFER	BEEMOTH LEVIATHAN	MALEFICI APOSTATAE INFIDELES

Fig. 14.—Some Medieval Tables of Correspondences: Ones, Twos, Threes
(Selected and adapted from Agrippa 1970, pp. 161ff)

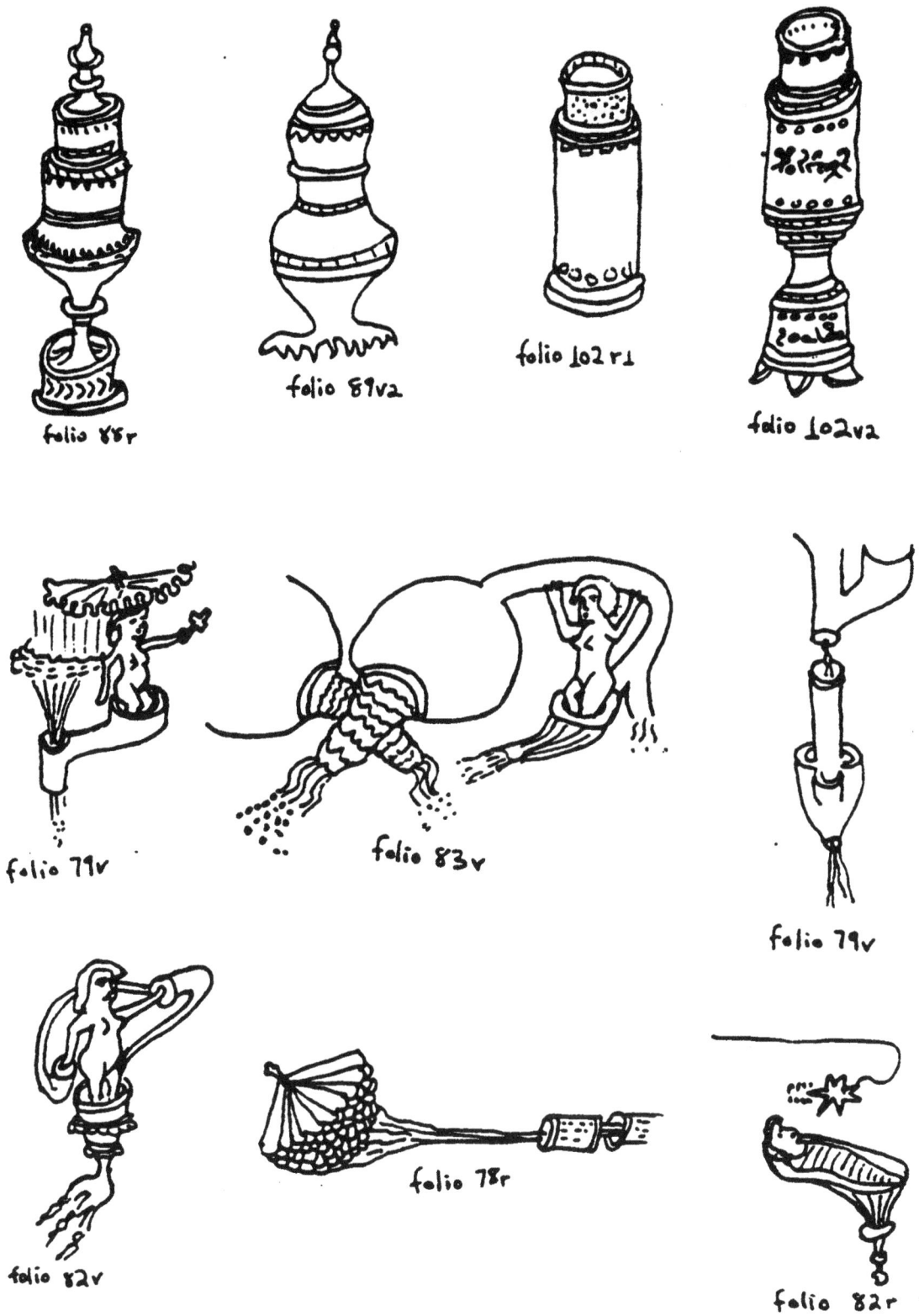

folio 88r

folio 89v2

folio 102r1

folio 102v2

folio 79v

folio 83v

folio 79v

folio 82v

folio 78r

folio 82r

Fig. 15—Details from Pharmaceutical and "Human Figure" Folios

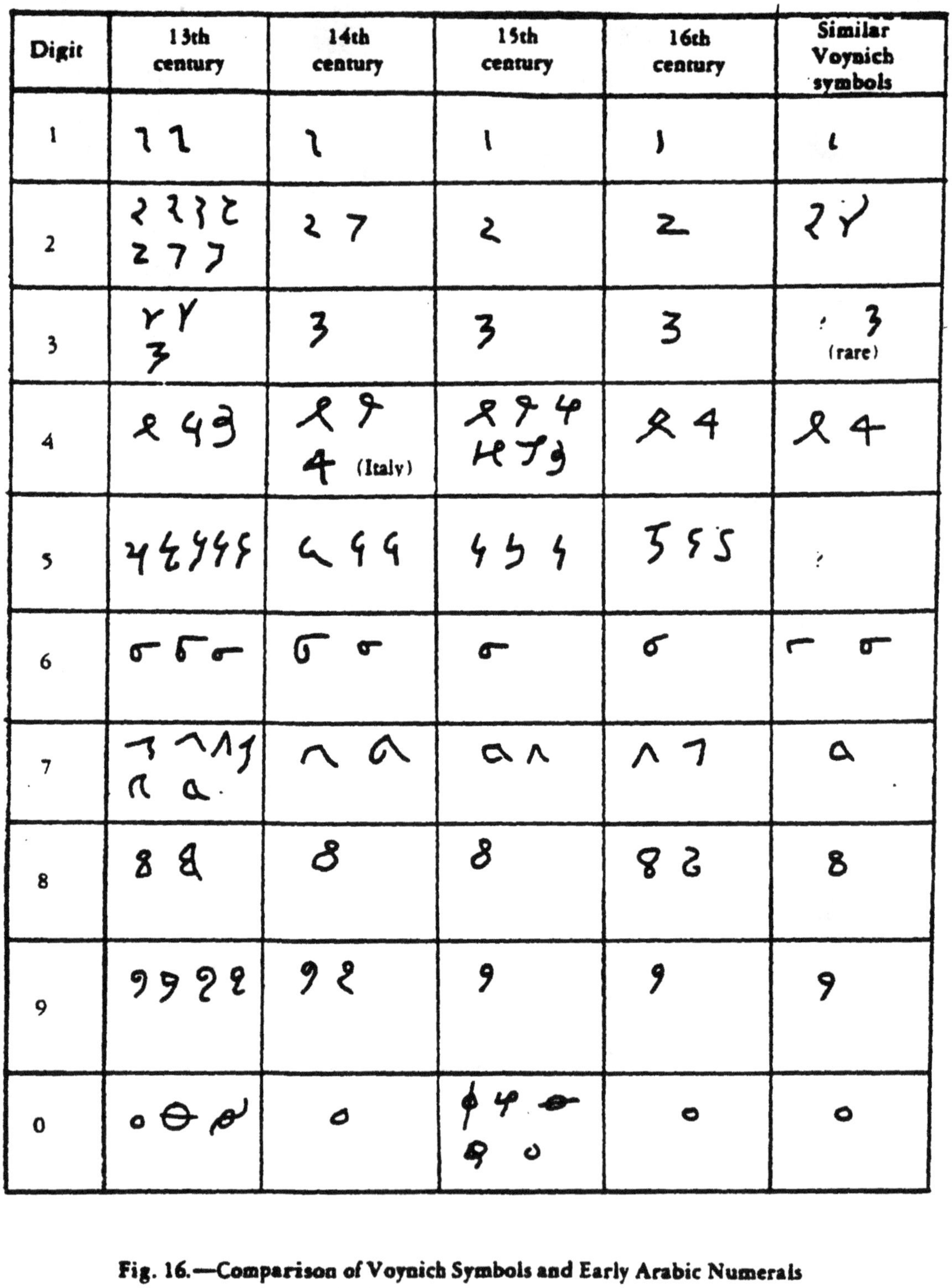

Digit	13th century	14th century	15th century	16th century	Similar Voynich symbols
1	7 7	7	1	1	ı
2	2 2 3 2 2 7 7	2 7	2	2	2 Y
3	r Y 3	3	3	3	3 (rare)
4	8 4 3	8 9 4 (Italy)	8 9 4 4 7 9	8 4	8 4
5	4 4 9 4 5	4 9 9	4 5 4	3 5 5	?
6	6 6 6	6 6	6	6	6 6
7	7 1 1 1 1 α	1 α	α 1	1 7	α
8	8 8	8	8	8 8	8
9	9 9 2 2	9 2	9	9	9
0	o θ ø	o	ø 4 o 9 o	o	o

Fig. 16.—Comparison of Voynich Symbols and Early Arabic Numerals
(Numeral forms redrawn from Hill 1915)

94

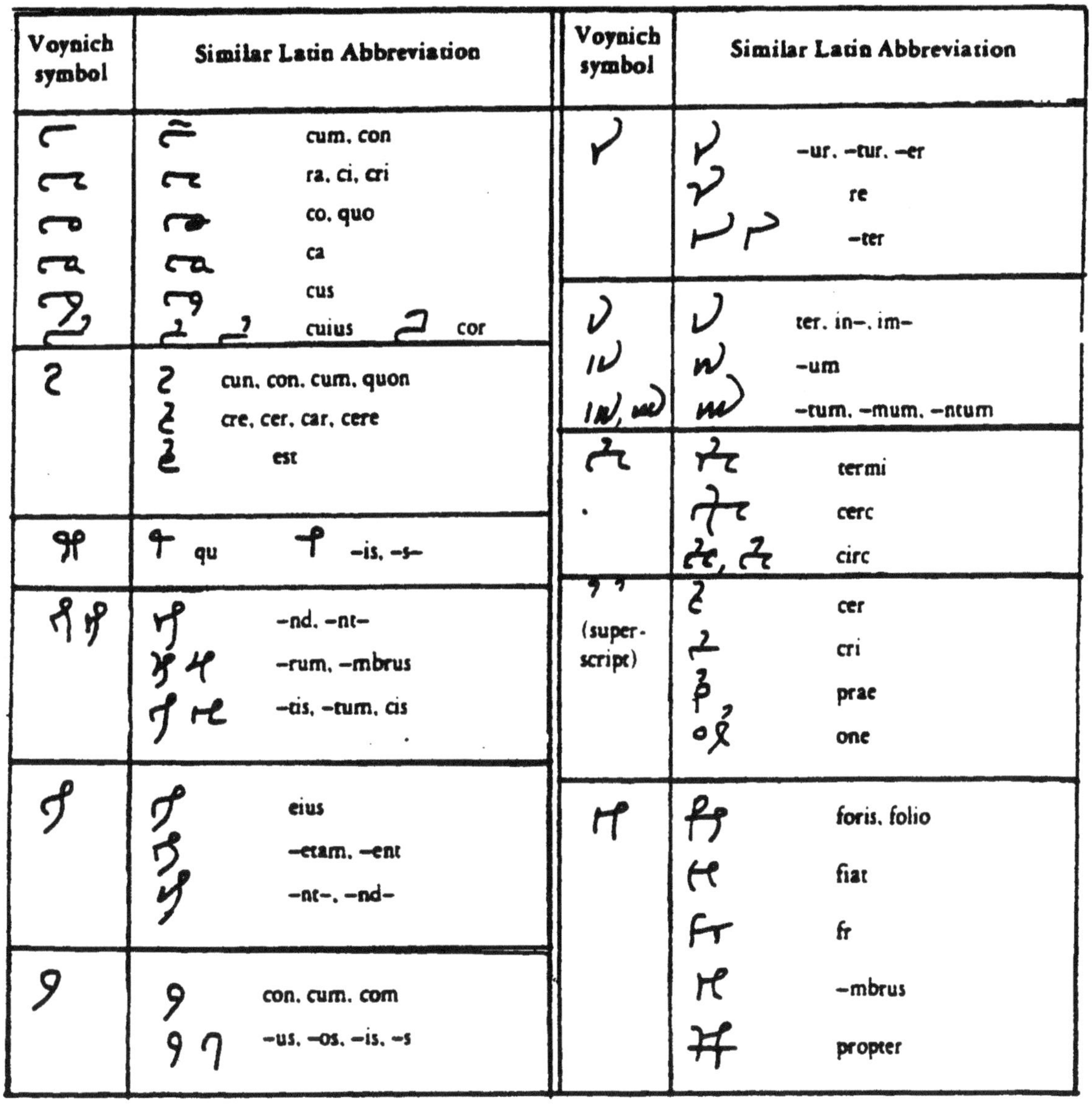

Voynich symbol	Similar Latin Abbreviation		Voynich symbol	Similar Latin Abbreviation	
		cum, con			−ur, −tur, −er
		ra, ci, cri			re
		co, quo			−ter
		ca			
		cus			ter, in−, im−
		cuius cor			−um
		cun, con, cum, quon			−tum, −mum, −ntum
		cre, cer, car, cere			termi
		est			cerc
	qu −is, −s−				circ
		−nd, −nt−	(super-script)		cer
		−rum, −mbrus			cri
		−tis, −tum, cis			prae
		eius			one
		−etam, −ent			foris, folio
		−nt−, −nd−			fiat
		con, cum, com			fr
		−us, −os, −is, −s			−mbrus
					propter

Fig. 17.—Comparison of Voynich Symbols with Latin Abbreviations

(Latin abbreviations adapted from Cappelli 1949)

95

Initial Symbol	Two Elements		Three Elements		Larger Compounds
	Final Symbol	Compound	Added Symbol	Compound	

Fig. 18.—Some Compound and Ligatured Forms

Miscellaneous Compound Forms:

96

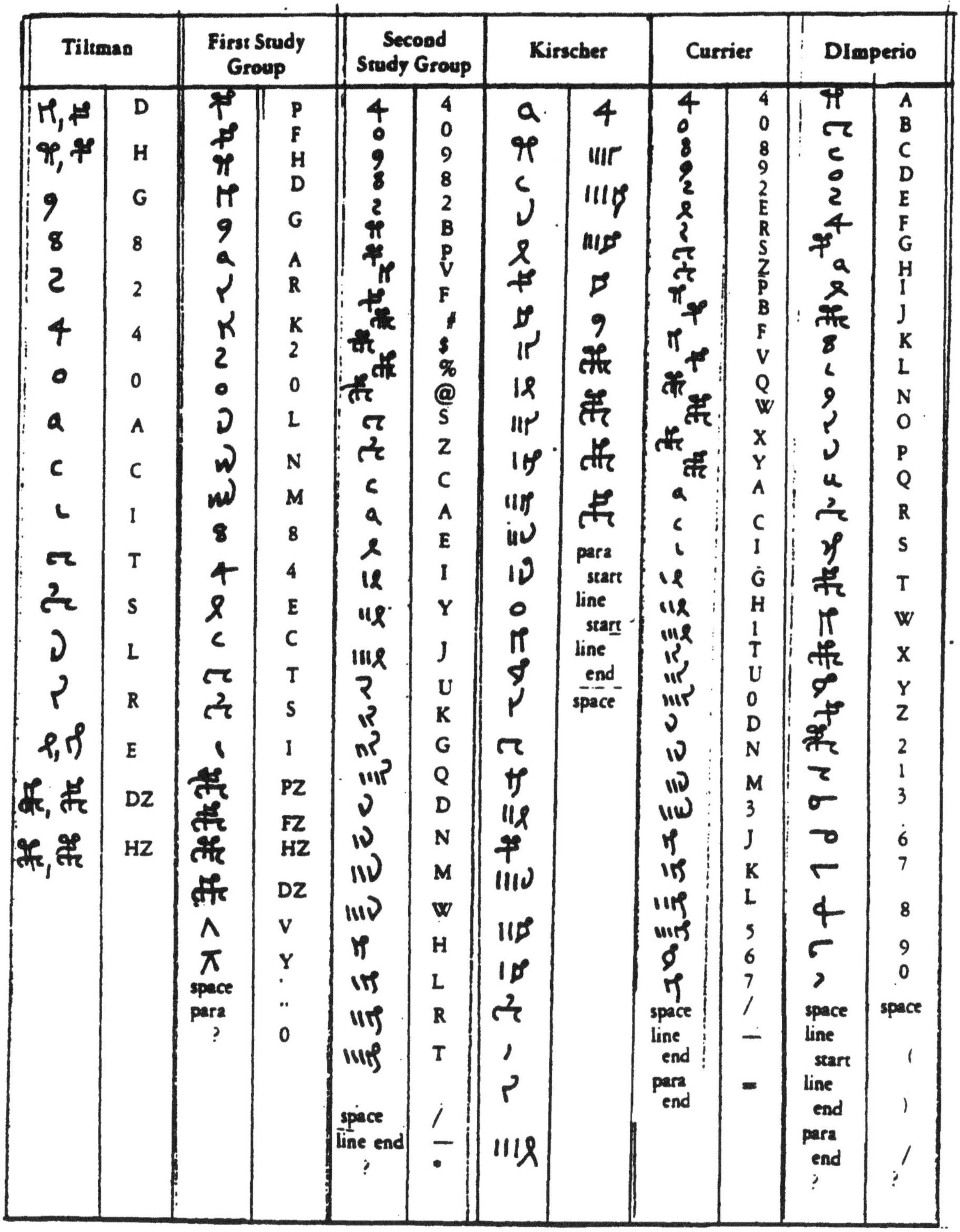

Fig. 19.—Transcription Alphabets of Several Researchers

Fig. 20.—Some Embellished and Variant Forms of Voynich Symbols

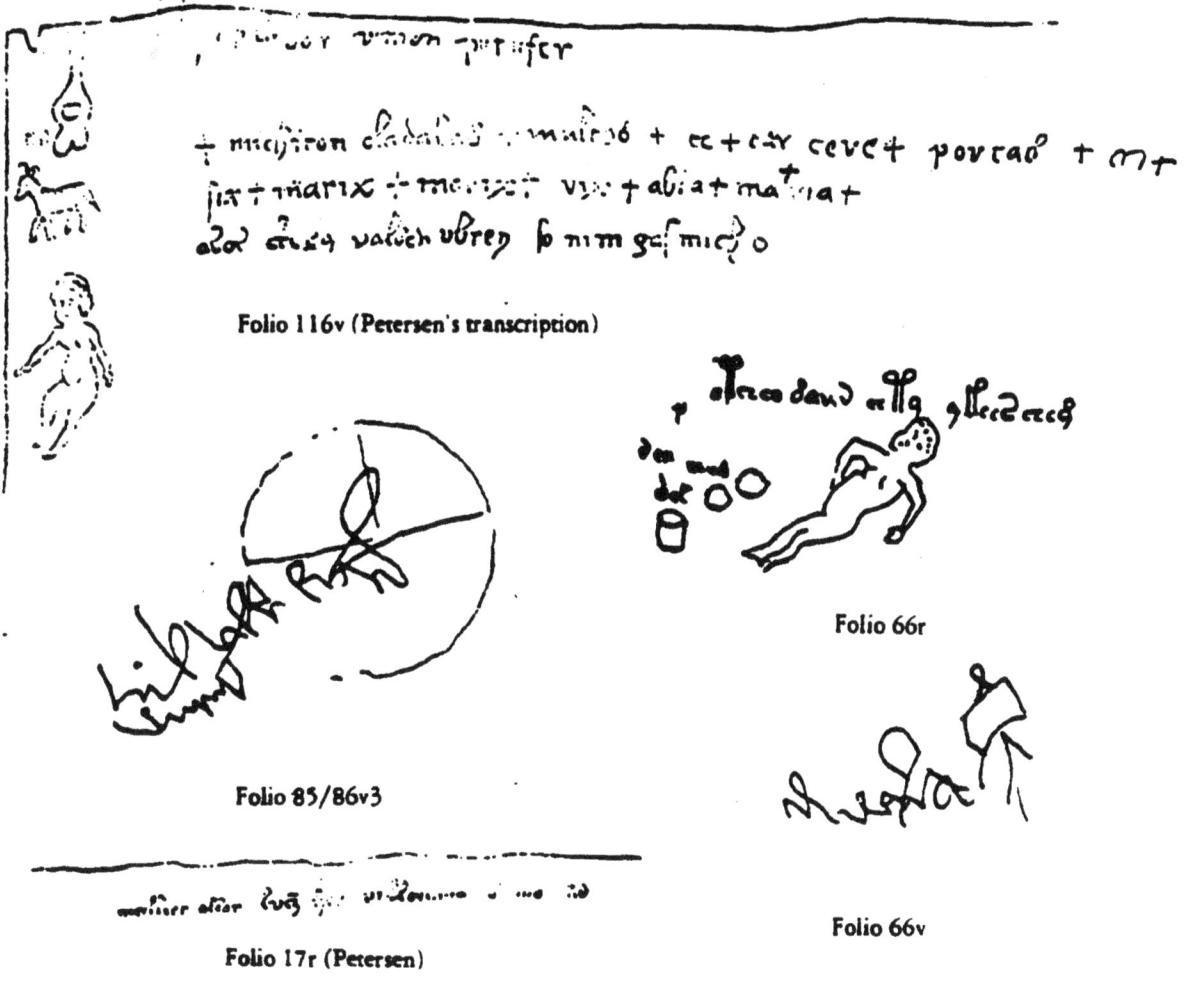

Folio 116v (Petersen's transcription)

Folio 85/86v3

Folio 17r (Petersen)

Folio 66r

Folio 66v

Fig. 21.—Details Showing Fragments of Writing in Extraneous Scripts

Folio	Marking	Interpretation
8v	Pⁿ9	first (primus)
16v	29	second
24v	39	third
32v	89	fourth
40v	5ᶜ9	fifth
48v	6ᵗ9	sixth
56v	Λᵐ9	seventh
66v	8ᵘ9	eighth
67r1	9ⁿ9	ninth
70v1	10ᵐ9	tenth
72v1	17ᵐ9	eleventh ?
83r	9	?
84v	13⁹	thirteenth
85/86v3	1▪4	fourteenth
90v1	17⁹	fifteenth
?	- - -	sixteenth
96v	1Λ⁹	seventeenth
?	- - -	eighteenth
102v1	19	nineteenth
103r	29	twentieth

Fig. 22.—Folio Gatherings

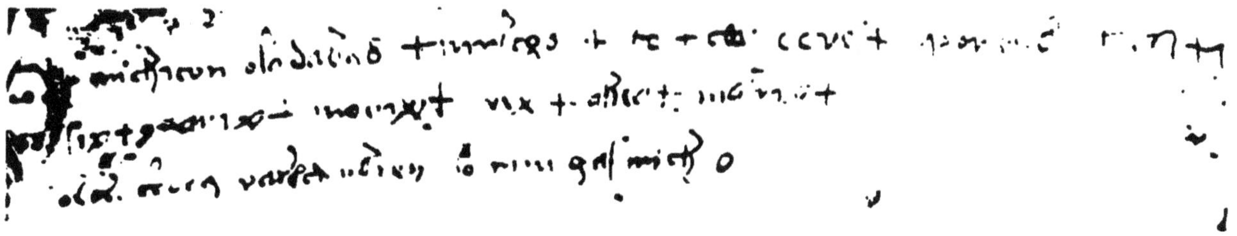

+ michiron oladaßaß. + miulrpß + re + rar cevc+ povraõ + m+
fix + marix + morixt vix + aßia + matria +
aiŵ circa valich ubren fo nim gafmich o

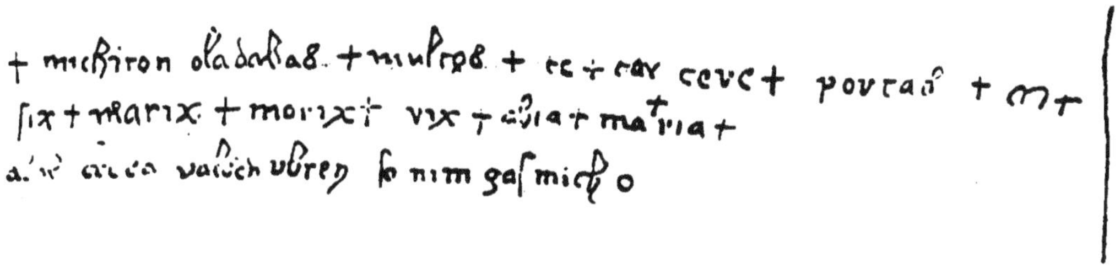

Petersen's Hand Transcript

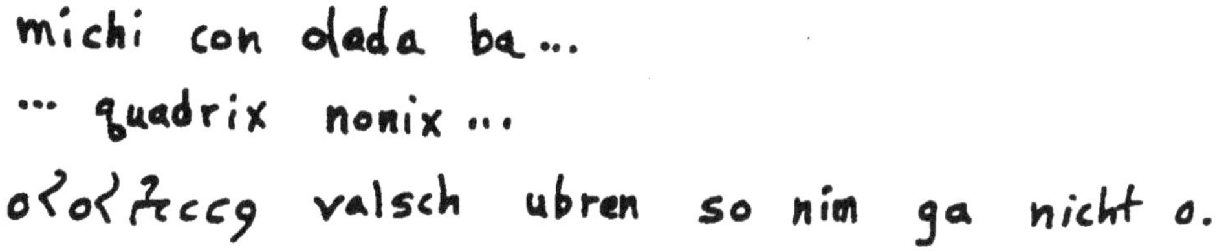

michi con olada ba...

... quadrix nonix ...

o⟨o⟨⟨cc9 valsch ubren so nim ga nicht o.

Brumbaugh's Reading (Brumbaugh 1975)

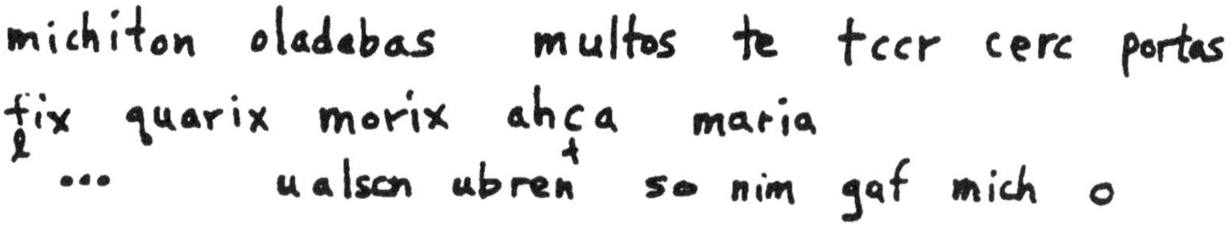

michiton oladebas   multos te tccr cerc portas
fix quarix morix ahça   maria
...   ualscn ubren   so nim gaf mich o

Newbold's First Reading (Newbold 1928. p. 73)

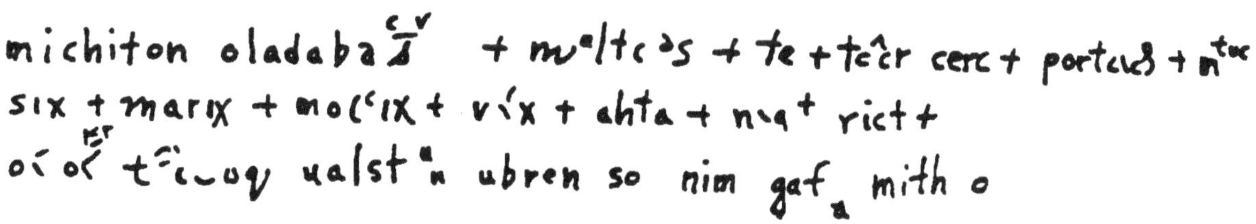

michiton oladabas̄   + multc⟩s + te + tccr cerc + portas + ntūc
six + marix + moc'ix + vix + ahta + nsa + rict +
oʃoʃ t̄c⟂oꝗ ualst̄n ubren so nim gaf mith o

Newbold's Second Reading (Newbold 1928. p. 108)

Fig. 23.—Some Different Readings of Folio 116v

101

Folio 69r

Cyclical Sequence. Folio 57v

Folio 76v

Folio 49v

Folio 66r

Fig. 24.—"Key"-Like Sequences

"Ovary" Labels (Folio 78r)

oℋccℰ⅍ℰ⅍o   oℋccℰ9

F E MM I N I N O   F E MM I N

Upper Tube Label

ℰaℓaℓo 荘 9

I S T S N F UNDU NTR   "Istis infunduntur"

Lower Tube Label

ℰccc ℰaℓ 9

I M M C I S N NTR   "Immiscuntur" or "Imcistinantur"

"Sack" Labels

oℋaℓoℰℓⅆgoℓoℓ9

F E S T O I N STN UT U T NTR   "Festo in(i)stio
utuntur"

oℋaℓaℓ

F E S T S N   "Festivi sunt"

ℓ	A	⅍	L	σ	U	ⅆ	ST
c	C	c	M	荘	ND	σて	UM
P	D	⅍,9	N(UNT)	荘	DER	⅍	TINC
ℋ	E	ⅆ	O(FVB)	荘	ER,RE.E	荘	UND
o	F (BVO)	ⅎ	P	荘	PER	荘	UNDR
⌒	G. H	9	R	룬	RUM	荘	PERM
⌢	H. G	a	S	룬 룬	HUM	荘	EM.ME
ℰ	I	ℓ	T	ℐ	ME	荘	MER
ℐ	NE	ℰ	EX	‖꒭	–M	꒭	–N

Fig. 25.—Feely's Initial "Clews" and Cipher Alphabet

(Adapted from Feely 1943, pp. 11, 34–35)

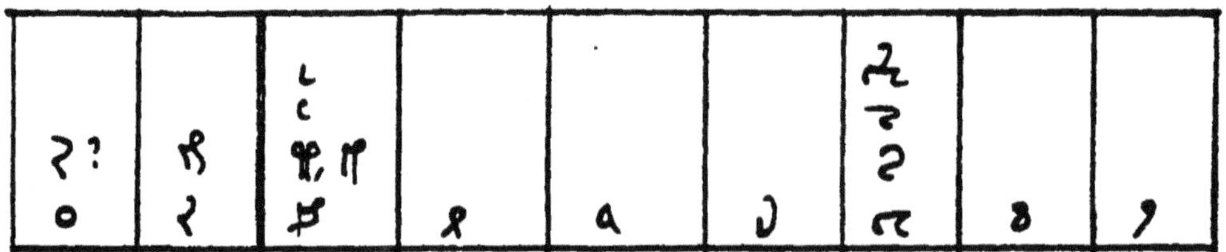

1	2	3	4	5	6	7	8	9
A J V	B K R	C L W	D M S (X)	E N X	F O T	G P Y	H Q U	I US Z

Deciphering Matrix

(Voynich symbols in upper rows reconstructed by the writer from Brumbaugh's text)

Plain:	A	B	C	D	E	F	G	H	I	J	K	L	M	N	O	P	Q
Cipher:	1	2	3	4	5	6	7	8	9	1	2	3	4	5	6	7	8

Plain:	R	S	T	U	V	W	X	Y	Z	US
Cipher:	2	4	6	8	1	3	5	7	9	9

(a?)

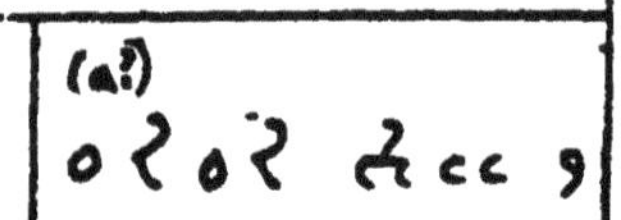

A R A B Y C C US

Enciphering Alphabet　　　　　From "Key" Sequence. Folio 116v

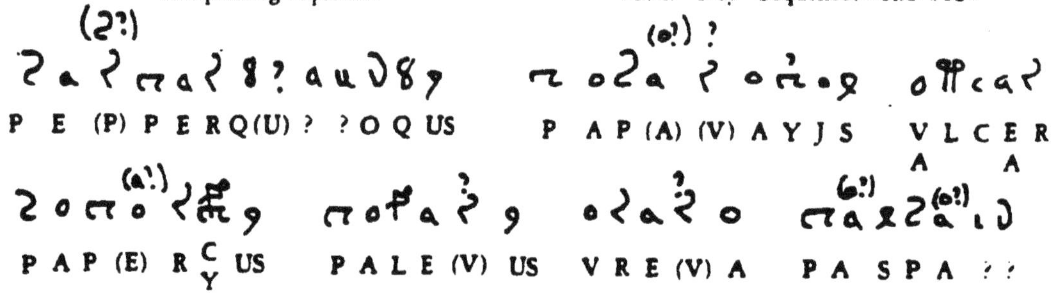

(2?)

P E (P) P E R Q(U) ? ? O Q US

(o?) ?

P A P (A) (V) A Y J S　V L C E R

(a?)

P A P (E) R C/Y US　　P A L E (V) US　　V R E (V) A　　P A S P A ? ?

P A C L US　　P J P E R H E L A C/Y　　G A L E R

Decipherments of Plant Labels on Folio 100r

Fig 26.—Brumbaugh's Results

(Brumbaugh 1974)

(Question marks and letters in parentheses indicate places where there is some doubt as to interpretation of the characters by Brumbaugh. Voynich characters are as seen and transcribed by the writer)

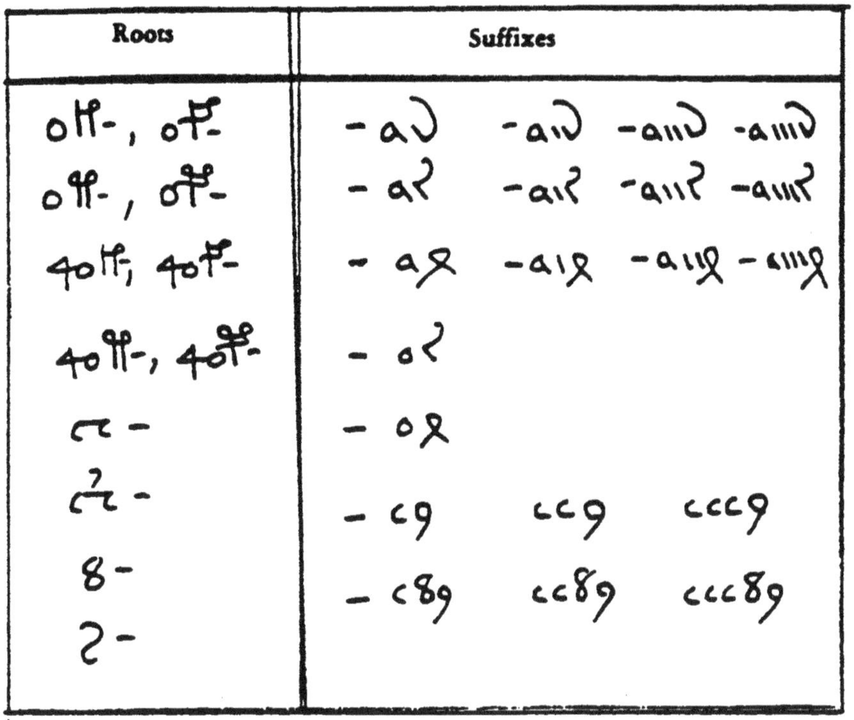

Fig. 27.—Tiltman's Division of Common Words into "Roots" and "Suffixes"
(Tiltman 1951)

Voynich Symbol	Currier Language A (Herbal)	Currier Language B (Herbal)	Krischer (fo. 103–116)	D'Imperio (Herbal, Astronom.)
4	290	257	233	368
O	2249	1373	729	3389
8	884	1250	406	1333
9	1231	1529	464	1893
ɔ	205	151	41	425
℞	663	496	250	(all) 1005
ʔ	531	495	201	(all) 971
ᴂ	1315	752	376	1373
ᴔ	415	289	93	557
ᵮ	516	376	187	734
ᵮ	75	108	47	154
ᵮ	595	801	267	865
ᵮ	21	63	6	53
ᵮ	165	51	13	266
ᵮ	42	12	7	49
ᵮ	86	100	15	106
ᵮ	7	9	2	29
ᴑ	900	1085	546	1470
c	769	1390	730	1094
ι	16	8	2	216
ιℛ	4	1	0	835
ιιℛ	1	0	0	167
ιιιℛ	0	0	0	23
ιↄ	22	45	35	689
ιιↄ	8	24	11	12
ιιιↄ	3	2	1	2
ɔ	38	3	4	0
ιɔ	82	73	38	7
ιιɔ	455	286	153	3
ιιιɔ	18	22	0	36
ƕ	78	99	23	13
ιƕ	6	5	1	
ιιƕ	1	1	1	
ιιιƕ	0	0	0	
♂	13	7	1	
♭	5	5	11	
ιιↄ			2	
Totals	11709	11168	4896	18137

D'Imperio (nested symbols and counts): ι 216, υ 835, ƍ 167, ƍ 23, u 689, ⌐ 12, ⌐ 2, ⌐ 0, ⌐ 7, ⌐ 3, ⌐ 36, ? 13

Fig. 28.—Monographic Frequency Counts of Some Students

Hermetic (Festugière 1944–54)	Agrippa (1970)	Hermetic (Festugière 1944–54)
Aldebaran	Caput Algol	Acharnahar
Alchoraya	Pleiades	Aldebaran
Caput Algol	Aldeboram	Hayok
Alhaiot	Hircus	Ascherhe Aljemaniya
Alhabor	Canis Major	Jed Algeuze
Algomeisa	Canis Minor	Rigel Algeuze
Cor Leonis	Cor Leonis	Sohel
Ala Corvi	Cauda Ursae	Ascherhe Asschemalija
Alchimech Alaazel	Ala Corvi	Cor Leonis
Alchimech Abrameth	Spica	Lion's Tail
Benenays	Alchameth	Alramech
Alfeca	Elpheya	Alahzel
Cor Scorpionis	Cor Scorpionis	Centaur
Vultur Cadens	Vultur Cadens	Vultur Cadens
Cauda Capricorni	Cauda Capricorni	Mouth of Southern Fish

Fig. 29.—Names of Fifteen Fixed Stars

107

	Picatrix (Ritter and Plessner 1962)	Agrippa (1970)
1	Al-Saratân	Alnath
2	Al-Butain	Allothaim
3	Al-Turaija	Athoraye
4	Al-Dabaran	Aldebram
5	Al-Haq'a	Alchataya
6	Al-Han'a	Alhanna
7	Al-Dira	Aldimiach
8	Al-Natra	Alnaza
9	Al-Tarf(a)	Alcharph
10	Al-Gabha	Algebh
11	Al-Zubra	Azobra
12	Al-Sarfa	Alzarpha
13	Al-'auwa'	Alhayre
14	Al-Simak	Azimeth
15	Al-Gafr	Algapha
16	Al-Zubana	Azubene
17	Al-Iklil	Alchil
18	Al-Qalb	Aljob
19	Al-Saula	Achala
20	Al-Na'a'aim	Abnahava
21	Al-Balda	Abeda
22	Sa'd Al-Dabih	Sadahacha
23	Sa'd Buta'	Sabadola
24	Sa'd Al-Su'ud	Chadezoad
25	Sa'd Al-Ahbija	Sadalabra
26	Al-Farj Al-Muqaddam	Pthagal Mocaden
27	Al-Farj Al-Mu'ahhar	Alhalgalmoad
28	Al-Risa'	Alchalh

Fig. 30.—Stations of the Moon

Zodiac Sign		Egypt (Roman Times)	Hermetic (200–300BC)	Coptic (400AD)
Aries	1	Xont-Har	χεντάχωρί	χοντɑρέ
	2	Xont-Xre	χοντɑρέτ	χοντɑχρέ
	3	Si-Ket	σίκέτ	σίκέτ
Taurus	1	Xau	σώου	χώου
	2	Arat	ἁρῶν	ἕρω
	3	Remen-Hare	δυμενώς	ϩομβρόμɑρε
Gemini	1	Thosalk	ξοχά	θοσόλκ
	2	Uaret	οὐɑρί	οὔκρε
	3	Phu-Hor	πεπισώθ	φοῦορι
Cancer	1	Sopdet	σωθείρ	σωθίς
	2	Seta	οὐφισίτ	σίτ
	3	Knum	χνοῦφος	χνοῦμίς
Leo	1	Xar-Knum	χνοῦμος	χɑρχνοῦμις
	2	Ha-Tet	ἰπί	ἥπη
	3	Phu-Tet	φɑτιτι	φουτήτ
Virgo	1	Tom	ἀθοόμ	τώμ
	2	Uste-Bikot	βρυσούς	οὔεστερκύτ
	3	Aposot	ἀμφɑτάμ	ɑφόσο
Libra	1	Sobxos	σφουκοῦ	σουχωέ
	2	Tra-Xont	νεφτίμης	πτηχοὔτ
	3	Xont-Har	φοῦ	χοντɑρί
Scorpio	1	Spt-Xne	βῶς	στωχγηνί
	2	Sesme	οὖστιχος	τετɑέ
	3	Si-Sesme	ἄφηβίς	τίσιλɛέ
Sagittarius	1	Hre-Ua	σέρος	ϩηουώ
	2	Sesme	τεὖχνος	τετɑέ
	3	Konime	χθισάρ	κομɑέ
Capricorn	1	Smat	τɑῖρ	σμάτ
	2	Srat	ἐπίτεκ	τρώ
	3	Si-Srat	ἐπιχνɑῦς	ἰσρώ
Aquarius	1	Tra-Xu	ἰσύ	πτιάν
	2	Xu	σοσορνῦ	ἀεύ
	3	Tra-Biu	χονουμοῦς	πτιριοῦ
Pisces	1	Biu	τετιλɑώ	βίου
	2	Xont-Har	σοπφί	χοντɑρέ
	3	Tpi-Biu	συρώ	πτιριοῦ

Fig. 31.—Names of the Thirty-Six Decans

(Gundel 1936. pp. 77ff.)

Third Pentacle of Saturn
(From The Keys of Solomon. Mathers 1974)

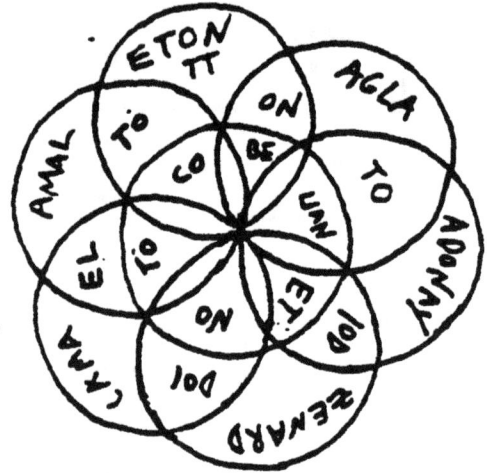

Pentacle for Conjuring Infernal Spirits
(de Givry 1971)

A charm to cause any
spirit to appear in the
form of a serpent

Square for use during
angelic invocation

A charm for divers
visions

Three Magic Squares from Abramelin
(Mathers 1975)

Fig. 32.—Some Magical Seals and Talismans

110

Some of John Dee's Angel Names (Deacon 1968)			Spirits of the Hours (Agrippa 1970)	
Aethyrs	Governors	Seven Great Angels	Day	Night
1. Lil	Occodon Pascomb Valgars	Sabathiel	Yayn	Beron
		Madimiel	Ianor	Barol
		Semeliel	Nafnia	Thami
		Nogahel	Salca	Athir
2. Ain	Doagnis Pascasna Dialiva	Corabiel	Sadedali	Mathon
		Lavanael	Thamor	Rana
		Zedekiel	Ourer	Netos
3. Zom	Samapha Virooli Andispi (etc.) (90 in all)	(Governors of the "watchtowers" or seven circles of heaven)	Tamic	Tafrac
			Neron	Saffur
			Iayon	Aglo
(etc.) (30 in all)			Abai	Calerva
			Natalon	Salam

Names of Planetary Spirits			Abramelin (Mathers 1975)	
	de Givry (1971)	Picatrix (Ritter-Plessner 1962)	4 Superior Spirits	8 Sub-Princes
Saturn	Aratron	Asbil	Lucifer	Astaroth
Jupiter	Bethor	Rufija'il	Leviathan	Magoth
Mars	Phaleg	Rubija'il		Asmodeus
Sun	Och	Ba'il	Satan	Beelzebud
Venus	Hagith	Bita'il		Oriens
Mercury	Ophiel	Harqil	Belial	Paimon
Moon	Phuel	Salja'il		Ariton
				Amaymon

Fig. 33.—Some Demon and Angel Names

111

Humors	Elements	Qualities	Conditions	Temperaments	Colors	Seasons	Ages	Winds	Zodiac Signs
Blood	Air	Hot-Moist	Liquid	Sanguine	Red	Spring	Childhood	S	Aries Taurus Gemini
Yellow Bile	Fire	Hot-Dry	Gaseous	Choleric	Yellow	Summer	Youth	E	Cancer Leo Virgo
Black Bile	Earth	Cold-Dry	Dense	Melancholic	Black	Autumn	Maturity	N	Libra Scorpio Sagittarius
Phlegm	Water	Cold-Moist	Solid	Phlegmatic	White	Winter	Old Age	W	Capricorn Aquarius Pisces

Fig. 34.—Elements of Galenic Medicine

112

Sephiroth	Attributes of God	Spheres
Kether	The Supreme	Primum Mobile
Hokhmah	Wisdom	Ogdoad (Fixed Stars)
Binah	Intelligence	Saturn
Hesod	Love, Mercy	Jupiter
Gevurah	Power, Wrath	Mars
Rahimin	Compassion	Sol
Netseh	Eternity	Venus
Hod	Majesty	Mercury
Yesod	Basis	Luna
Malkuth	Kingdom, Glory	Elements

Fig. 35.—Some Elements of Cabala

The Herb Lunaria
(Ashmole 1652, p. 348)

Spiritus, Anima, Corpus.

(Ashmole 1652, p. 350)

Fig. 36.—Two Alchemical Drawings

114

Fig. 37.—Some Costume Elements in Voynich Manuscript Drawings

115

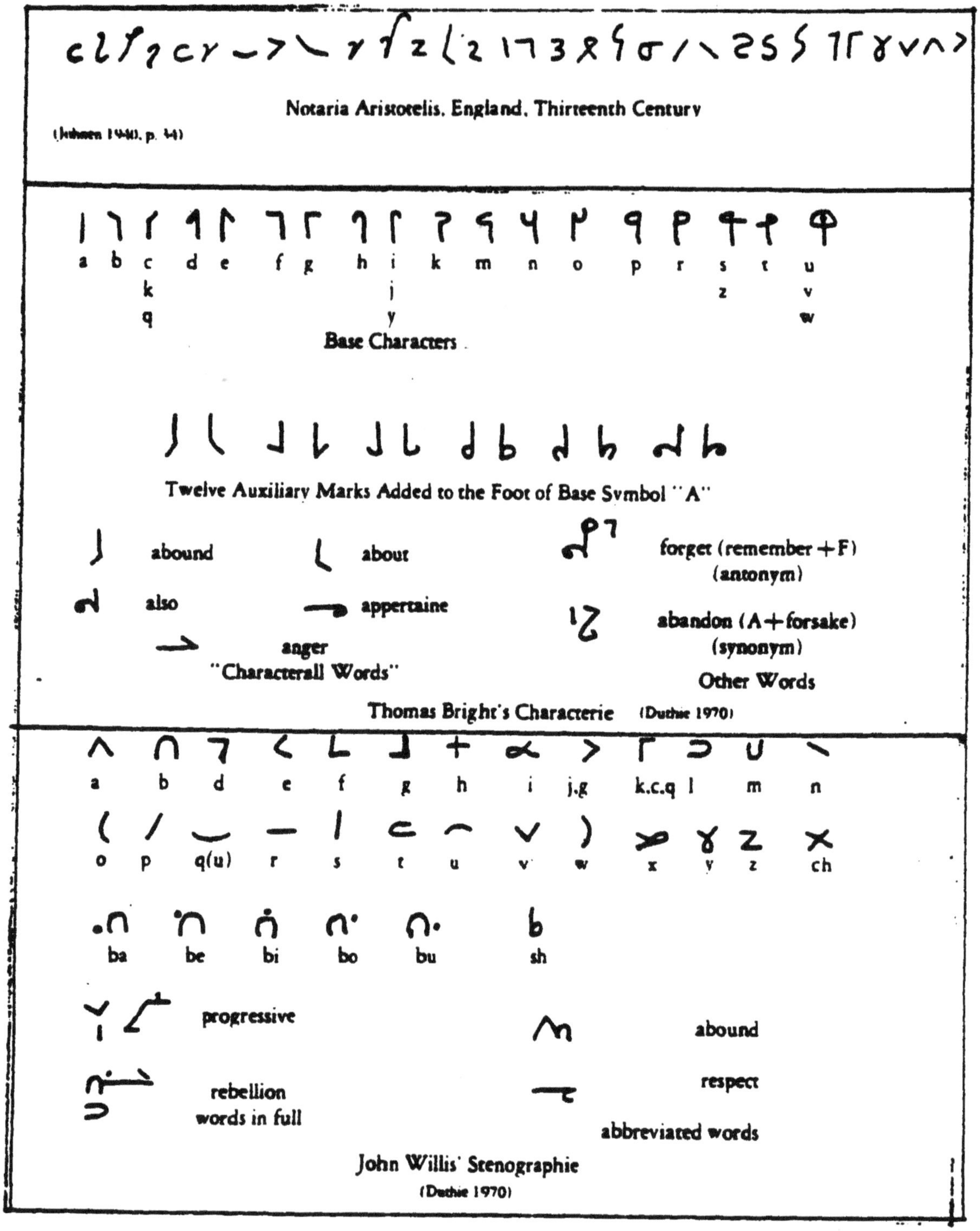

Notaria Aristotelis. England. Thirteenth Century

(Johnen 1940). p. 54)

Base Characters

Twelve Auxiliary Marks Added to the Foot of Base Symbol "A"

abound | about | forget (remember + F) (antonym)

also | appertaine | abandon (A + forsake) (synonym)

anger

"Characterall Words" | Other Words

Thomas Bright's Characterie   (Duthie 1970)

a   b   d   e   f   g   h   i   j.g   k.c.q   l   m   n

o   p   q(u)   r   s   t   u   v   w   x   y   z   ch

ba   be   bi   bo   bu   sh

progressive | abound

rebellion
words in full | respect

abbreviated words

John Willis' Stenographie
(Duthie 1970)

Fig. 38.—Early Shorthand Systems

116

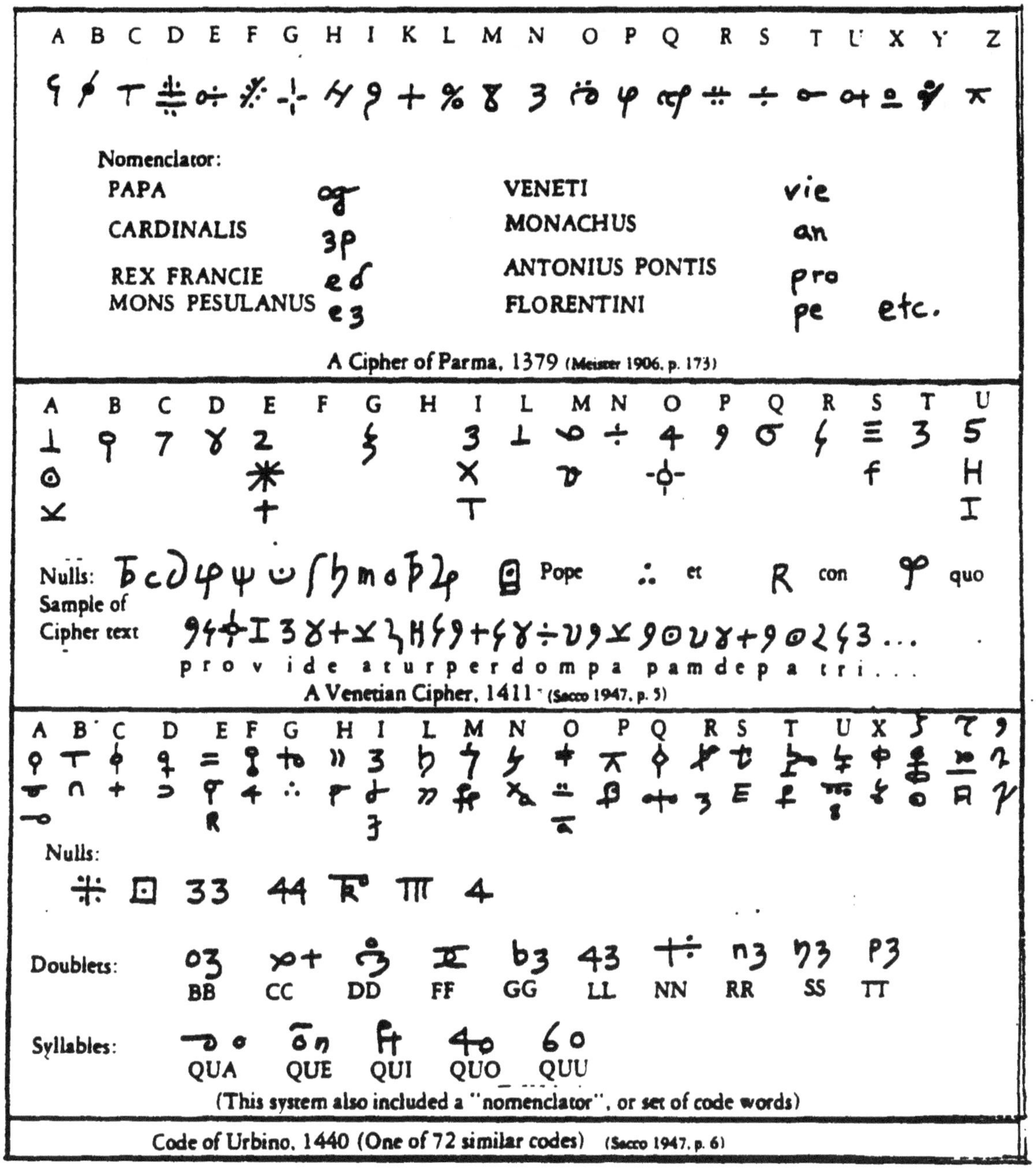

The figure below shows three early Italian cryptographic systems.

A Cipher of Parma, 1379 (Meister 1906, p. 173)

Nomenclator:

PAPA		VENETI	vie
CARDINALIS		MONACHUS	an
REX FRANCIE		ANTONIUS PONTIS	pro
MONS PESULANUS		FLORENTINI	pe etc.

A Venetian Cipher, 1411 (Secco 1947, p. 5)

Nulls: ... Pope ∴ et R con quo

Sample of Cipher text:

p r o v i d e a t u r p e r d o m p a p a m d e p a t r i ...

Code of Urbino, 1440 (One of 72 similar codes) (Secco 1947, p. 6)

Nulls:

Doublets:

BB	CC	DD	FF	GG	LL	NN	RR	SS	TT

Syllables:

QUA	QUE	QUI	QUO	QUU

(This system also included a "nomenclator", or set of code words)

Fig. 39.—Some Early Italian Cryptographic Systems

Word Designator	Word Matrix or Chart: Column Designators					
	I, BD	II, AF	III, DL	IIII, CL	V, AC	VI, BA
i	AUDIO	BONUM	CEDO	DILIGO	EXPELLO	FALLO
ij	AMO	BELLUM	CONFERO	DORMIO	EXPLICO	FALSUM
iij	ASPICIO	BENEFICIO	CONCLUD	DONO	EXTOLLO	FALLACIO
iiij	AGNOSCO	BIS	COMMENDO	COCEO	EXIMO	FRAUS
v	ALEXANDER	BESTIA	CONSIGNO	DOCTRINA	EMO	FORSAN
vi	AMOR	BELLIGERO	CONDEMNO	DOLUS	EMULO	FORIS
vij	APPETO	BACULUS	COMMODO	DOLOR	EQUUS	FORAMINA
etc.	etc.	etc.	etc.	etc.	etc.	etc.

Ending Codes

Nouns:

Case and Number

	Singular	Plural
Nominative	A	G
Genitive	B	H
Dative	C	I
Accusative	D	K
Vocative	E	L
Ablative	F	M

Gender

Masculine	BB
Feminine	CC
Neuter	DD

Verbs:

Mood

Indicative	N
Passive	O
Imperative/Optative	P
Subjunctive	Q
Infinitive	R

Tense

Present	S
Imperfect	T
Perfect	V
Pluperfect	X
Future	Z

Person

1 sg.	ℰ
2 sg.	Y
3 sg.	θ, Ɔ
1 pl.	Ʀ
2 pl.	YY
3 pl.	θθ, ƆƆ

Samples of Coded Text:

F a . G. Bnvθ. Ed.

Pontifex   semper   amavit   justitiam.

AF. i . DL. xix .g.dd. BA. x. n. s. ƆƆ. CL. viij. AF. xv. K. bb.

Bona   consilia   faciunt   dominos beatos

Fig. 40.—Jakob Silvester's Code

(Silvester 1526, folios 24–31)

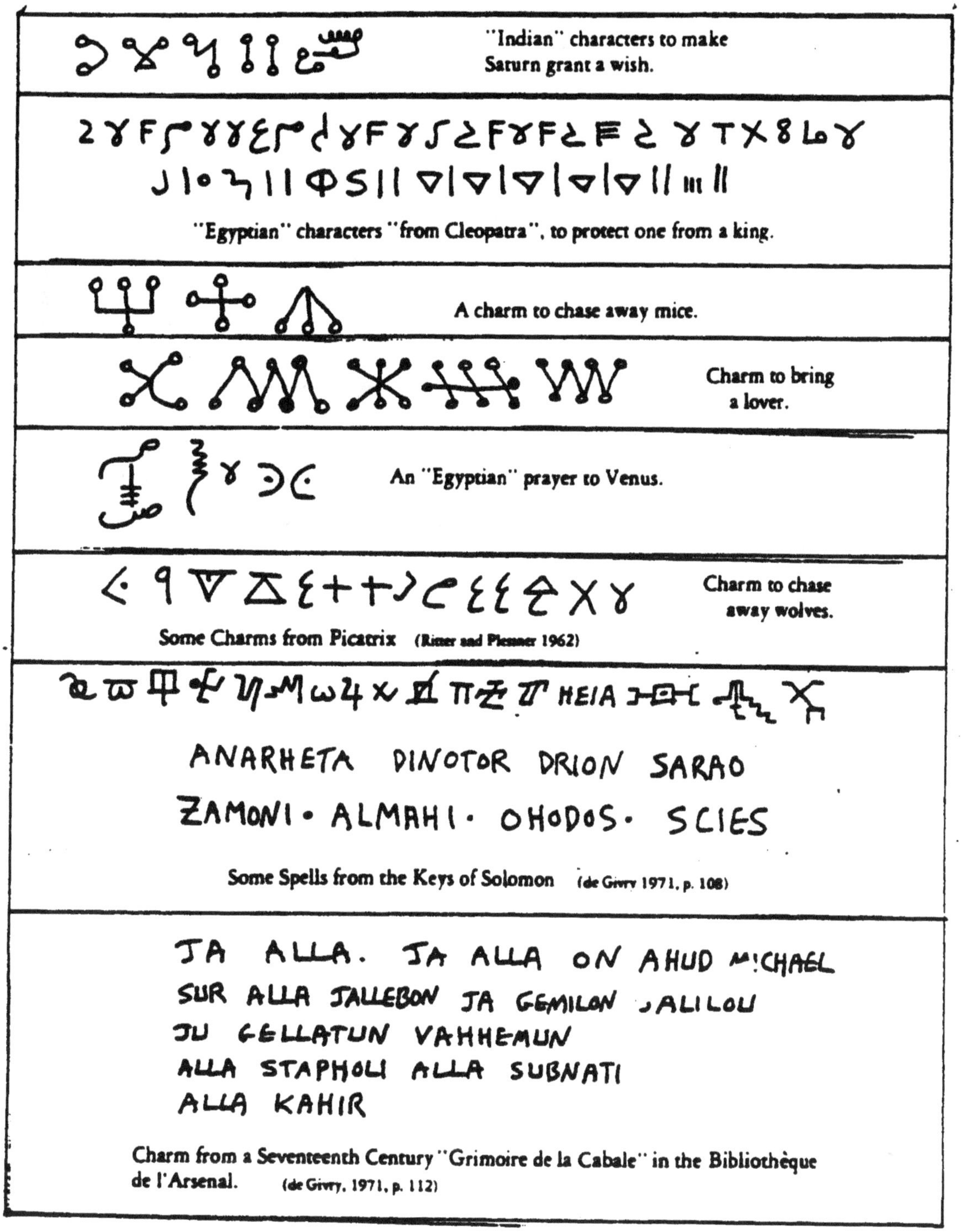

"Indian" characters to make Saturn grant a wish.

"Egyptian" characters "from Cleopatra", to protect one from a king.

A charm to chase away mice.

Charm to bring a lover.

An "Egyptian" prayer to Venus.

Charm to chase away wolves.

Some Charms from Picatrix (Ritter and Plessner 1962)

ANARHETA DINOTOR DRION SARAO

ZAMONI · ALMAHI · OHODOS · SCIES

Some Spells from the Keys of Solomon (de Givry 1971, p. 108)

JA ALLA. JA ALLA ON AHUD MICHAEL
SUR ALLA JALLEBON JA GEMILON JALILOU
JU GELLATUN VAHHEMUN
ALLA STAPHOLI ALLA SUBNATI
ALLA KAHIR

Charm from a Seventeenth Century "Grimoire de la Cabale" in the Bibliothèque de l'Arsenal. (de Givry, 1971, p. 112)

Fig. 41.—Some Magical Spells and Invocations

119

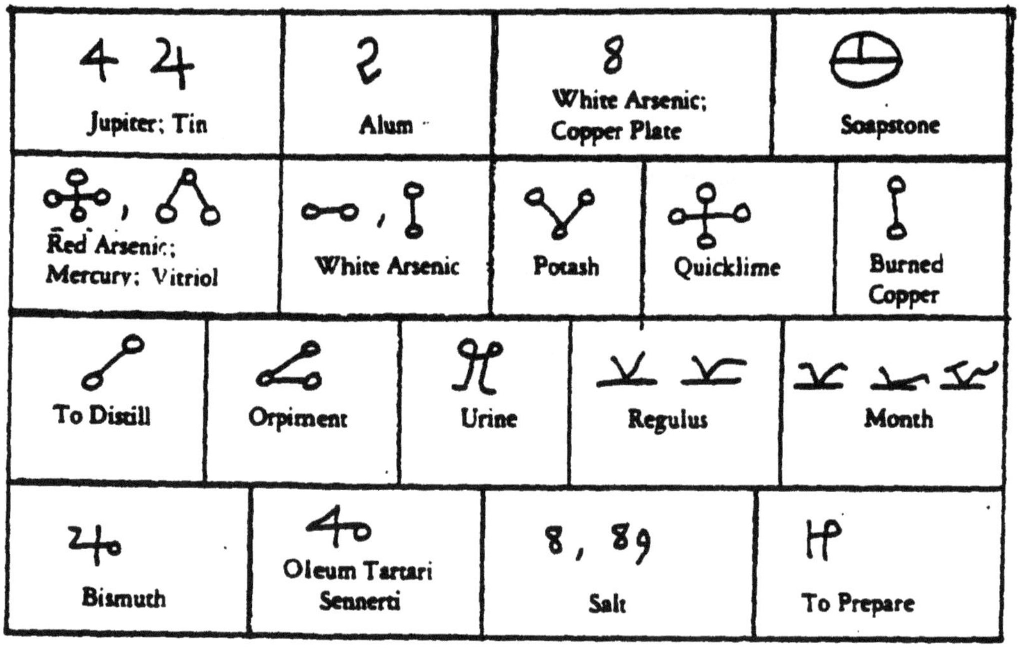

4 4 Jupiter; Tin	2 Alum	8 White Arsenic; Copper Plate	⊕ Soapstone

Red Arsenic; Mercury; Vitriol	White Arsenic	Potash	Quicklime	Burned Copper

To Distill	Orpiment	Urine	Regulus	Month

Bismuth	Oleum Tartari Sennerti	8, 89 Salt	To Prepare

Fig. 42.—Some Alchemy Symbols
(Gessmann 1922)

120

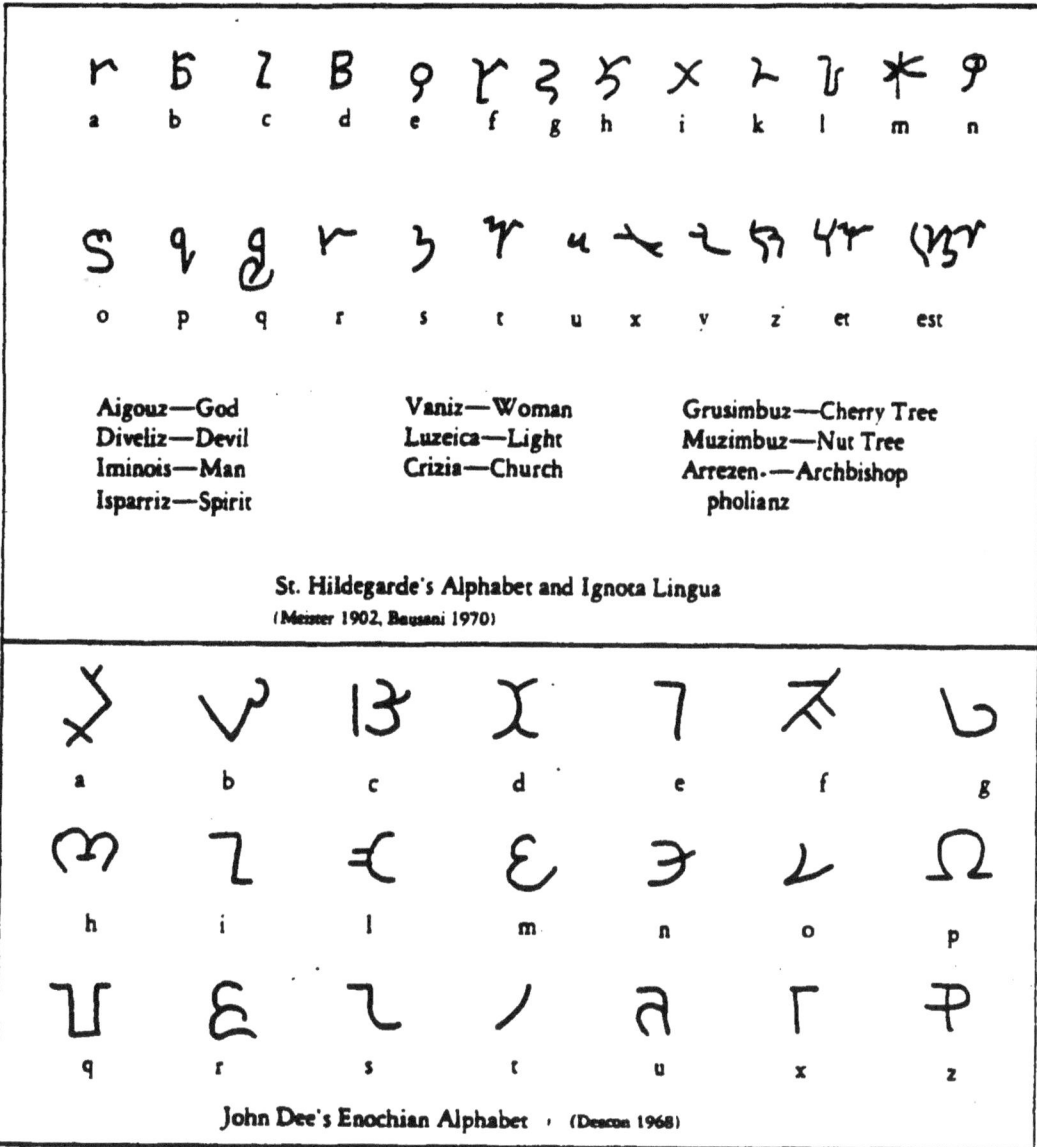

St. Hildegarde's Alphabet and Ignota Lingua
(Meister 1902, Baussani 1970)

Aigouz—God
Diveliz—Devil
Iminois—Man
Isparriz—Spirit

Vaniz—Woman
Luzeica—Light
Crizia—Church

Grusimbuz—Cherry Tree
Muzimbuz—Nut Tree
Arrezen.—Archbishop
  pholianz

John Dee's Enochian Alphabet · (Deacon 1968)

Fig. 43.—Two Mystical Religious Languages

MICMA	Behold,	HOMIL	the true ages
GOHO	Faith	COCASB	of time;
PIAD	your God	FAFEN	to the intent that,
ZIR	I am;	IZIZOP	from the highest vessels
COMSELH	a circle	OD	and
AZIEN	on whose hands	MIINOAG	the corners
BIAB	are	DE	of your governments,
OS LON DOH	12 kingdoms:	GNETAAB	you might work
NORZ	six	VAUN	my power,
CHIS	are	NANAEEL	pouring down
OTHIL	the seats	PANPIR	the fires of life
GI GI PAH	of living breath;	MALPIRGI	continuously
UNDL	the rest	CAUSG	on the earth.
CHIS	are	PILD	Thus
TA PU IN	as sharp sickles,	NOAN	you are become
Q MOS PLFH	or the horns	UNALAH	the skirts
TELOCH	of death;	BALT	of justice
QUIIN	wherein	OD VOOAN	and truth.
TOLTORG	creatures of the earth	DO OI AP	In the name
CHIS	are,	MAD	of the same, your God
I CHIS GE	to are not (sic)	GOHOLOR	lift up,
(E)M	except	GOHUS	I say,
OZIEN	mine own (hand)	AMIRAN	yourselves
DST	which	MICMA	Behold
BURGDA	sleep	JEHUSOZ	His mercies
OD	and	CACACOM	flourish
TORZUL	shall rise.	OD DOOAIN	and name
ILI	In the first	NOAR	is become
EOL	I made you	MICAOLZ	mighty
BALZARG	stewards	A AI OM	amongst us;
OD	and	CASARMG	in whom
HAALA	placed you	GOHIA	we say
THILN OS	in seats 12	ZODACAR	move,
NETAAB	of government:	UNIGLAG	descend
DLUGA	giving	OD	and
VOMZARG	unto any one of you	IM UA MAR	apply yourselves unto me
LONSA	power	PUGO	as unto
CAPMIALI	successively,	PLAPLI	the partakers
VORS	over	ANANAEL	of his secret wisdom
CLA	456	QAAN.	in your creation.

Fig. 44.—A Sample of Enochian Text
(Casaubon 1659, p. 94)

122

YARRY	To the providence	LNIBM	One season
ID OIGO	of him that sitteth	OUCHO	let it confound
	on the Holy Throne	SYMP	another
OD	and	OD	and
TORZULP	rose up	CHRISTGOS	let there be
IAODAF	in the beginning	AGTOLTORN	no creature
GOHOL	saying	MIRC	upon.
CAUSGA	the earth.	Q	or
TABAORD	let her be governed	TIOBL	within her
SAANIR	by her parts:	LEL	the same.
OD	and	TON	All
CHRISTGOS	let there be	PAOMBD	her members
YRPOIL	division	DILZMO	let them differ
TIOBL	in her	ASPIAN	in their qualities
BUSDIRTILB	that the glory of	OD	and
	her	CHRISTGOS	let there be
NOALN	may be	AGLTOLTORN	no one creature
PAID	always	PARACH	equal
ORSBA	drunken	A SYMP	with another.
OD	and	CORDZIZ	The reasonable crea-
DODRMNI	vexed		ture of the earth.
ZYLNA	in itself.		or man.
EL ZAP TILB	Her course	DODPAL	let them vex
PARM GI	let it run	OD FIFALZ	and weed out
PIRIP SAX	with the Heavens.	LS MNAD	one another.
OD	and		
TA	as		
QURIST	an handmaid		
BOOAPIS	let her serve them.		

Fig. 45.—Another Sample of Enochian Text

(Casaubon 1659. p. 203)

(The absence of Y and J from the alphabet of fig. 43 is not explained)

Bibliography

(It has been suggested to me by a colleague that I should add a note to this bibliography telling where the books may be found. Most of the books may be obtained either from the Library of Congress (including the Rare Book Room), Widener Library at Harvard University, or the Main Library at Catholic University. Some are recent reprints which I saw in the Yes Bookstore in Washington, D.C. The purpose of this bibliography is to make the literature as accessible as possible to any serious student of the Voynich manuscript; hence I have provided information on currently available reprints and facsimile editions of some older works. Personal communications and other unpublished materials are preserved in a collection of Voynichiana, and may be examined by arrangement with me.)

Agrippa, Henry Cornelius. 1970. *Opera*. London: ?1531. (Reprinted 1970.)

Agrippa, Henry Cornelius. 1651. *Three Books of Occult Philosophy*. Translated by J. French. London.

Aguirre y Respaldiza, Andres. 1935. *Rogerio Bacon*. Barcelona-Buenos Aires: Editorial Labor s.a.

Alberti, Leon Battista. 1568. *Opuscoli Morali*. Edited by C. Bertolli. Venezia.

Alessio, F. 1957. *Mito e Scienza in Ruggero Bacone*. Milan: Ceschina.

Alessio, F. 1959. "Un Secolo di Studi su Ruggero Bacone (1848–1957)." *Revista Critica di Storia della Filosofia* 14.

Allen, Don Cameron. 1941. *The Star-Crossed Renaissance: The Quarrel About Astrology and Its Influence in England*. Durham, North Carolina: Duke University Press.

Allen, Thomas William. 1889. *Notes on Abbreviations in Greek Manuscripts*. Oxford: Clarendon.

Alston, R. C. 1956. *Treatises on Shorthand*. Leeds: Printed for the author by E. J. Arnold.

Altick, Richard D. 1950. *The Scholar Adventurers*. New York: Macmillan.

Arber, Agnes. 1953. *Herbals, Their Origin and Evolution, 1470–1670*. Cambridge: The University Press.

Ashbrook, Joseph. 1966. "Roger Bacon and the Voynich Manuscript." *Sky and Telescope* (April). pp. 218–219.

Ashmole, Elias. 1652. *Theatrum Chemicum Britannicum*. London: Nath. Brooke. (Reprinted Hildesheim: 1969.)

Askham, Anthony. 1548a. *An Almanacke a Prognosticacyon*. London: W. Powell.

Askham, Anthony. 1548b. *A Pronosticacion Made for the Yere MDXLVIII*. London: W. Powell.

Askham, Anthony. 1550. *A Little Herball of the Properties of Herbes*. London: W. Powell.

Askham, Anthony. 1552. *A Lytel Treatyse of Astronomy*. London: W. Powell.

Askham, Anthony. 1553. *A Prognostication for the Yere MCCCCLIII*. London: W. Powell.

Atwood, Mary Anne. 1960. *Hermetic Philosophy and Alchemy*. New York: Julian Press.

Bacon, Roger. 1659. *De Mirabili Potestate Artis et Naturae, or Friar Bacon His Discovery of the Miracles of Art, Nature and Magick*. London.

Bacon, Roger. 1603. *Sanioris Medicinae Magistri Rogeri D. Baconis Angli de Arte Chymiae Scripta*. Frankfort.

Bacon, Roger. 1683. *The Cure of Old Age, and Preservation of Youth*. Translated by Richard Browne. London: Printed for Tho. Flesher and Edward Evets.

Bacon, Roger. 1859. *Fr. Rogeri Bacon Opera Quaedam Hactenus Inedita*. Edited by John S. Brewer. London: Green, Longman and Roberts.

Bacon, Roger. 1893. *Lettre sur les prodiges de la nature et de l'art*. Translated and commented by A. Poisson. Paris: Chamuel.

Bacon, Roger. (1897–1900). *The 'Opus Majus' of Roger Bacon*. Edited by John H. Bridges. Oxford: Clarendon Press. (Reprinted Frankfurt/Main: Minerva-Verlag. 1964.)

Bacon, Roger. 1902. *The Greek Grammar of Roger Bacon and a Fragment of His Hebrew Grammar*. Edited by Edmond Nolan and S. A. Hirsch. Cambridge: The University Press.

Bacon, Roger. 1909. *Un fragment inédit de l'opus tertium de Roger Bacon*. With preface by Pierre Duhem. Quaracchi: St. Bonaventure College Press.

Bacon, Roger. 1909–1940. *Opera Hactenus Inedita*. Edited by Robert B. Steele. Oxford: Clarendon Press.

Bacon, Roger. 1911. *Compendium Studii Theologiae*. Edited by A. G. Little. Aberdeen: University Press. (Reprinted 1966.)

Bacon, Roger. 1912. *Part of the Opus Tertium of Roger Bacon*. Edited by A. G. Little. Aberdeen: University Press.

Bacon, Roger. 1923. *Roger Bacon's Letter Concerning the Marvelous Power of Art and of Nature*. Translated by Tenney L. Davis. Easton, Pa: The Chemical Publishing Co.

Bacon, Roger. 1928a. *Fratris Rogeri Bacon 'De Retardatione Accidentium Senectutis'*. Edited by A. G. Little, with preface by E. Withington. Oxford: Clarendon Press.

Bacon, Roger. 1928b. *The Opus Majus of Roger Bacon*. Translated by Robert B. Burke. Philadelphia: University of Pennsylvania Press. (Reprinted New York: Russell & Russell. 1962.)

Baeumker. Clemens. 1916. *Roger Bacons Naturphilosophie*. Münster: I. W.

Bales. Peter. 1597. *The Arte of Brachygraphie*. London: Imprinted by G. Shawe and R. Blower. for T. Charde Reprinted New York: DaCapo Press. 1972.)

Bardon. Franz. 1962. *Initiation into Hermetics*. Translated by A. Radspieler Kettig über Koblenz: Osiris-Verlag.

Bardon. Franz. 1975. *The Practice of Magical Evocation*. Wuppertal: Victor Rüggeberg.

Bauer. H. 1963. *Die wunderbare Mönch: Leben und Kampf Roger Bacons*. Leipzig: Koehler & Amelang.

Bausani. Alessandro. 1970. *Geheim und Universalsprachen*. Stuttgart.

Beck. Cave. 1657. *The Universal Character*. London: Printed by Tho. Maxey. for William Weekley.

Bettoni. Efrem. 1962a. "Ruggero Bacone in Alcune Recenti Pubblicazione Italiane." *Revista di Filosofia Neoscolastica* 54. p. 3.

Bettoni. Efrem. 1962b. "San Bonaventura e Ruggero Bacone." *Studi Francescani* 59. p. 12.

Bettoni. Efrem. 1966. "L'Aristotelismo di Ruggero Bacone." *Revista di Filosofia Neoscolastica* 58. p. 5.

Bettoni. Efrem. 1967. "La Dottrina della Conscienza di Ruggero Bacone." *Revista di Filosofia Neoscolastica* 59. p. 3.

Biedermann. Hans. 1972. *Medicina Magica. Metaphysische Heilmethoden in spätantiken und mittelalterlichen Handschriften*. Graz: Akadem. Druck-Verlaganst.

Bigalli. Davide. 1971. *I Tartari e l'Apocalissi. Ricerce sull' Escatologia in Adamo Marsh e Ruggero Bacone*. Firenze: La Nuova Italia.

Bird. Malcolm. 1921. "The Roger Bacon Manuscript: Investigation into its History. and the Efforts to Decipher It. *Scientific American Monthly* 3 (June). pp. 492–496.

Bishop. William Warner. 1950. *A Checklist of American Copies of "Short-Title Catalogue" Books*. 2nd ed. Ann Arbor University of Michigan Press.

Blau. Joseph Leon. 1944. *The Christian Interpretation of the Cabala in the Renaissance*. New York: Columbia University Press.

Blish. James. 1971. *Doctor Mirabilis: A Novel*. New York: Dodd. Mead.

Bober. H. 1948. "The Zodiacal Miniature of the Très Riches Heures of the Duke of Berry." *Journal of the Warburg and Courtauld Institutes* 11. pp. 1–34.

Boge. Herbert. 1973. *Griechische Tachygraphie und Tironische Noten*. Berlin: Akademie-Verlag.

Boll. Franz and Bezold. Carl. 1931. *Sternglaube und Sterndeutung: Die Geschichte und das Wesen der Astrologie*. 4th ed. Leipzig: B. G. Teubner.

Bolton. Henry C. 1904. *The Follies of Science at the Court of Rudolph II. 1576–1612*. Milwaukee: Pharmaceutical Review Publishing Co.

Bouyges. M. 1930. "Roger Bacon a-t-il lu les livres Arabes?" *Archives d'histoire doctrinale et littéraire du moyen âge* 5. pp. 311–315.

Bregola. G. 1937. "Il Valore delle Lingue e delle Scienze nell' Apologetica di Ruggero Bacone." *La Scuola Cattolica* 65. pp. 372–391.

Bridges. John Henry. 1914. *Life and Work of Roger Bacon*. Oxford: Clarendon Press.

Brophy. Liam. 1963. *The Marvelous Doctor. Friar Roger Bacon*. Chicago: Franciscan Press.

Brumbaugh. Robert S. 1974. "Botany and the Voynich 'Roger Bacon' MS. Once More." *Speculum* 49. pp. 546–548.

Brumbaugh. Robert S. 1975. "The Solution of the Voynich 'Roger Bacon' Cipher." *Yale University Library Gazette* 49 (April). pp. 347–355.

Brumbaugh. Robert S. 1976. "The Voynich 'Roger Bacon' Cipher Manuscript: Deciphered Maps of Stars." *Journal of the Warburg and Courtauld Institutes XXXIX* (1976). pp. 139–150.

Bruno. Giordano. 1582. *De Umbris Idearum*. Paris.

Brusadelli. M. 1954. "Ruggero Bacone nella Storia." *Revista di Filosofia Neoscolastica* 6.

Burland. Cottie A. 1967. *The Arts of the Alchemists*. London: Weidenfeld and Nicholson.

Butler. Eliza M. 1948. *The Myth of the Magus*. Cambridge: University Press.

Butler. Eliza M. 1949. *Ritual Magic*. (Reprinted by Newcastle Publishing Co.. Inc.. 1971.)

Candler. Howard. 1907. "Roger Bacon and Francis Bacon: A Comparison." In *Royal Society of Literature of the United Kingdom, Essays by Divers Hands, Being the Transactions*. 2nd Series 27. pp. 171–195.

Cappelli. Adriano. 1949. *Lexicon Abbreviaturarum*. Milan: Ulrico Hoepli.

Carter. Albert H. 1946. "Some Impressions of the Voynich Manuscript." Unpublished notes. 10 September 1946.

Carton. Raoul. 1924a. "L'expérience physique chez Roger Bacon." *Études de philosophie médiévale* 2. Paris: J. Vrin."

Carton. Raoul. 1924b. "L'expérience mystique de l'illumination intérieure chez Roger Bacon." *Études de philosophie médiévale* 3. Paris: J. Vrin.

Carton, Raoul. 1924c. "La synthèse doctrinale de Roger Bacon." *Études de philosophie médiévale* 5. Paris: J. Vrin.

Carton, Raoul. 1929. "Le chiffre de Roger Bacon." Révue d'histoire de la philosophie 3. pp. 31–66, 165–179.

Casaubon, Meric. 1659. *A True and Faithful Relation of What Passed Between Dr. John Dee and Some Spirits*. London. Printed by D. Maxwell.

Cecchetti, Bartolomeo. 1868/69. "Le Scritture Occulte nella Diplomazia Veneziana." In *Atti del Real Istituto Veneto di Scienze, Lettere ed Arti*, Series III 14, p. 1185.

Charles, Émile. 1861. *Roger Bacon: sa vie, ses ouvrages, ses doctrines d'après des textes inédits*. Bordeaux: G. Gounouilhou.

Clement, Adolf. 1926. "Sur l'indication de la composition de la poudre a feu chez Roger Bacon." *Archivio de Storia della Scienza* 7. pp. 34–35.

Cockayne, T. O. 1866. *Leechdoms, Wortcunning and Starcraft of Early England*. London: Chronicles and Memorials 3.

Courtney, William L. 1892. "Roger Bacon." In *Studies at Leisure*. London: Chapman and Hall, Ltd.

Crowley, Theodore. 1950. *Roger Bacon, the Problem of the Soul in His Philosophical Commentaries*. Louvain: Éditions de l'institut supérieure de philosophie.

Crowley, Theodore. 1951–52. "Roger Bacon: The Problem of Universals in His Philosophical Commentaries." *Bulletin of the John Rylands Library* 34.

Currier, Prescott. 1970–1976. "Voynich MS. Transcription Alphabet; Plans for Computer studies; Transcribed Text of Herbal A and B Material; Notes and Observations." Unpublished communications to John H. Tiltman and M. D'Imperio. Damariscotta, Maine.

Dailey, William. 1975. *The Mirror of Alchimy, Composed by the Famous Friar, Roger Bacon, etc., with the Smaragdine Table of Hermes, Trismegistus, of Alchemy*. Los Angeles (facsimile).

Dalgarno, George. 1661. *Ars Signorum, Vulgo Character Universalis et Lingua Philosophia*. London: F. Hayes.

Dalgarno, George. 1680. *Didascalocophus*. Oxford: Printed at the Sheldonian Theater (Menston: Scholar Press, 1971, facsimile).

Deacon, Richard. 1968. *John Dee*. London: Frederic Muller.

Dee, John. 1664. *Monas Hieroglyphica*. Antwerp.

Dee, John. 1842. *The Private Diary of Dr. John Dee*. Edited by James Richard Halliwell. London: Printed for the Camden Society by J. B. Nichols and Son. (Reprinted New York: AMS Press, 1968.)

Dee, John. 1963. *Diary of John Dee*. Franklin, New Hampshire: Hillside Press.

Dee, John. 1964. "Monas Hieroglyphica." Translated by C. H. Josten. *Ambix* 12. pp. 84–221.

De Givry, Grillot. 1971. *Witchcraft, Magic and Alchemy*. Translated by J. Courtenay Locke. New York: Dover.

Delorme, F. M. 1911. "Un opuscule inédit de Roger Bacon O.F.M." *Archivum Franciscanum Historicum* 4.

DeRola, Stanislas Klossowski. 1973. *The Secret Art of Alchemy*. New York: Avon Publishers.

D'Imperio, M. E. 1976. "New Research on the Voynich Manuscript: Proceedings of a Seminar." Washington, D.C., 30 November 1976. Privately circulated.

Dioscorides. 1959. *The Greek Herbal of Dioscorides. Illustrated by a Byzantine, A.D. 512. Englished by John Goodyer, A.D. 1655*. New York: Hafner.

Duhem, Pierre M. M. 1913–1959. *Le système du monde: histoire des doctrines cosmologiques de Platon a Copernic*. Paris: A. Hermann.

Duthie, George Ian. 1970. *Elizabethan Shorthand and the First Quarto of King Lear*. Folcroft, Pa.: Folcroft Press.

Easton, Stewart C. 1952. *Roger Bacon and His Search for a Universal Science*. Oxford. (Reprinted New York: Russell & Russell, 1971.)

Evans, Robert John Weston. 1973. *Rudolph II and His World: A Study in Intellectual History, 1576–1612*. Oxford: Clarendon Press.

Feely, Joseph M. 1943. *Roger Bacon's Cipher: The Right Key Found*. Rochester, New York: n.p.

Fell-Smith, Charlotte. 1904. *John Dee*. London: Constable and Co., Ltd.

Feret, P. 1891. "Les imprisonnements de Roger Bacon." *Revue des questions historiques* 50. pp. 119–142.

Festugière, André Marie Jean. 1944–1954. *La révélation d'Hermès Trismégiste*. Paris: Lecoffre.

Festugière, André Marie Jean. 1967. *Hermétisme et mystique païenne*. Paris: Aubier-Montaigne.

Folkingham, William. 1620. *Brachigraphy: or the Art of Short Writing*. Amsterdam: Theatrum Orbis Terrarum.

Frankowska, Malgorzata. 1971. *Scientia as Interpreted by Roger Bacon*. Translated by Ziemislaw Zienkiewicz. Warsaw. U.S. Department of Commerce, National Technical Information Service, Springfield, Va. (Original publication Warsaw: 1969.)

French. Peter J. 1972. *John Dee*. London: Routledge and Kegan Paul.

"Friar Bacon." *The Nation* (New York) 123 (December 22, 1926), p. 656.

Friedman. Elizebeth. 1962. "The Most Mysterious MS.—Still an Enigma." *Washington D.C. Post.* 5 August. E1. E5.

Friedman. William F. and Elizebeth S. 1959. "Acrostics. Anagrams. and Chaucer." *Philological Quarterly* 38 (January). pp. 1–20.

Garland. Herbert. 1921. "The Mystery of the Roger Bacon Cipher MS." *Bookman's Journal and Print Collector* (London) 5, New Series (October). pp. 11–16.

Geissler. H. 1959. *Comenius und die Sprache*. Heidelberg.

Gemelli. Agostino. 1914. *Scritti Vari Pubblicati in Occasione del VII Centenario della Nascita Di Ruggero Bacone*. Florence: Libraria Editrice Florentina.

Gerard. John. 1633. *The Herball*. London: Adam Islip Joice Norton and Richard Whitakers (Reprinted by Dover. 1975).

Gessman. Gustav W. 1922. *Die Geheimsymbole der Alchymie. Arzneikunde und Astrologie des Mittelalters*. Berlin: Verlag von Karl Siegismund.

Gilson. Étienne. 1928. (Review of the Newbold-Kent Book) *Révue critique d'histoire et de littérature* (Paris) 95 New Series (August). pp. 328–383.

Giulietti. Francesco. 1968. *Storia delle Scritture Veloci*. Firenze: Giunti. G. Barbèra.

Goldsmith. Edmund. ed. 1886. *Bibliotheca Curiosa. The Famous History of Fryer Bacon*. Edinburgh.

Grattan. John H. G.. and Singer. Charles J. 1952. *Anglo-Saxon Magic and Medicine. Illustrated Specially from the Semi-Pagan Text 'Lacnunga'*. London: Oxford University Press.

Graubard. Mark Aaron. 1953. *Astrology and Alchemy: Two Fossil Sciences*. New York: Philosophical Library.

Greene. Robert. 1594. *The Honourable Historie of Friar Bacon and Friar Bungay*. London: Printed for Edward White (Reprinted New York: AMS Press. 1970).

Groves. Edward. 1846. *Pasilogia: An Essay Towards the Formation of a System of Universal Language. both Written and Visual*. Dublin: James McGlashan.

Gundel. Wilhelm. 1936. *Dekane und Dekansternbilder*. Studien der Bibliothek Warburg 19.

Hajdu. Helga. 1936. *Das mnemotechnische Schrifttum des Mittelalters*. Vienna.

Hall. Manly Palmer. 1964. *The Mystical and Medical Philosophy of Paracelsus*. Los Angeles: Philosophical Research Society.

Hall. Manly Palmer. 1971. *Codex Rosae Crucis*. Los Angeles: Philosophical Research Society.

Heck. Erich. 1957. *Roger Bacon: ein mittelalterlicher Versuch einer historischen und systematisch Religionswissenschaft*. Ph.D. Dissertation. Bonn.

Held. Gustav. 1881. *Roger Bacons praktische Philosophie*. Jena.

Hildegardis.. 1913. *Die Kompositionen der Heil.* Published by Joseph Gmelch. Dusseldorf: L. Schwann (facsimile).

Hill. Sir George Francis. 1915. *The Development of Arabic Numerals in Europe*. Oxford: Clarendon Press.

Hime. Henry W. L. 1904. "Friar Bacon." In *The Origin of Gunpowder*. London: Longmans. Green and Co. p. 141.

Hime. Henry W. L. 1914. "Roger Bacon and Gunpowder." In *Roger Bacon Essays*. Edited by A. G. Little. Oxford: Clarendon Press. pp. 321–335.

Hime. Henry W. L. 1915. "Friar Bacon." In *The Origin of Artillery*. London: Longmans. Green and Co.. pp. 102–116.

Hoffmans. Hadelin. 1906. "Une théorie intuitioniste de la connaissance du XIII siècle." *Revue néoscolastique de philosophie* 13. pp. 371–391.

Hoffmans. Hadelin. 1907. "La synthèse doctrinale de Roger Bacon." *Archiv für Geschichte der Philosophie* 14. pp. 196–224.

Hoffmans. Hadelin. 1908. "La genèse des sensations d'après Roger Bacon." *Revue néoscolastique de philosophie* 15. pp. 32–46.

Hoffmans. Hadelin. 1909a. "La sensibilité et les modes de la connaissance d'après Roger Bacon." *Revue néoscolastique de philosophie* 16. pp. 32–46.

Hoffmans. Hadelin. 1909b. "L'intuition mystique et la science." *Revue néoscolastique de philosophie* 16. pp. 370–397.

Hoffmans. Hadelin. 1926. "L'expérience chez Roger Bacon." *Revue néoscolastique de philosophie* 27. pp. 170–190.

Hugo. Herman. 1617. *De Prima Scribendi Origine et Universa Rei Literariae Antiquitate*. Auvers.

James. Montague Rhodes. 1903. *Ancient Libraries of Canterbury and Dover*. Cambridge: The University Press.

James. Montague Rhodes. 1921. *MSS Formerly Owned by Dr. John Dee*. London: Bibliographical Society "Transactions" (Supplement).

Johnen. Chr. 1940. *Geschichte der Stenographie*. Berlin: H. Apitz.

Josten. C. H. "An Unknown Chapter in the Life of John Dee." *Journal of the Warburg and Courtauld Institute* 28. pp. 223-257.

Jourdain. C. 1888. "Discussions de quelques points de la philosophie de Roger Bacon." In *Excursions historiques et philosophiques.* Paris: Firmin-Didot et Cie.. pp. 129-145 (Reprinted Frankfurt/M.: Minerva-Verlag. 1966).

Kahn. David. 1967. *The Codebreakers: The Story of Secret Writing.* New York: Macmillan. pp. 863-872. 1120-1121

Keicher. O. 1913. "Der Intellectus Agens bei Roger Baco." In *Studien der Geschichte der Philosophie.* Supplement I. Münster: I. W.. pp. 297-308.

Kipling. Rudyard. 1926. "The Eve of Allah." In *Debits and Credits.* London: Macmillan.

Kircher. Athanasius. 1663. *Polygraphia Nova et Universalis ex Combinatoria Arte Detecta.* Rome.

Kocher. Paul. 1953. *Science and Religion in Elizabethan England.* San Marino. California: The Huntingdon Library.

Kraus. Hans P. n.d. *Thirty-Five Manuscripts.* Catalogue 100.

Krischer. Jeffrey P. 1969. *The Voynich Manuscript.* Harvard University.

Liebeschütz. H. 1930. *Das alegorische Weltbild der heilige Hildegard von Bingen.* Leipzig and Berlin: B. G. Teubner.

Little. Andrew G. 1892. *The Grey Friars in Oxford.* Oxford: Clarendon Press.

Little. Andrew G. 1914. *Roger Bacon Essays.* Oxford: Clarendon Press. (Reprinted New York: Russell & Russell. 1972.)

Little. Andrew G. 1929. *Roger Bacon: Lecture on a 'Master Mind'.* London: H. Milford.

Longpré. E. 1938. "La summa dialectica de Roger Bacon." *Archivum Franciscanum Historicum* 31. pp. 204-205.

Longwell. H. C. 1908. *The Theory of Mind of Roger Bacon.* Ph.D. Dissertation. Emperor William University. Strasbourg.

Lutz. Edward. 1936. *Roger Bacon's Contribution to Knowledge.* New York: J. F. Wagner. Inc.

Maccagnolo. Enzo. 1955. "Ruggero Bacone e la Metafisica Classica." *Studi Francescani* 52.

Maffre. Camille. 1863. *Roger Bacon.* Paris.

Mandonnet. P. 1910. "Roger Bacon et le 'Speculum Astronomiae'." *Révue néosolastique de philosophie.*

Mandonnet. P. 1913. "Roger Bacon et la composition des trois 'Opus'." *Révue neoscolastique de philosophie.*

Manly. John M. 1921a. "Roger Bacon's Cipher Manuscript." *American Review of Reviews* 64 (July). pp. 105-106.

Manly. John M. 1921b. "The Most Mysterious Mansucript in the World: Did Roger Bacon Write It and Has the Key Been Found?" *Harper's Monthly Magazine* 143 (July). pp. 186-197.

Manly. John M. 1931. "Roger Bacon and the Voynich MS." *Speculum* 6 (July). pp. 345-391.

Massa. Eugenio. 1953. "Ruggero Bacone e la 'Poetica' di Aristotele." *Giornale Critica della Filosofia Italiana* 32.

Massa. Eugenio. 1955a. *Ruggero Bacone—Etica e Poetica nella Storia dell' Opus Maius.* Rome: Edizioni di Storia e Litteratura.

Massa. Eugenio. 1955b. "Vita Civile e Crisi Latina in Ruggero Bacone." *Rassegna di Politica e di Storia* I.

Massie. Mitford C. 1934. *The Roger Bacon or R. R. Dee Chess Code.* n.p.: Press of Fremont Payne. Inc.

Mathers. S. L. MacGregor. 1951. *The Kabbalah Unveiled.* London. (Reprinted New York: S. Weiser. 1968.)

Mathers. S. L. MacGregor. 1974. *The Key of Solomon the King (Clavicula Solomonis). Now First Translated and Edited from Ancient MSS. in the British Museum.* New York: Samuel Weiser. Inc.

Mathers. S. L. MacGregor. 1975. *The Book of the Sacred Magic of Abramelin the Mage. As Delivered by Abraham the Jew unto His Son Lamech. A.D. 1458.* New York: Dover.

Matrod. H. 1927. "Sur Roger Bacon (1214-1294)." *Études franciscaines* 29.

May. J. 1929. *Die heilige Hildegard.* München.

McCracken. George E. 1948. "Athanasius Kircher's Universal Polygraphy." *Isis* 39 (November). pp. 215-228.

McKaig. Betty. n.d. "The Voynich Manuscript—Cipher of the Secret Book." Reprinted courtesy Independent Newspapers Inc.. San Diego. California.

McKeon. Richard. 1928. "Roger Bacon." *The Nation* 127 (August 29). pp. 205-206.

Meister. Aloys. 1896. "Zur Kenntnis des venetianischen Chiffrenwesens." *Historisches Jahrbuch* 17 pp. 319-330.

Meister. Aloys. 1902. *Die Anfänge der modernen diplomatischen Geheimschrift.* Paderborn: F. Schoningh.

Meister. Aloys. 1906. *Die Geheimschrift im Dienste der päpstlichen Kurie.* Paderborn: F. Schöningh.

Miano. Vincenzo. 1960. "Tradizionalismo e Umanesimo in Ruggero Bacone." In *L'homme et son destin d'apres les penseurs du moyen âge. actes du premier congres internationale de philosophie médievale.* Louvain-Paris.

Moorsel. Gerard von. 1955. *The Mysteries of Hermes Trismegistus.* Utrecht.

Moses. Montrose J. 1921. "A Cinderella on Parchment: The Romance of the New 600-Year-Old Bacon Manuscript." *Hearst's International.* pp. 16-17. 75.

Newbold. William Romaine. 1921. "The Cipher of Roger Bacon." *Transactions of the College of Physicians of Philadelphia* 43 (1921). pp. 431-474. Read April 20. 1921.

Newbold. William Romaine. 1928. *The Cipher of Roger Bacon.* Edited with foreword and notes by Prof. Roland Grubb Kent. Philadelphia: University of Pennsylvania Press.

Nock. A.D., and Festugière, A. M. J. 1945. *Hermès Trismégiste.* Paris.

O'Neill. Hugh. 1944. "Botanical Observations on the Voynich MS." *Speculum* 19 (January). p. 126.

Panofsky. Erwin. 1954. "Answers to Questions for Prof. E. Panofsky." Personal communication to William F. Friedman. March 19. 1954.

Pasini. Luigi. 1873. *Delle Scritture in Cifra L'sate dalla Repubblica Veneta.* Venezia: Regio Archivio Generale di Venezia. p. 291.

Peers. Edgar Allison. 1929. *Ramon Lull, a Biography.* New York: Macmillan.

Pelzer. A. 1919. "Une source inconnue de Roger Bacon. Alfred de Saraschel." *Archivum Franciscanum Historicum* 12. p. 45.

Petersen. Theodore C. 1953. "Notes to Mr. Tiltman's [1951] Observations on the Voynich Cipher MS." Unpublished. April 23. 1953.

Petersen. Theodore C. 1966. Hand Transcript and Concordance of the Voynich Manuscript and Other Working Papers In the Friedman Collection. George Marshall Library. Lexington. Virginia.

Philalethes. Aevrenaeus. 1678. *Ripley Reviv'd.* London: Printed by T. Ratcliff and N. Thompson. for W. Cooper.

Poisson. Albert. 1890. *Cinq traités d'alchimie.* (Paracelsus. Albertus Magnus. Roger Bacon. Ramon Lull. Arnold de Villanova.) Paris: Bibliothèque Chacornac.

Pollard. A. W., and Redgrave. C. R. 1969. *A Short-Title Catalogue of Books Printed in England and Ireland and of English Books Printed Abroad 1475-1640.* London: The Bibliographical Society.

Porta. Giovannie Battista. 1563. *De Furtivis Literarum Notis Vulgo de Ziferis.* Naples.

Porta. Giovanni Battista. 1644. *Magia Naturalis.* Levden.

Powys. John Cowper. 1956. *The Brazen Head.* London: MacDonald.

Pratt. Fletcher. 1942. *Secret and Urgent.* Garden City. N.J.: Blue Ribbon Books (see especially pp. 30-38).

Redgrove. Herbert Stanley. 1920. *Roger Bacon. the Father of Experimental Science and Medieval Occultism.* London: W. Rider & Son. Ltd.

Reitzenstein. Richard. 1904. *Poimandres.* Leipzig: B. G. Teubner.

Reventlow. Carl Otto (Carl Christian Otto). 1843. *Lehrbuch des Mnemotechnik.* Stuttgart: Tübingen.

Review of "The Cipher of Roger Bacon (Newbold)." *Quarterly Review of Biology* (Baltimore. Md.) 3 (December 1928). pp. 595-596.

Reville. John C., S. J. 1921. "Friar Roger Bacon and Modern Science." *America: A Catholic Review of the Week* 25 (May 21). pp. 101-102.

Ripley. George. 1591. *The Compound of Alchymy.* London: T. Orwin.

Ripley. George. 1756. *Georgii Riplaei . . . Chymische Schriften. etc.* Translated by Benjamin Roth-Scholtzen. Wienn: Zu finden bey J. P. Krauss.

Ritter. H. and Plessner. M. 1962. *Picatrix.* Studies of the Warburg Institute 27.

"The Roger Bacon Manuscript: What It Looks Like. and a Discussion of the Possibilities of Decipherment." *Scientific American.* May 28. 1921. p. 421.

Rohde. Eleanour S. 1971. *The Old English Herbals.* (1922) Reprinted New York: Dover Publications.

Rose. Valentin. 1874. "Tironische Noten in Stenographie im 12ten Jahrhundert." *Hermes* 8. p. 303.

Rossi. Paolo. 1960. *Clavis Universalis.* Milan-Naples.

Rossi. Paolo. 1961. "The Legacy of Ramon Lull in Sixteenth-Century Thought." *Warburg Institute. Medieval and Renaissance Studies* 5. pp. 182-213.

Rossi. Paolo. 1974. *Francesco Bacone: Dalla Magia alla Scienza.* Torino: G. Einaudi.

Sacco. Luigi. 1947. "Un Primato Italiano: La Crittografia nei Secoli XV e XVI." *Bolletino dell' Istituto di Coltura dell' Arma del Genio* 26 (December).

Saisset. Émile Edmond. 1862. *Précurseurs et disciples de Descartes.* Paris: Didier et Cie.

Saisset. M. 1861. "Roger Bacon." *Revue des deux-mondes* 314. p. 369.

Salomon. Richard. 1934. Review of Manly's Critique of Newbold's Decipherment. *Bibliothek Warburg. Kulturwissenchaftliche Bibliographie zum Nachleben der Antike* 1. p. 96.

Salomon. Richard. 1936. *Opicinis de Canistris. Weltbild und Bekenntnisse eines avignonischen Klerikers des XIV JH.* London: Warburg Institute.

Sandys. Sir John E. 1914. *Roger Bacon*. Oxford: University Press.

Saxl. Fritz. 1915. 1927. "Verzeichnis astrologischer und mythologischer Handschriften des lateinischen Mittelalters. In *Sitzungsberichte der heidelberger Akademie der Wissenschaften (philosophisch-historische Klasse)* 6 and 16.

Scott. W. 1924-36. *Hermetica*. Oxford.

Seligmann. Kurt. 1948. *Magic, Supernaturalism and Religion*. New York: Random House, Pantheon.

Seznec. J. 1953. *The Survival of the Pagan Gods*. Translated by B. F. Sessions. New York: Bollingen, Pantheon.

Sharp. D. E. 1930. *Franciscan Philosophy at Oxford in the 13th Century*. Oxford: Clarendon Press. (Reprinted New York: Russell & Russell, 1964.)

Shulman. David. 1976. *An Annotated Bibliography of Cryptography*. New York: Garland Publishing, Inc.

Shumaker. Wayne. 1972. *The Occult Sciences in the Renaissance: A Study in Intellectual Patterns*. Berkeley, California: University of California Press.

Silvester. Jakob. 1526. *Opus Novum, Praefectis Arcium: Imperatoribus Exercituum, etc.* Rome.

Singer. Charles Joseph. 1927. *The Herbal in Antiquity*. Bungay, Suffolk: Printed by R. Clay & Sons, Ltd. (Also in *Journal of Hellenic Studies* 47.)

Singer. Charles Joseph. 1928. *From Magic to Science*. New York: Boni and Liveright (Reprinted by Dover, 1958).

Singer. Charles Joseph. 1959. *A History of Biology*. 3rd rev. ed. London and New York: Abelard-Schuman.

Singer. Charles Joseph. 1975. "The Scientific Views and Visions of Saint Hildegard." In *Studies in the History and Method of Science*. (Oxford: 1921) Reprinted New York: Arno Press (vol. 1, pp. 1-58).

Singer. Charles Joseph, and Underwood. E. A. 1962. *A Short History of Medicine*. 2nd ed. Oxford: Clarendon Press.

Singer. Dorothea Waley. 1928-31. *Catalogue of Latin and Vernacular Alchemical Manuscripts in Great Britain and Ireland, Dating from Before the Sixteenth Century*. Brussels: M. Lamartin.

Singer. D. W. 1932. "Alchemical Writings Attributed to Roger Bacon." *Speculum* 7.

Smith. David Eugene, and Karpinski. Louis Charles. 1911. *The Hindu-Arabic Numerals*. Boston and London: Ginn and Company.

Steele. Robert. 1928a. "Luru Vopo Vir Can Utriet." *Nature* 121 (February 11), pp. 208-209.

Steele. Robert. 1928b. "Science in Medieval Cipher." *Nature* 122 (October 13), pp. 563-565.

Steele. Robert. 1933. "Roger Bacon as Professor: A Student's Notes." *Isis* 20, pp. 53-71.

Steele. Robert. 1975. "Roger Bacon and the State of Science in the Thirteenth Century." In *Studies in the History and Method of Science*. Edited by Charles Joseph Singer. (Oxford: 1921.) Reprinted New York: Arno Press.

Storms. Godfrid. 1975. *Anglo-Saxon Magic*. (The Hague: M. Nijhoff, 1948.) Reprinted by Folcroft Library Editions.

Strong. Leonell C. 1945. "Anthony Askham, the Author of the Voynich MS." *Science* (Lancaster, Pa.) 101 (June 15), pp. 608-609.

Strong. Leonell C., and McCawley. G. L. 1947. "A Verification of a Hitherto Unknown Prescription of the 16th Century." *Bulletin of the History of Medicine* (Baltimore, Md.) 21 (November-December), pp. 898-904.

Taylor. Henry Osborne. 1922. *Greek Biology and Medicine*. Boston: Marshall Jones Company.

Thomson. S. H. 1937. "An Unnoticed Treatise of Roger Bacon on Time and Motion." *Isis* 27, pp. 219-224.

Thorndike. Lynn. 1916. "The True Roger Bacon." *American Literary Review* 21, pp. 237-257 and 468-480.

Thorndike. Lynn. 1921. Letter in Correspondence Column. *Scientific American*, June 25, p. 509.

Thorndike. Lynn. 1923-58. *A History of Magic and Experimental Science*. New York: Macmillan.

Thorndike. Lynn. 1929. "Roger Bacon." *American Historical Review*. (Lancaster, Pa.) 34 (January), pp. 317-319.

Thorndike. Lynn. 1963. *Science and Thought in the 15th Century: Studies in the History of Medicine and Surgery, Natural and Mathematical Science, Philosophy and Politics*. New York: Hafner.

Tiltman. John H. 1951. "Interim Report on the Voynich MS." Personal communication to William F. Friedman. 5 May 1951.

Tiltman. John H. 1967. "The Voynich MS." Script of an address presented to the Baltimore Bibliophiles. March 4. 1951.

Tiltman. John H. 1968. "The Voynich Manuscript, the Most Mysterious Manuscript in the World." Paper privately circulated. Baltimore.

Top. Alexander. 1603. *The Olive Leafe: Or Universall ABCE. Wherein is Set Foorth the Creation of Letters*. London.

Trithemius. Joannes. 1564. *Polygraphiae Libri Sex*. Coloniae.

Trithemius. Joannes. 1606. *Steganographia*. Frankfurt.

Vanderwalle. C. B. 1929. *Roger Bacon dans l'histoire de la philologie*. Paris.

Volkmann. Ludwig. 1929. "Ars Memorativa." *Jahrbuch der kunsthistorischen Sammlung in Wien* N.F. Sonderheft 30. Vienna. pp. 111-203.

Von Aretin. J. Chr. Freiherr. 1806. *Theorie der Mnemonik*. Salzbach.

Von Boehn. Max. 1964. *Die Mode: Menschen und Moden im 16. Jahrhundert*. Munich: F. Bruckmann K. G.

Voynich. Wilfrid M.; Voynich. Ethel; and Nill. A. M. 1917?–196?. Notes concerning the history of the cipher manuscript. Voynich Archives. Library of the Grolier Club of New York.

Voynich. Wilfrid M. 1921. "A Preliminary Sketch of the History of the Roger Bacon Cipher Manuscript." *Transactions of the College of Physicians of Philadelphia* 43. pp. 415–430. Read April 20. 1921.

Waite. Arthur Edward. 1929. *The Holy Kabbalah*. London: Williams and Norgate Limited (Reprinted New Hyde Park. N. Y.: University Books. 1960).

Waite. Arthur Edward. 1961. *The Brotherhood of the Rosy Cross*. New York: University Books.

Walker. Daniel Pickering. 1958. *Spiritual and Demonic Magic from Ficino to Campanella*. London: The Warburg Institute.

Walsh. James J. 1921. "Vindication of Medieval Science." *America: a Catholic Review of the Week* 25 (September 10). pp. 488–490.

Walz. Rudolf. 1928. *Das Verhältnis von Glaube und Wissen bei Roger Baco*. Freiburg (Schweiz): St. Paulusdruckerei.

Warburg Institute. University of London. 1967. *Warburg Institute Library Catalogue*. 2nd ed. Boston: G. K. Hall. (And Suppl.. London: 1971.)

Wedel. Theodore Otto. 1920. *The Medieval Attitude Toward Astrology*. New Haven: Yale University Press.

Welborn. M. C. 1932. "The Errors of the Doctors According to Fr. Roger Bacon." *Isis* 18. pp. 26–62.

Werner. Alfred. 1963. "The Most Mysterious Manuscript." *Horizon* 5 (January). pp. 4–9.

Werner. Karl. 1879a. *Die Psychologie. Erkenntnis- and Wissenschaftslehre des Roger Baco*. Wien. (Reprinted Frankfurt/Main: Minerva-Verlag. 1966.)

Werner. Karl. 1879b. "Die Kosmologie und algemeine Naturlehre des Roger Baco." In *Wiener Akademie. Sitzungsberichte* 94. pp. 484–612.

Westacott. Evalyn. 1953. *Roger Bacon in Life and Legend*. London: Rockliff. (Reprinted Folcroft. Pa.: Folcroft Library Editions. 1974.)

Wilkins. John. 1641. *Mercury. or the Secret and Swift Messenger*. London: Printed by I. Norton. for John Maynard. and Timothy Wilkins. etc.

Wilkins. John. 1668a. *An Essay Toward Real Character. or a Philosophical Language*. London: Printed for Sa. Gellibrand. and for John Martyn. printer to the Royal Society.

Wilkins. John. 1668b. *An Alphabetical Dictionary. etc*. London: Printed by J. M. for Samuel Gellibrand and John Martin.

Willis. John. 1602. *The Art of Stenographie*. London.

Wilson. Grove. 1942. "Roger Bacon." In *Great Men of Science: Their Lives and Discoveries*. New York: The New Home Library. pp. 72–79.

Woodruff. Francis Winthrop. 1938. *Roger Bacon. a Biography*. London: J. Clarke & Co.. Ltd.

Yates. Frances. 1954. 1960. "The Art of Ramon Lull." *Journal of the Warburg and Courtauld Institutes* 17. pp. 115. 23. p. 1.

Yates. Frances. 1964. *Giordano Bruno and the Hermetic Tradition*. London: Routledge and Kegan Paul.

Yates. Frances. 1966. *The Art of Memory*. Chicago: University of Chicago Press.

Yates. Frances. 1968. "The Hermetic Tradition in Renaissance Science." In *Art. Science and History in the Renaissance*. Edited by C. H. Singleton. Baltimore.

Yates. Frances. 1969. *Theatre of the World*. Chicago: University of Chicago Press.

Yates. Frances. 1972. *The Rosicrucian Enlightenment*. London: Routledge and Kegan Paul.

Zimansky. Curt A. 1970. "William F. Friedman and the Voynich MS." *Philological Quarterly* 49. pp. 433–443.

135

www.ingramcontent.com/pod-product-compliance
Lightning Source LLC
Chambersburg PA
CBHW050642150426

42813CB00054B/1161